BUILDING A LIFE

TED LUSTIG'S STORY

Best wishes

Building a Life
Ted Lustig's Story

By Ari Unglik

Hardie Grant Books

First published in Australia in 2001
by Hardie Grant Books
12 Claremont Street
South Yarra Victoria 3141

Copyright © Ted Lustig, 2001

All rights reserved. No part of this publication may be reproduced, stored in a retrieval system or transmitted in any form by any means, electronic, mechanical, photocopying, recording or otherwise, without prior written permission of the publishers and copyright holders.

National Library of Australia Cataloguing-in-Publication Data:
    Unglik, Ari
    Building a life : Ted Lustig's story.

    ISBN 1 74064 004 7.

    1. Lustig, Ted. 2. Lustig and Moar Group – History. 3. Real estate developers – Victoria – Biography. 4. Immigrants – Victoria – Biography. 5. Architects – Victoria – Biography. I. Title.

    333.33092

By Ari Unglik of The Wilder Group Pty Ltd
Edited by L. Elaine Miller of Otmar Miller Consultancy Pty Ltd
Cover and text design by Phil Campbell
Typeset in Aldine 401 by J&M Typesetting
Printed and bound by Griffin Press in Australia

All photographs are from Ted Lustig's personal collection.

I WISH TO DEDICATE THIS BOOK TO THE MEMORY OF MY PARENTS, LUCIA AND SAMUEL LUSTIG, AND TO MY FAMILY AND FRIENDS WHO MADE MY LIFE SO INTERESTING AND THIS BOOK POSSIBLE.

TED LUSTIG WILL DONATE HIS PROCEEDS FROM SALES OF THE BOOK TO THE ALZHEIMER'S ASSOCIATION, VICTORIA

Foreword

The autobiography of Ted Lustig will strike a resonant chord with many of his generation, particularly those who lived through the Second World War. It should also be read by younger individuals needing motivation when life's trials seem overwhelming.

It reflects a youthful spirit, and its ingredients are values passed down and observed as a boy; profound loss; the challenge of surviving independently and establishing a foothold for life ahead; success in employment, in love, and in dealing with a period of lesser fulfilment—all of this before Ted Lustig and his family chose to emigrate to Australia.

Unlike many new settlers in Australia after the war, Ted did not immediately embark on a course that would lead him to financial success and independence. In fact it was not until he reached 50 years of age that Ted Lustig started to invest in his own worth, education and experiences.

By any measure Ted Lustig has lived a remarkable life, particularly the last 30 years here in Victoria.

Over the approximately 25 years I have known Ted, I have often considered him a 'cantankerous old bastard', but nonetheless a very successful one. Some of the seeds of that attitude are evident in the account of Ted's early life. But so too are some of the gentler moments that are not so apparent to his acquaintances.

Ted Lustig over the last 30 years did much to change the face of Melbourne and some of its suburbs. While his results and triumphs are briefly referred to, there is no detail of the trials, the intrigue, the deals with governments and unions that preceded each official opening. It was Ted's faith in his projects and in himself that led to the battles producing the 'cantankerous old bastard' reputation. He has always tenaciously pursued his objectives.

This autobiography is an easy and genuinely interesting read, although I get the feeling it is only Volume One of a two-volume production. If that volume has not been written, then it should be—for it would be part of the historical and architectural development of Melbourne in the last third of the twentieth century, and Ted Lustig was a major contributor to that period.

The Hon Jeff Kennett
Premier of Victoria 1992–1999

Contents

Preface	1
Acknowledgements	3
Prologue	5

Part I Poland

1	In the Right Place at the Wrong Time	11
2	My Neighbourhood	17
3	Discovering Judaism	24
4	Anselm	28
5	School Days	33
6	An Awakening	43
7	Hard Times	53
8	Across the Seas, Another World Away	60

Part II Israel

9	Life in the Holy Land	69
10	Student of Life in Haifa	79
11	The Storm Clouds Gather	92
12	Leaving the Past Behind	100
13	A World at War	108
14	A 'Working-Class' Man	117
15	Engineering a New Fate	125
16	For King and Country	136
17	Sarah	145
18	The Tender Age	155
19	The Tide Turns	165
20	War of Independence	175
21	A Grand Design	187
22	All for One? One for All.	196

Part III Australia

23	Alone in the Most Isolated City in the World	207
24	Back to the Beginning	217
25	Home at Last	229
26	How to Make a Million	246
27	Shopping Around	258
28	To Be Frank	271
29	My Love Lost	279
30	Raising the Stakes	286
Epilogue		299
Index		304

Preface

I am a builder, a man of business. My life's work has been the design and construction of solid structures for practical uses. So why publish a book? Why have I tried to capture in print something as intangible as the story of a life lived in three very different parts of the world over more than four-fifths of the twentieth century? I suppose the reader may be asking these questions. Let me try briefly to answer them.

Reminiscences rely on memory. The greatest pleasure in the course of work on this book has been the revival of pleasant memories: of childhood friends, of the intensity of young love, of the energy that drives a man in the early stages of his career, and of the satisfactions that success brings. Perhaps the greatest difficulty was the effort required to bring memories accurately to the fore and to convey the feel and the flavour of times and places that are long past. It was a struggle to piece together the story of my 84 years. The project began as fun, but it developed into a serious matter. After all, I was looking my life in the face, and I was going to make it public.

Parkinson's disease has robbed me of the opportunity to write the story with my own hand. A raconteur works best in the presence of his audience, like a solo performer on a theatre stage. But I am pinned now to a printed page. I trust the reader will sense the personality behind the typed words. Storytelling is the fundamental motivation for this book. I have always enjoyed telling stories.

I arrived in Australia in 1956 with the usual apprehensiveness of the migrant. Can a man start again at 40? Could a Jew succeed in Australia? Would anti-Semitism in Australia be as virulent as it had been in Europe? Thankfully, I can say it was not.

We settled initially in Perth, later moving to Melbourne. I worked very hard, mainly in residential development as a designer, structural engineer and quantity surveyor all in one. Fifteen years in the difficult environment of Palestine—later Israel—were a solid preparation for the challenge of establishing myself in the design and construction business in Australia.

After we moved to Melbourne and as my business reputation grew, we gradually widened the group of friends and acquaintances who came to our home and joined in my passion for the game of bridge. People wondered about the various stories that were being told about me. Was I really a man whose hard-heartedness competed with granite? How had I come from Central Europe via Palestine, Damascus and Israel to Australia? The playing cards were laid aside late in the evenings, refreshments were served and I found myself being asked to relate different episodes from my life.

Now I have compiled the stories into this book, and while it is not as grand or substantial as a hotel, such a book has its practical use as a tangible record of a life.

Ted Lustig
Melbourne, February 2001

Acknowledgements

I have discovered these past few years that in one sense producing a book is like constructing a building. You cannot do it alone. I wish to thank a number of people who, in their different ways, have made a contribution to this book.

First, credit should be given to the writer, Ari Unglik, of The Wilder Group Pty Ltd, to whom I narrated many episodes from my life. He distilled them, added historical detail and wrote the manuscript.

The publisher, Sandy Grant, and his team at Hardie Grant Books worked coolly under a demanding deadline. They included managing editor Tracy O'Shaughnessy, project manager Kirsty Manning and designer Phil Campbell. Special thanks to Elaine Miller of Otmar Miller Consultancy Pty Ltd, whose skilled editing improved the book.

Many people read the manuscript and made suggestions. I acknowledge the time and thought that each of them invested. My thanks to the former Premier of Victoria, Jeff Kennett, for his typically forthright foreword.

The architect David Cole assisted me by researching and preparing building designs relating to my career in Australia and I thank him. Many of the detailed tasks associated with any autobiography, including preparation of correspondence and collation of materials and photographs, were undertaken with great professionalism by my secretary, Kerry Sutton. To her and to other staff and advisers, including Marlene Blewett, my secretary for 35 years, I express my appreciation.

I wish to pay tribute to Sarah, my companion from 1942 when we married in Damascus until 1982 when Alzheimer's claimed her life. When Heather and I married we both had known the experience of being widowed. Heather's charm and intelligence have enriched my life. Her companionship is a constant support to me.

Prologue

THE HEAVY, CLASSICAL furnishings that decorated our modest apartment belied our social standing. Much to her chagrin, my mother had little power to improve our address, but she was nevertheless determined to adorn the interior as if it were a palace. Twelve elegantly upholstered chairs sat proudly around a solid mahogany dining table, with four extras placed at the corners of the room. A plush, formal chaise lounge extended across the length of one wall, and a teak desk was carefully placed beside the set of large French windows, dressed with rich, heavy drapes.

The French windows were set 22 centimetres above the floor and opened out onto a small terrace. This windowsill became *my* spot, my favourite place to sit, despite the abundance of more accommodating alternatives. Each Saturday, I would set the radio beside me on the sill, open the doors, and tune in. I would continue to adjust the dial until I came across some music that best suited my prevailing mood. As a teenage boy, my mood was usually romantic and sentimental, so I would settle on the old American standards, or sometimes a dose of jazz.

'*Radiofonika Italiana, Milano, Firenze ...* ' my favourite announcer would begin, her melodic Italian immediately waking me from my reverie. The mellifluous tones of her seductive monologue spoke directly and only to me. Frankly speaking, I was in love with her voice. It was music in itself. In my mind, I pictured her face and body, and as in all fantasies, no reality could possibly match the image I had conjured of my perfect female.

On a more earthly level, my newly aroused emotions found some degree of expression in the direction of Renata Himmel, my neighbour, who lived with her family on the large estate next door. I would position the radio and adjust the volume in order that she might hear it, and hoped that, possibly by osmosis, she would share my enjoyment and feeling for the music.

Renata was constantly practising the piano—from two until five, seven days a week—and in an attempt to impress her, or at the very least establish a common interest between us, I would take out my violin, stand by the window, and try to reproduce the songs I had just heard on the radio. Given my distinct lack of expertise on the instrument, this may well have been exactly where I went wrong. Or perhaps not. Renata and I were of the same age, but she was interested only in older boys (if interested at all), and as it turned out, any romantic future I may have had with her was as much a pipedream as a rendezvous with my Italian radio announcer.

My father would return home from the office for lunch, after which he insisted on taking an afternoon nap. At least once each week, he would complain that my activities were disturbing him, and each week my mother would come to my defence. After all, my learning the violin was her idea. In her eyes, it was a most civilised and sophisticated pursuit, and one befitting a young man in an important social position. She would do everything in her power to encourage me. I would have preferred to learn the piano, like Renata, but we could not afford a piano. The violin was an affordable alternative.

'I'll shut all the doors,' she would snap at my father, 'so stop complaining.'

More than sixty-five years had passed since I sat at the window, violin in hand. Now, as I stood in front of 36 Mickiewicza Street, before the dilapidated, neglected old building I once called 'home', the memories began to flood back.

I had been determined never to return to the land of my childhood. As far as I was concerned, Poland had nothing to offer me. When I left in 1938, the country was disintegrating in the face of simmering nationalist sentiment and racial hatred. And yet so many of my Jewish brethren seemed to remain unaware, or chose to carry on with their daily routines in blithe ignorance of what was about to befall them. As I left my parents to return to my studies in Palestine, I had sensed that this was a final farewell. Above all, I had felt impotent—powerless to save my parents and friends from the tempest on the horizon. If I had screamed with as much force as I could muster, *'Don't you people see what is happening? Get out of here!'*, I suspected that I would have found I had no voice. Or they had no ears.

No, Poland had nothing to offer me. I stubbornly refused to believe otherwise. My decision to return to Drohobycz came only after much persuasion on the part of my wife Heather, who felt that at the age of eighty, it could be time for me to 'make peace with my past'. I had never intended to do this, nor indeed did I have any idea what this meant. Throughout my life, I had travelled extensively, and my appointment as Honorary Consul of Hungary had provided the opportunity to visit central Europe on a number of occasions. But despite my proximity, I had never entertained the thought of returning to the *pipiduvka* (piss-hole) that was once my home and source of culture.

I had now reluctantly decided to do so, but had deliberately limited the duration of the visit to a single day. It was a protective measure. After all, how much could happen in twenty-four hours? I remained determined not to allow my return to evoke any emotion at all. This was not to become a 'voyage of self-discovery', nor a pilgrimage to my past. Yet I had not counted on the fact that sixty years could be reduced to an instant in the presence of unreconciled ghosts of the past. As hard as I tried, I could not hold back the memories of those people who had been around me and the events that had transpired, each in its way contributing to shape my future without my even being aware of it.

I had always perceived myself as being a victim of the prevailing currents, blown from one place to another by forces greater than myself. The events that took place at the end of the First World War had deprived me of a Viennese upbringing and had sent me instead into Poland. The Second World War put paid to my plans of studying medicine in Vienna and, with little choice in the matter, I ended up as a civil engineer in Palestine. Finally, Israeli party politics, as well as my wife's hunger for the antipodean, propelled me towards Australia, where I would spend more than half of my life.

All this time, I had felt utterly devoid of guidance, left to grope my way through. But now I could sense that certain people and events had shaped my values and my personality, and had set in place my most essential desires and priorities in life. All this now stood before me, in Drohobycz, and it was inescapable.

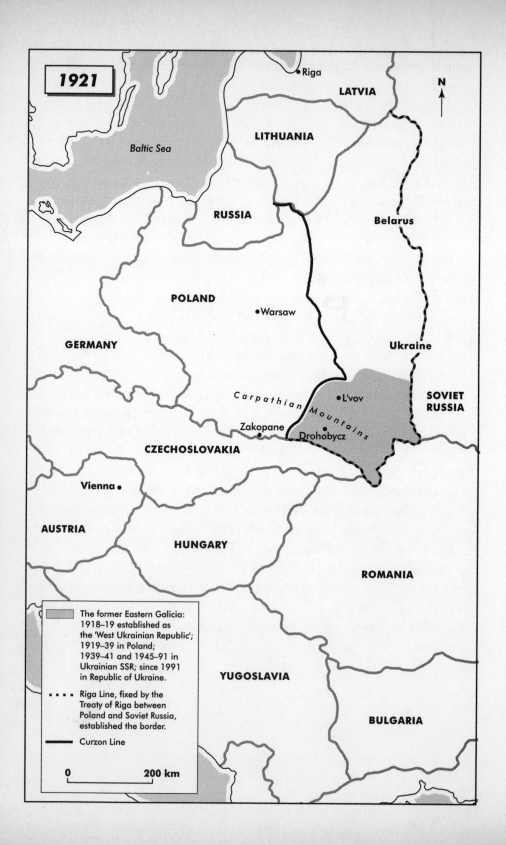

Part I

POLAND

1 In the Right Place at the Wrong Time

Fashion can be bought. Style one must possess.
EDNA WOOLMAN CHASE

I WAS BORN in Vienna in 1917. One might suggest that I was born in the right place at the wrong time. The tide of events around me would determine that ultimately I would not be raised in this glorious city. Rather, I would be moved to Drohobycz, a small town in Eastern Galicia which would become a part of Poland soon after the conclusion of the First World War. This would set a pattern for much of my life, a life that would be periodically redirected by the forces of the twentieth century's ever-changing political and social landscape.

After the turmoil of the Napoleonic Wars, the nineteenth century had been relatively tranquil in Europe. As the capital of the powerful and wealthy Austro-Hungarian Empire under the Habsburgs, Vienna had been at the centre of European culture. In the early part of the twentieth century, the city burgeoned with artists, musicians, writers and thinkers, and provided a fertile environment for the development of radical, modernist perspectives.

Vienna was the home of Sigmund Freud, the neurologist who, in the first decade of the century, fathered modern psychoanalytic theory. At around the same time, in neighbouring Germany, physicist Albert Einstein was threatening solid ground with his radical new ideas on relativity. In the field of philosophy, Vienna was at the forefront of new developments in scientific and logical empiricism with the 'Vienna Circle', led by the German philosopher Moritz Schlick and attended in the 1920s by the young Ludwig Wittgenstein.

The visual arts in Vienna were flourishing, nurturing the bright new ideas of young artists through the *'Vienna Sezession'* founded in 1897 and led by Gustav Klimt. These artists introduced modernism and anti-authoritarian expressionism, developing the *Jugendstil* style of German art nouveau.

These new ideas soon found their way into the famous Viennese theatres. The early twentieth century saw the emergence of drama that concerned itself less with classical verse and more with the psychology of characters: works by Friedrich Hebbel and Gerhart Hauptmann. Josef Jarno, the manager of Theatre in der Josephstadt, brought in plays by internationally popular writers such as Ibsen, Chekov, Strindberg, Shaw and Wilde. Even Vienna's more conservative theatre, the Burgtheater, broke with tradition to embrace a more modern repertoire. Audiences could see Expressionist works by local playwrights such as Oskar Kokoschka (also a painter) and Georg Kaiser, performed by a new breed of avant-garde and Expressionist actors such as Fritz Kortner.

The home of Haydn, Mozart, Schubert and Wagner was also nurturing exciting developments in music around this time. The Vienna Opera, directed by Gustav Mahler, was producing works that were more vast, complex and emotionally charged than ever before, including Mahler's own seventh symphony. In 1904, a scandal was caused by *Salome*, the 'obscene' and 'blasphemous' Richard Strauss opera inspired by the work of Oscar Wilde. In 1908, Arnold Schoenberg introduced a new innovation, his dissonant and expressionist atonal music. Alban Berg would develop this concept to extremes over the course of the next fifteen years.

I might have been far too young to be aware of the beauty and vitality of early twentieth-century Vienna, but my mother, Lucia Kuhrmärker, certainly was not. Had she had her way, the family would have remained in Vienna and I would have been raised in this exhilarating intellectual and artistic centre. My mother was somewhat of an intellectual snob. She had an insatiable appetite for social and cultural acceptance and longed to become an indistinguishable part of secular society, through assimilation.

To be Viennese in the early part of this century was one thing; to be a Viennese Jew was quite another. After all, Gustav Mahler, the genius once referred to as 'that Jew', had to be baptised a Catholic before he could gain the post of Director of the Vienna Opera. The city was unashamedly anti-Semitic.

That said, Vienna was also a magnet for Jews from central and eastern Europe in search of culture and a modern education. As the metropolitan centre for the Austro-Hungarian Empire, it was also a world city. Between 1848 and 1914, while Vienna's overall population multiplied five times, its Jewish population increased 35 times, from 5000 to 175,000, rising to almost 10% of the population by 1914. Jews played a hugely disproportionate role in the arts, education and the professions. By 1910, Jews composed 43% of the university teaching faculty; by 1936 62% of Vienna's lawyers and 47% of its doctors were of Jewish origin.

Although not Viennese herself, it was not unreasonable for my mother to see herself as a product of Austrian culture. The same can be said of my father, Dr Samuel Lustig, PhD in law. They were both raised in the town of Drohobycz, situated in the region of Galicia, which had been under Austrian rule since the partitions of Poland in the late eighteenth century. Indeed, during the First World War, my father faithfully served in the Austrian Army with the rank of captain, albeit as an advocate and later a judge in the military courts.

The story of how my parents met set the tone for their relationship. My mother was born into a reasonably wealthy family, and was a strikingly beautiful and highly opinionated woman. My father, who was still a law student at the time, was employed to tutor her through matriculation. He was not from an affluent background and was tutoring to pay his way through university, which he attended in nearby L'vov.

In time, he became smitten with my mother, with her irresistible, smiling hazel eyes, her rich auburn hair, and her youthful exuberance. A true gentleman, he waited until he had graduated and begun practising as a lawyer before he felt it appropriate to propose marriage. He was twenty-six years of age, and she was just eighteen.

My mother was greatly impressed by the fact that this academic, a considerably older man, should want to spend his life with her. Her mother suggested that she should wait for a man with better financial prospects, but Lucia felt strongly that Samuel would build a substantial career for himself. Indeed, she pinned her hopes on it. They were married in Drohobycz and my elder brother Anselm was born a year later, in 1908. Another son, Ludwig, was born in 1912, but he died less than twelve months later.

My father's opportunity to move to Vienna resulted from his marriage to my mother. Her uncle, Dr Pachtmann, ran a highly successful law firm in the capital and invited my father to join him. My father rented a small apartment in Marie Hilfe Strasse for himself, my mother and Anselm. Dr Pachtmann's practice specialised in advising the foreign investors involved in Austria's oil industry, which centred around the rich oil and natural gas fields of Galicia. This was big business, and the move represented a significant step forward for my father's career. While in Vienna, he also took the opportunity to complete his doctorate in law. My mother's ambitions for my father seemed to be on track, but would soon be interrupted by the far-reaching effects of the First World War.

The period prior to the First World War might be described as a progression from international competition, to international tension, to international war. The age of 'New Imperialism' from 1870 to 1914, in which hitherto isolationist countries such as Germany, the United States and Japan acquired a taste for empires, led to a situation in which preservation of empire itself became a reason for extending authority to new areas. This ensured conflict with other imperial powers. The era was peppered with occasions that threatened war—the confrontation between Britain and France for control of the Nile, the Russo-Japanese War, the Boer War, and the incident at Agadir that almost resulted in war between Germany and Britain. In the end, it was a challenge to Austrian imperialism by Serbian nationalism that triggered the world war: the assassination of the heir to the empire, Archduke Francis Ferdinand, in Sarajevo on 28 June 1914.

I was born in April 1917. Six months later the President of the United States, Woodrow Wilson, declared war on Austria, and within eighteen months the reign of the Habsburgs was over. The Austro-Hungarian and Ottoman empires fell, the Habsburg, Romanov and Hohenzollern dynasties vanished, and the Bolsheviks triumphed in Russia. The entire map of Europe was redrawn.

With the collapse of the Habsburg empire, four new nations came into being: Hungary, Czechoslovakia, Yugoslavia, and the Republic of Austria. Poland regained its independence for the first time since 1795 (apart from a brief period, 1807 to 1814, when Napoleon neutralised Russia and Prussia), but the status of oil-rich Galicia remained undecided. Disputes over the area would lead to a war between Poland and Russia. The fate of my father's career and the future of my family would hang in the balance while Poland and the Soviets fought over the source of wealth.

The rise of the Ukrainian nationalist movement meant that by 1918, Poland was fighting the Ukrainians of Eastern Galicia (the

Ruthenians). In November of that year, the Ukrainians seized the predominantly Polish city of L'vov (which had been the capital of the medieval Ukrainian state of Halich before it was annexed to Poland in the mid 1300s) and proclaimed a Ukrainian Republic. By December, however, the city had been retaken by Polish troops, initiating a war with the West Ukrainian army.

In the spring of 1919, as the Supreme Council of the Allied Powers debated the status of Galicia, the Curzon Line was proposed as a plan to settle the future of the region. Western Galicia would be allocated to Poland while Eastern Galicia would be granted the right to self-determination, as a Polish protectorate. It was not anticipated, however, that Eastern Galicia would fall into the hands of the Bolsheviks, whom the Allies were trying to wipe out in Russia. The allies sanctioned a Polish advance east on the grounds that this would weaken the Bolsheviks. Thus the Poles took over all of Galicia.

The Red Army attacked Poland in April of 1920. The Polish head of state, Jozef Pilsudski, signed an alliance with the head of the East Ukrainian government, General Semyon Petlyura, envisaging the creation of an independent Ukraine which would be allied with Poland. In return for Polish help against Russia, Petlyura agreed to give up claims to the territory of East Galicia, which would become a part of Poland.

The Polish and Ukrainian troops entered Kiev in May, but the Soviets counterattacked in June, sending the Poles and Ukrainians in full retreat and threatening Warsaw. Faced with a Soviet victory and the possibility of the Red Army rolling into Germany, the Allied powers pushed for an armistice. They offered a revised Curzon Line, with L'vov and the adjoining Drohobycz and Boryslaw oilfields on the Soviet side. It was rejected by the Bolsheviks, who offered the Poles more land if they accepted other Soviet terms. A Polish provisional revolutionary committee, *Polvekrom* (in effect an embryonic communist government for Poland), was established in July. However, Pilsudski upset the Soviet plan by bold military actions, and by August, he had won the Battle of Warsaw.

Peace talks began at Riga in March 1921, leading to the establishment of a new Polish–Soviet boundary. Poland extended recognition to Soviet Ukraine, and Galicia, including my parents' home town of Drohobycz, would become a part of Poland.

The Galician oil industry would continue to be dominated by the multinationals operating out of Vienna, but with Galicia now Polish territory, the Polish government would be involved, claiming royalties that would have to be negotiated. Dr Pachtmann's firm would be required to open a branch office in Drohobycz, and he felt that my father was the right man to do it.

To the great disappointment of my mother, her time in Vienna had come to an end. And so had mine. By late 1920, when I was just three years old and my brother Anselm was twelve, our family moved back to Drohobycz. When my parents had left there seven years earlier, it had been a part of Austria. Now they were returning home—only 'home' was now a part of Poland.

2 My Neighbourhood

Of all animals, the boy is the most unmanageable.
PLATO, *LAWS*

THE REGION OF Galicia had seen countless rulers over the centuries. In the twelfth century it was one of the chief principalities of Russia; Hungary ruled the region for a short time before it was sacked by the Mongols in 1240. There followed a period of alternating Polish and Hungarian rule before Poland's King Jagiello took control in the middle of the fourteenth century. Upon the first partition of Poland in 1772, Galicia became an Austrian territory, but the Polish nobles maintained political pressure to ensure that the rights of the Polish population would remain paramount.

Historically, this meant that Galicia enjoyed a relatively liberal society, as the Austrian government sought to head off the revolutionary demands of the Polish nobles by winning the support of the peasants with land reforms. Revolutions in Europe affected circumstances within Austria. By 1848, war with the Magyars resulted in Hungary being granted considerable autonomy. The *Wiosna Naroduv* ('Spring of Nations') resulted in a flurry of liberal reforms: the end of censorship, a promise of a national constitution and the end of serfdom in Galicia. The Governor of Galicia formed an alliance with the Ruthenians and by the late 1860s, a number of freedoms and opportunities had been extended to other minorities, including Jews. By 1868, the *Augsleich* agreement between Austria and Hungary to form the Austro-Hungarian empire, providing Austria with a constitution and parliament, also granted Galicia provisional autonomy and a legislative assembly.

Despite these freedoms, a social hierarchy was firmly in place in Galicia. The Austrians, Germans and Magyars represented the elite, with the Poles a distant second and the Ukrainians and Jews well below them.

Set in the foothills of the Carpathian Mountains about one hundred kilometres south-south-west of L'vov, my home town of Drohobycz dated back to the eleventh century. It had grown significantly in size and wealth during the latter part of the nineteenth century with the discovery of oil.

Two Polish pharmacists, Ignacy Lukasiewicz and Jan Zeh, had developed the technology that led to the establishment of a new industry based on petroleum. They created a method of distilling crude oil, and then in March 1853, they constructed the first kerosene lamp. As early as July of the same year, their new lamp was used to illuminate the public hospital in L'vov. Their discoveries marked the beginnings of the rapid search for petroleum in the Carpathians, especially in the eastern sector of the mountain chain where deposits rich in oil were uncovered. By the 1890s, the Kracow daily newspaper *Czas* ('Time') spoke regularly of new oil discoveries in eastern Galicia.

The oil industry had transformed Drohobycz from a small town into a very attractive, compact bourgeois city with a population of around 45,000 residents. Forty per cent of these were Jewish, thirty-five per cent were Polish gentiles, and the remainder were Ukrainian, with a spattering of Germans, Austrians, Hungarians and Czechs.

Drohobycz boasted a number of fine restaurants and hotels. The streets of the city centre were lined with a broad range of elegant shops and boutiques, which were owned almost exclusively by Jewish families—Schwartz sold shoes, Binstock was the town photographer, Fischmann ran the bookstore, and Schulz's coffee house (the Kawiarnia) was one of the city's favoured meeting places. One of the most memorable was a cheese shop on the *Rynek*, the market square—memorable because the Jewish owner went under the unlikely name of Apollo, but also because the smell of the cheese was abominable. Indeed, the smell of the cheese was so foul that my Aunt Mila's mother was declared a public nuisance for her habit of taking slabs of it into the local cinema to snack on during the movie.

My family lived at 36 Mickiewicza Street, named after Adam Mickiewicz, the nineteenth-century Polish poet and leader of the Romantic movement. Mickiewicza Street was where the rich folk lived, primarily Jewish families who had made colossal amounts of money from the oil business.

We occupied one storey of a large house on the property. The apartment consisted of a drawing room, a dining room, a kitchen and two bedrooms, one for my parents and the other for Anselm and me. Before long, we moved into a larger abode in an adjacent apartment block. The whole property, approximately two hectares in size including the house, apartments and surrounding grounds, was owned by Dr Wilder, a general practitioner who was also a professional investor in real estate. He was a big man, a gruff, masculine fellow with a permanent five o'clock shadow. I could always tell when Dr Wilder had been in the vicinity because in his wake he left the stench of cigar smoke. Indeed, it seemed to me that a cigar was permanently, possibly surgically, attached to his lips—a situation of some benefit to him since it left both his hands free to fondle the bodies of the local domestic staff, particularly our maid Marysia.

Dr Wilder had four children. His son, Staszek, was five years my senior and I would become close friends with him as I grew older. Mrs Wilder was a tiny woman, and as a young boy, I always wondered how a woman of her stature could possibly bear four children, especially when the sizeable Dr Wilder was the father.

The buildings on the Wilders' property were surrounded by gardens and a meticulously cultivated orchard. Beside the orchard stood the stables and the garage that housed Dr Wilder's pride and joy, a collection of vintage cars and a brand new 1920-model Ford. At school I would brag about the fact that a Ford was parked at the back of our house—of course it did not belong to my family, but I wasn't lying.

One of my earliest memories is of Dr Wilder's stables. One summer Sunday morning, my mother dressed me in one of those sailor suits that every child of my generation seems to have been subjected to, and sent me into the yard to play. Dr Wilder's groom was amusing himself by tormenting Dr Wilder's dog. Then, when the hound reached a feverish state of excitement, he turned it onto me. If the manservant was seeking blood, he would have been severely disappointed because the dog knew me well. Instead of biting me, the dog jumped up and licked me with ardour.

From an upper storey window, my father had witnessed this series of events. He descended to the yard and confronted the man. Father was not a big man—in fact he was short—but he was muscular, fit and extremely strong. Without uttering a word, he raised one hand and struck the groom across the jaw, sending him flat on his back and knocking him out cold. I was impressed.

At the front of our apartment building, facing the street, was a pharmacy run by Dr Yedick. My recollections of him are vague, except that he was an elderly man and, like Dr Wilder, he was on call day and night. More memorable was his lady assistant, who was of such unenviable facial disposition that her portrait was shown to some children by their governesses as a bizarre form of punishment. A drawing room above the pharmacy was made available to the residents of the building for music practice and social pursuits, and above the drawing room was an apartment used by Dr Wilder for his medical practice.

Dr Wilder's property was a substantial one, but it paled into insignificance next to the property of our neighbours, the Himmel family. Their home was set on fifteen hectares of land. Like ours, the grounds included a fine orchard with an impressive variety of fruits, as well as a substantial vegetable garden. The front of the house boasted a manicured garden modelled on one of the gardens at the Palace of Versailles.

Dr Himmel was a radiologist, and therefore a man of some substance. But it was Mrs Himmel's wealth that set their family apart from others in Drohobycz. Indeed, Mrs Himmel was widely recognised as one of the wealthiest women in Europe at the time. Lola Himmel was the daughter of a *Baal Agalah*—a Yiddish word meaning 'owner of a two-wheeled cart'. Her father was referred to in this way because this was virtually all he owned ... once.

Throughout the 1880s and 1890s, Lola's father worked as a water carrier, selling fresh water from house to house in Drohobycz and the nearby town of Boryslaw. One day in 1895, he was digging for a spring outside Boryslaw when suddenly a malicious black jet of liquid shot out at him. Ignorant of the nature of his find, he fled and consulted a rabbi to ask what had brought about this curse to strike him. The Rabbi answered that he should be thanking God—he had in fact struck oil. The illiterate water carrier then formed the Galicia Petroleum Company and subsequently became fabulously wealthy selling his oil to the sophisticates in Vienna, and from there, across Europe.

Lola was a highly intelligent woman, and she had cannily invested much of her oil fortune in real estate, primarily tenanted buildings in L'vov. Her investments there had resulted in the creation of entire streets.

I spent much of my childhood playing in the gardens at the Himmels', with their two children Zigmund and Renata. Ziggy was three years my senior, but Renata was my age and over time we developed a close friendship that would last all our lives. Young children could not possibly appreciate the effort and care that had been put into creating the paradise where we played. Exotic fruits and wild berries at our fingertips, the sun's rays dappling through the trees, the Himmels' garden was an Eden for our frolics and our daydreams.

Dr Himmel had been a close friend of my father's from their university days. On weekends, the two could often be found playing chess together, or skittles in Dr Himmel's tenpin bowling alley in the garden. The Himmels employed three or four gardeners to tend to their expansive grounds, and one of their jobs was to train the fruit trees horizontally so that their fruit would be within easy reach of lazy bowlers.

When I was about ten years old, Dr Himmel died of radiation poisoning, at the age of forty-two. He had not taken the appropriate precautions in his X-ray rooms, and the radiation had destroyed his immune system. His death was a tremendous loss for Lola and the children. Our families remained close, and my father took responsibility for overseeing the legal side of Lola's affairs.

I started my schooling at a local preschool for boys when I was about four years of age. I knew from the very first moment that I did not like the headmistress, Pani Fichmanowna (Miss Fichman, the suffix 'owna' denoting that she was unmarried). Her ugliness offered some explanation as to her marital status. She was particularly grotesque when she smiled, and so we all remained deliberately sombre for fear of exacerbating the sight. Furthermore, Pani Fichmanowna was short, and being short for my own age (and already conscious of it), I was not impressed by her lack of imposing presence. She also wore some kind of headband that somehow blended with her hair. Not being acquainted with matters of ladies' attire, I had no idea what it was. But I knew that I did not like it, nor did I like her.

It was at this preschool that I met Tadek Chciuk and Milek Tauchner, my closest friends for the next twelve years. We attended the local primary school together, and would meet after school to play and to embark on various adventures. The forests and the open areas of farmland on the outskirts of Drohobycz made for a wonderful playground, with their hiding spots and their endless supply of raspberries, blackberries and wild mushrooms. But most of the adventures— the games of cops and robbers or cowboys and Indians—took place in the abandoned quarries in the grounds of the old brick factories. The production of bricks was conducted on the site of large areas of suitable clay. After plumbing the depths, the entire factory would be relocated, leaving a large number of appropriately filthy, abandoned quarries, perfect for our boyhood romps. We duly exploited each and every one.

Drohobycz had a comparatively modern jail on its outskirts, and from a certain vantage point, I could see the prisoners in the yard. Seeing these inmates had a tremendous impact on me. I would have loved to know what each of them had done to land himself there, and my imagination made a regular point of running riot.

The movies were another important part of my childhood. I began to visit the cinema regularly by about the age of seven. I would attend with my mother, or with Ziggy and Renata Himmel, accompanied by Linda, their governess. I grew up sympathising with the Indians, unable to tolerate the concept of all of the Indians being killed by a few omnipotent cowboys, as usually happened in the movies. Life in Europe would imitate art in a few short years, with players far more sinister than cowboys.

My parents' social scene was made up of people from Mickiewicza Street. They were educated, professional people. For the most part, the husbands were lawyers like my father, and their wives, like my mother, were professional shoppers. It was, after all, unseemly for a woman to return home from a trip to the town centre without some sort of beautifully wrapped, readily identifiable package tucked under her arm. A cake from the most exclusive *kaffehaus* was an acceptable purchase. It was rarely clothing, for a woman could not possibly buy 'off the rack'; clothing had to be original, whether tailor-made or fashioned by the woman herself.

Giselle Hahn, the wife of Dr Hahn the lawyer, was a regular companion for my mother on her outings. It always baffled me how a woman with the legs of a piano could go by such a name, for she bore no resemblance whatsoever to a 'gazelle'. My friend Tadek Chciuk came to take on the role of 'straight man' in my comic routines. I taught him to feed me lines by always asking 'In what respect?' Thus, in the case of Mrs Hahn:

'She has legs like a gazelle.'

'In what respect?'

'The hair.'

The number of lawyers in Drohobycz was in absolute disproportion to the number of clients. My father had the advantage of representing

Galicia Petroleum, as did a number of his friends. After the First World War, however, business was poor due to drops in production in the refineries. The competition was fierce, and while most of my father's friends were lawyers, he remained wary of them as rivals.

Dr Hahn was one such 'friend'. Another was Dr Kaufman. In contrast to my father, who was an academic and a philanthropist, the short, plump, silver-haired Dr Kaufman was an aggressive self-marketer. His image was his selling tool and the perpetual bachelor saw profit in the wide range of salacious rumours that surrounded—and were quite possibly started by—him. While my father taught him the basics of law, Kaufman was able to build a profitable practice by means of his fanatical salesmanship. I could see that this was disconcerting for my father, who was well aware that he was himself a superior practitioner but possessed neither the business acumen nor the materialist mentality to earn the amount of money Kaufman made. My mother's capacious desire for the good life no doubt contributed to his frustrations.

Kaufman's greatest claim to fame was his light cream-coloured convertible sports car, a 'Prague' imported from Czechoslovakia. The perennial question around town was how he could afford such a magnificent vehicle. Kaufman would recline in the plush red leather upholstery of the back seat while his Polish chauffeur drove him around the town. Even in bad weather, Kaufman insisted that the roof stay down so that he could be admired by the multitudes. He took on the persona of a Hollywood screen idol and waved to his fans accordingly.

I would occasionally run messages for Kaufman, and in return, he would allow me to ride with him in his car. I liked to be the centre of attention. It may have been at this early stage that I developed my own taste for creature comforts. Unlike my father, I certainly came to believe that life was more interesting if you had a wad of zlotys in your pocket.

3 Discovering Judaism

If you go to church, and like the singing better than the preaching, that's not orthodox.
EDGAR WATSON HOWE

I DID NOT realise that I was Jewish until I was twelve years old. There was simply no reference to it in our family. Like most of the Jews who lived in our neighborhood and belonged to my parents' social circle, our home life was bourgeois, genteel and secular.

Many of my mother's friends thought she was in fact a Christian, so regularly did she attend the church on Sunday mornings with me in tow. In truth, she was attracted to the aesthetic qualities of Christianity rather than its theology. Her visits were expressly to listen to the choral music, which she so loved.

At home we spoke German. My father was fluent in Yiddish, but my mother considered it vulgar, so there was no Yiddish to be heard in my house. My father displayed the double standards common to many assimilated central European Jews of that period. He considered himself a middle-class, middle-of-the-road Zionist, but he didn't involve himself in any Jewish cultural or religious practices, and attended synagogue only on high holidays. That is not to say that my parents were not pious. While they were not at all partial to organised religious ritual, I believe that they shared a faith in God. After all, my own name Theodore means 'a gift from God'. The choice of my name, shared with Theodore Hertzl, may also have reflected my father's sympathy for Zionism.

My mother wanted me to assimilate and blend into the greater society. To her profound dismay, my brother Anselm, nine years my senior, had aligned himself with the extreme left-wing Zionist youth movement, *Hashomer Hatzair*, during his high school days. He was a temperamental young man, and his patriotism and involvement with this group had landed him in all sorts of trouble. My mother's disappointment with Anselm only served to strengthen her conviction to raise me in a secular environment.

It was my mother's family who introduced me to the sophisticated world of German Jewry. Her mother, Anna Elbaum, could well have been a model for the title character in *Travels with my Aunt*. She was an elegant, formidable woman with striking looks and commanding eyes, who spent much of her time in Vienna, Switzerland, and northern Italy. While she was fond of my father, she wasn't reticent about the fact that she thought my mother foolish for marrying him. She too had made a foolish decision in marrying her first husband, Kuhrmärker, but had made up for her error through her second husband's sizeable portfolio of oil shares, and her third husband's industrial empire.

My father's family starkly contrasted with my mother's. His parents had belonged to the *Ostjuden*—those Jews who chose to live in *shtetl* communities, relatively segregated from the greater society. My father was one of four sons. However, his elder brother, Abraham Lustig, was shot dead in the Rynek in 1908, during a demonstration against unemployment organised by Ukrainian university students and workers' groups.

The ethnic conflict in Galicia had deepened around the turn of the century. Massive peasant strikes against Polish landlords had occurred in 1902. The introduction in 1907 of universal male suffrage in elections to the Austrian parliament intensified pressures for a similar reform at the provincial level. Ukrainian students engaged in demonstrations and clashes with the Poles, and in 1908 a student assassinated the Galician governor. On that fateful day in the Rynek, Abraham, who was working as a journalist for the daily Jewish newspaper, *Chwila*, wandered into the thick of the demonstration. When the Polish police were instructed to curb the mob by firing their rifles into the air, somebody aimed low and Abraham became a proletarian martyr.

My paternal grandfather, Anselm, had died many years before, and my father, now the eldest brother, took it upon himself to take care of his two younger brothers, Moses and Shimon. With his support, they both studied law at the University of L'vov as he had done, and upon graduation they completed their articles in my father's law firm.

In 1929, when I was twelve, my father took a stand against my mother's determination to give us a secular upbringing. On Christmas

Eve, he returned home to find a decorated tree standing in the parlour. It was not our usual practice, but perhaps my mother thought he would not notice this latest innovation in her mission to assimilate the family. In a fit of fury, my father grabbed the tree and hurled it out the front door, down each flight of stairs in the apartment block, and out of the building. He hauled it around the corner and to the rear of the building, out of sight of the neighbours.

He returned a few minutes later, grim-faced and covered in pine needles. Mother burst into tears, but they did not soften my father's resolve this time. Pointing in my direction, while looking my mother squarely in the eye, he announced, 'Tedek is having his bar mitzvah this year.' Whereupon my mother took the next step in attempting to get her way: one of her celebrated fainting spells. The salts were brought out, but the decree stood.

For my bar mitzvah, I would have to read from the Torah—in Hebrew—before the congregation of the Drohobycz synagogue. The rabbi, Professor Dr Rabbi Schrier, sent a *Shamash* to our home to give me lessons. While I had already proven adept at other languages—Latin, German, Polish, Ukrainian, and even ancient Greek—I did not excel in learning Hebrew.

The *Shamash* wore an Assyrian beard, highly cultivated, cut, trimmed and adjusted to perfection. I did not like his beard. I did not like him, nor did I like his instruction. With the tacit approval of my mother and with the help of our maid, I concentrated my efforts towards finding a way to get rid of him. My master plan was far from original: balancing a bucket of white chalk dust atop the door that the tutor was about to enter.

Needless to say, my teacher subsequently excused himself from giving me further instructions for my bar mitzvah. My father was not impressed. He sternly assured me that my bar mitzvah would proceed, but how I managed with the Hebrew was no longer his concern.

The day of my bar mitzvah was the first time I had seen the inside of a synagogue. I read from the Torah, though to a certain extent I merely mimicked the rabbi's words. What would have taken a normal bar mitzvah boy ten minutes took me almost half an hour. My father stood beside me, proudly pointing to the 'hieroglyphics' that wobbled before my eyes.

Mother commented only on the absence of any dignitaries to shake my hand after the ceremony. She hadn't wanted the ceremony to take place, but resigned to its inevitability, she was now only concerned that it should be *the* social event of the Drohobycz Jewish calendar. She was duly disappointed. Upon our arrival home, she broke down once more. 'How could you let this happen?' she cried.

'He was praying to God,' my father replied. 'He wasn't being circumcised.'

I was somewhat traumatised by this deferred knowledge of my Jewish identity. It seemed that the protective wall my mother had tried to construct around me suddenly collapsed. In being given this new, alien heritage, I began to notice certain things for the first time.

I had never before encountered, or been aware of, racial demarcation in the schoolyard. Of course I knew that my friend Chciuk was ardently Polish; that Pioter Ilnitzki, whose father was a good friend of my father and a fellow lawyer, was Ukrainian; and even that I was neither Polish nor Ukrainian—but it had never mattered. Yet soon after my bar mitzvah, Pioter pulled me aside in the playground and began to explain to me how to eliminate Jews. Unaware that I was one of their number, he proceeded to draw his hand across his throat and crow the word '*risat*'—Ukrainian for slitting a throat.

I found myself most distressed by his performance. When I spoke of the incident with my father, he reassured me. 'Tedek,' he explained, 'whatever Pioter might say, that is not going to happen. For one thing, we will never have the Ukrainians running the show here. The Poles will always be in charge.' Little did he know.

I don't know whether this incident was indicative of my newfound Jewish sensibility, or truly reflected a growing anti-Semitism in Drohobycz, but from then on, I began to notice it more and more. Of course it was the 1930s and with the world in a severe economic depression, the environment was ripe for hatred and jealousy. I would never be on fire with patriotism as my brother was, but the discovery of my Jewish identity would certainly open my eyes to a world I had not seen before.

4 Anselm

After all, blood is thicker than water. But then so is soup.
LENNIE LOWER, 'HERE'S LUCK'

LIKE MY FATHER, my elder brother Anselm was of small stature and strong build, with dark brown hair. The similarities ended there. His restless brown eyes often revealed the temperamental nature that lay behind, a lighthouse warning nearby craft to steer clear of perilous waters. In personality, my brother was in such contrast to my stoic and composed father that my mother often joked that she wondered about the true identity of Anselm's sire.

As it is for most younger brothers, Anselm was my boyhood hero.

I was seven years old and the local cinema had most young boys fascinated with the culture of America's 'Wild West'. To my knowledge, there were not too many cowboys in the immediate vicinity of our Polish town, nor were there native American tribes. But such films were immensely popular, and were also responsible for the widespread use of bows and arrows among local youth.

I was particularly entranced by the archery skills of a group of older boys who were friendly with the caretaker of our building. One day I was sitting on the downpipe watching these boys at play, when one of them turned to me sharply from about twenty metres away and called 'Tedek, look here!' As I did, an arrow whistled past me, grazing the side of my head. This immediately inspired the other boys to follow their leader in assigning me the role of enemy, and using me for target practice. I had little recourse but to roll myself into a ball and weather the storm.

Like the Lone Ranger, Anselm the hero appeared on the horizon to save the day. (Actually, he appeared from behind the garage.) 'Stop!' he cried. They did, momentarily, but sensing safety in numbers, they soon turned their aim upon this fourteen-year-old Gary Cooper-like figure who sought to foil their conquest. Foolish they were, considering that many of them had known, and suffered, the wrath of this hero on previous occasions. A lesser man might have turned and fled their attack, but Anselm charged at them, seizing their weapons and causing them to beat a hasty retreat. I was saved.

Anselm tutored me in the art of knife-throwing, another useful skill I had taken an interest in while watching cowboy movies in Drohobycz. I spent many hours practising this art at the expense of the large oak tree that stood outside our bedroom window at 36 Mickiewicza Street.

Within a few years, however, Anselm's attentions had turned to more adult pursuits: to girls, to sport, to Zionist politics, and to mischief (not necessarily in that order) and he had little time for a 'kid brother'. We were never particularly close; our age difference was simply too great. I knew more about my brother's life from the endless concerns expressed by my parents than from my brother himself. During his teen years and beyond, he was more than a handful for them.

Indeed, on one occasion he proved, quite literally, to be a headache for my mother. A patron of the classical arts, she was hardly enamoured of sport, a 'trivial' activity in her opinion. Nevertheless, with two sons, she would be unable to avoid it completely. She had never attended a soccer match, but with Anselm involved in the 'big match' between *Betar* (the local Jewish team) and the Polish team, I managed to convince her to accompany me to watch it. For the first half of the match, my mother's sympathies lay with the ball. She wondered what ghastly deed it had performed in order to be attacked so viciously by members of both teams. Her sympathy subsided early in the second half when the ball sailed across the fence and hit her squarely on the head. Of course, she fainted. That was enough football for my mother for one day—indeed for one lifetime.

Anselm's game was marred as usual by his vast repertoire of fouling techniques. An awareness of his social status within Drohobycz had given rise to an arrogant belief that nobody would dare question his behaviour on the field.

This arrogance was not restricted to the football field. My brother had always displayed a certain imperious haughtiness: as the son of Dr Lustig, he believed himself to be clearly superior to others in every way.

Perhaps spending much of his boyhood in Vienna before moving to Drohobycz had contributed in some way to his disposition. During his teen years, when he took up the cause of Zionism as a member of the *Hashomer Hatzair* movement, his identity as a proud Jew further set him apart from the rest of society. Armed with this 'us and them' mentality, he would seek out potential targets for hostile actions. Arrogance and rebelliousness mixed with patriotism would prove to be a dangerous cocktail.

Professor Kravczyshyn taught mathematics and physics at the King Jagiello Gymnasium, where my brother attended high school. He was a tall man, upright and rigid in his posture. The school prohibited pupils from appearing unaccompanied on the streets after six o'clock in the evening. Furthermore, the students were obliged to wear their uniform in public at all times. Kravczyshyn was responsible for enforcing these rules. Since he was Ukrainian, he was immediately branded an anti-Semite by Anselm and a number of his malcontent compatriots. They embarked on a campaign of terror against the Professor, hiding in the shadows of evening and ambushing him as he strode past on his way home. The boys would hurl all kinds of objects in his direction, including bricks, which fortunately never managed to strike him. As this was a regular practice, it was inevitable that they would eventually be caught.

Anselm's geography teacher, Professor Einleger, a particularly unattractive-looking man who went under the nickname 'Magellan', was another who suffered at the hands of my brother. Anselm did not like him at all, and 'Magellan' was well aware of this. Their differences reached a crisis point while the class was on a geography excursion, travelling by train through L'vov and further east towards the Russian border. Anselm had practised the art of leaning out of the train window and tossing a rucksack so that it flew through the window of the next carriage and landed on the window seat. On this occasion, my brother knew that 'Magellan' would be positioned in that seat, and he proceeded with the planned operation. Not possessed of a mind for covert warfare, however, Anselm had neglected to cover his tracks. He used his own readily identifiable rucksack for ammunition, and while he had scored a king-hit, he was immediately held responsible for the attack.

As Anselm descended deeper and deeper into trouble with the authorities at the Gymnasium, my parents realised that they would have to take action. They had fervently hoped that this was just a passing phase in my brother's life, but it now appeared that even if this was true, he might well damage his future irreparably. A close friend of my father's was a professor at the high school in nearby Sambor. He had a daughter of Anselm's age, and my parents felt that she might be capable of exerting a positive influence on their errant son. My brother was sent to Sambor to complete his schooling.

There must have been some improvement in my brother's attitude toward his studies: although he was forced to repeat two school years along the way, Anselm finally completed school at the age of twenty, and with surprisingly high grades. Indeed, his grades were sufficient to ensure his acceptance into the technical school in Vienna. He lived in Vienna for twelve months before my mother's uncle (and Anselm's guardian) Dr Pachtmann discovered that Anselm had not attended the school at all during that year. In fact, he did not even know where the technical school was located. To my parents' horror, they learned that he had been living the good life in Vienna on the monthly allowances sent to him by our father.

Anselm was ignominiously retrieved from Vienna and my father had him enrolled at an officers' training school in Poland. Here, yet again, my brother's insolence would prove to be his undoing. One day on the parade ground, he overheard a junior lieutenant make disparaging remarks about Jews. He stepped forward and asked permission to speak. When this was granted, he informed the officer that he was Jewish, and proceeded to accuse his superior of being an anti-Semite. When the lieutenant tried to pull rank, Anselm lunged forward and knocked him to the ground. As penance, my brother had to serve in the Polish Army for twelve months. Miraculously, he emerged intact a year later, and was sent to a technical school in L'vov. My parents had all but given up hope.

Anselm's passionate patriotism may have indicated an overwhelming urge to love something, or someone. This need was also evidenced by a continuous string of 'fiancées'. About every six months he would bring home an unattractive young woman wearing an equally unattractive (and inexpensive) engagement ring. Mother would always faint on the spot, as was her wont, but my father seemed to know that it would not last. And sure enough, six months later, there would be another.

When I was sixteen, in 1933, Anselm brought home a young girl named Helena (which by way of 'Helusia' was called 'Lusia'), and this time the engagement was for real. Lusia was nowhere near as unattractive as those who came before her and, relatively speaking, my mother took quite a shine to her. Like my brother, Lusia counted herself among the adherents of the Zionist movement, but she was also a staunch communist. By this time, my brother had abandoned *Hashomer Hatzair* for a more conservative political stance, but within a short period of time, Lusia managed to draw Anselm back to his earlier sympathies.

By the end of that year, Anselm and Lusia were married and they decided to make *aliyah*: to leave Poland and settle in Palestine. My parents were clearly shocked, particularly my mother, who perceived Palestine as a wild frontier, an uncultured backwater peopled with Philistines. But at the same time, she was pleased that there was finally a purpose in Anselm's life, and she harboured some hope that his wife would encourage him to make something of himself.

Anselm's letters had given us all the impression that he was living the good life in Palestine. When I arrived in Palestine three years later, I soon realised that this was hardly the case, and that my mother's hopes had been in vain. In fact, life had become extremely difficult for Anselm and Lusia.

Neither my brother nor his wife spoke Yiddish or Hebrew, and in the course of three years, neither had been willing to make the effort to learn. Anselm spoke Polish and German, which helped them to get by on a fundamental level, while Lusia spoke only Polish.

Anselm had found a job as an unskilled factory worker, where he worked for the first two and a half years performing various menial tasks. He earned six pounds a month, but was able to supplement this meagre wage with money sent by my father.

Despite the fact that he was once again a member of *Hashomer*, and by definition sympathetic to collectivist socialist principles, Anselm was still the son of Dr Lustig, and in his mind at least, superior to his workmates. Inevitably, the factory foreman grew tired of his arrogant behaviour and had him sacked. He would not work again for more than four years.

5 School Days

About teaching: If you are going to be any good, you have got to like the little swine.
J.R. DARLING, HEADMASTER, GEELONG GRAMMAR

I ATTENDED THE King Jagiello state school, which was located just one block away from our home, a short stroll across the park. As its name suggests, the school was based on a Polish education system, with Polish as the language of learning. Material with a pro-Polish bias formed a significant portion of the curriculum.

History records that following the revolution that swept Austria in 1848, the imperial regime reached an agreement with the Polish nobility that in effect ceded political control of Galicia to the Poles. The local Polish authority was little affected by the reforms of the 1860s that gave Galicia its provincial authority and diet (legislature). The governors appointed by Vienna were exclusively Polish aristocrats. The civil service and the major public schools, which had been Germanised in the early years of Habsburg rule, were now 'Polonized'. Following the First World War, although the Allied powers accepted the Polish annexation of Galicia on the basis of its regional autonomy, the Polish government proceeded to dismantle the remaining institutions of self-government inherited from the Habsburg period. Eastern Galicia, officially termed Eastern *Malopolska* or 'Eastern Little Poland', was administered by governors and local prefects appointed by Warsaw.

More than sixty-five per cent of my teachers were Polish, while only twenty per cent were Jewish. Most of my Jewish professors harboured support for German and Austrian, rather than Polish, culture.

Jews had been generally considered throughout eastern and central Europe as bearers of German culture. In Habsburg Galicia, Jews referred to the Austrian Kaiser Franz Josef as 'Froyim Yossel' and looked to him for protection. During the First World War, as German troops entered Jewish pockets of Polish territory, they were sometimes welcomed as cultural liberators. At home, my father had us singing 'Deutschland Uber Alles', and like so many who counted themselves among those sympathetic to the Germanic way, he suffered profoundly from *Reichschmerz* (literally 'empire grief'), the German psychological condition that arose from their defeat in World War I. Interestingly, Catholic Poles in Poland were referred to as Poles (never simply as Catholics), yet Jewish Poles were always referred to simply as Jews. It was a matter of the Poles and the non-Poles. Jews were not seen as part of the Polish nation, which explains how we were to be so easily cut adrift in the years to come.

I was a conscientious student. Each year level at King Jagiello was divided up by skill and talent. The most capable students were placed in Class A, the less capable in Class B, and so on. I was placed into Class A, though I must admit that Class A was not as intellectually acute as such a system might suggest. If a Class A student failed, he repeated the year in Class A of the following year level. The same applied for Classes B, C, and D. The repeating students in Class D were a sorry lot.

At the back of each classroom, two rows were reserved for the slow learners. This seemed paradoxical to me, for surely these students would have benefited from being placed at the front, closer to the teacher. Some of the students in the back rows had been there for two or three years, but if the fourth year came along and they had not progressed, they were removed from school.

Within the classroom, these two rows represented another world. There was no communication between them and the students at the front, and these 'backbenchers' seemed to have their own systems in place, their own way of life. From time to time we would be subjected to an outburst from their quarter. It never arose as a result of academic revelation; rather, it was usually the effect of someone cheating another at cards. In some cases, a backbencher might manage to pass, and escape to the year above, but this was not a common occurrence.

Being of small stature, like my parents, I had no inclination towards bullying. Rather, I would make my presence felt by way of wit—not overly sophisticated repartee, but wit nonetheless. This was my preferred method for getting the better of my teachers, for catching them on the back foot. I quickly gained a reputation among my fellow students for my quick retorts.

On occasion, I would receive such credit where no credit was due. Our German literature professor, Dr Mantel, was in many ways a stereotypical Jewish intellectual. He was unremarkable: average in height, in weight, in looks. He was a particularly nervous man, and this expressed itself through a series of pronounced body movements and strange facial twitches. The boys at school had dubbed him 'Dr Schmuck', which translates from Yiddish as Dr Penis. But Dr Mantel commanded respect, and no one would dare call him that to his face.

Dr Mantel had set an assignment: each of us was to read a short German novel before presenting a report before the class. My book, *Die Journalisten*, was so entirely dull that I could make little sense of it apart from the name of its protagonist—and this minor detail had implications too frightening to contemplate.

My day had arrived.

'Lustig,' Dr Mantel said, 'what about your story?'

'I don't think the class will be interested, sir,' I replied. 'I fear that I will not be able to convey it properly.'

'Nonsense. Just try.'

'Well,' I stammered, 'in this story a group of journalists band together under the leadership of one journalist.'

'So,' interrupted the Professor, 'what is his name?'

'Dr Schmuck.'

As I had anticipated, the class erupted. The other boys, laughing hysterically—some were even rolling on the floor—were marvelling at my show of daring. It was a misunderstanding on all counts, for they did not realise that I had no choice in the matter.

For a moment, I wondered whether Dr Mantel had deliberately assigned me this book, to put me in my place. I was embarrassed, and wanted the floor to open up and swallow me whole. Dr Mantel turned to me and asked, 'What is the reason for this uproar? What did you say? You must have said something.'

I could not bring myself to explain. Instead I simply continued: 'There is a Dr Schmuck and he gives direction to a group of journalists.'

More uproar.

Following this incident, my luck with Dr Mantel seemed to worsen. No doubt with suspicions firmly implanted in his mind, he began to single me out.

'Lustig,' he addressed me one day, 'do you play any musical instruments?'

'Oh yes,' I replied.

'In an orchestra?'

'Yes.'

'Perhaps you will tell me which instrument?'

'The cymbals.'

Our school orchestra featured almost every instrument known to man. We did not necessarily *perform* together, but at least we were all playing our instruments at the same time. In consideration of my musical talent, or lack thereof, the large cymbals had been allocated to me. I would wait half an hour for the maestro's signal, and then: BOOM. That was about the extent of it.

This was not Dr Mantel's idea of musical talent, however. 'The cymbals. Is that all you play?'

'Well, sir,' I explained reluctantly, 'at home, my parents are pushing me to play the violin.'

He appeared most impressed, and so I felt compelled to clarify my statement. 'I don't exactly *play* the violin, sir. In fact, I have been trying to undermine my violin teacher for years.' Indeed, whenever I prepared to practise the violin at home, my family would batten down the hatches, close all the windows and doors, and even go so far as to plug their ears with cotton wool.

This did not deter the resolute Dr Mantel. My inability to hold my tongue, to keep secret my decidedly second-rate ability to pluck a fiddle, had already sealed my fate. There was no escape.

'Lustig, I have a brief piece of music for the violin, *Heilige Nacht*, and I would like you to play it for the class. You shall perform in a month. It is a beautiful piece.'

I took the sheet music home and explained the predicament to my violin tutor. Try as he might, there was no hope of my acquiring the necessary proficiency in the time allotted, and as each tuneless scrape foreshadowed the embarrassment that lay before me, I became increasingly frustrated by my tutor's inability to perform the requisite miracle. I certainly did not want to fail in this task, for I suspected that Dr Mantel would interpret my ineptitude as a further attempt to taunt him in front of the class. This was not my intention at all.

The big day arrived, and I was instructed to stand before the class. Dr Mantel addressed the students. 'Today we will start with Lustig, who will play a beautiful piece of music that he has been practising.' From the expressions on the faces of my classmates, I could see that they were expecting some of Lustig's famous trickery, some ruse that would provide them with comic entertainment for the afternoon.

In desperation, I had devised a series of stunts that I hoped would delay the start of my performance to such an unacceptable hour that Dr Mantel would abandon it in disgust. Plan 'A' was truly lame. Plan 'B' was somewhat inspirational. There was no Plan 'C'.

Plan 'A' involved my arriving for the performance with no stand for my music. 'Perhaps,' I suggested to Dr Mantel, 'I am inconveniencing the class. I could try again next week, when I have the music stand.'

'No, no,' insisted my professor, 'carry on.'

I had to improvise, had to keep wasting time. Another student would be required to assist me with the sheet music. I selected the slowest, clumsiest oaf to step forward and hunch over in front of me with the music pinned to his back. Where were the pins? I had to find them, which took even more time, as did the process of pinning them to my human music stand. I would pin one, and then drop the rest, pick them up and repeat the procedure.

Throughout this ordeal, Dr Mantel remained inordinately patient, far too patient for my liking. Plan 'A' had not deterred him. Finally, he stepped in. 'Enough, Lustig! You will now play your piece. Place your music on a chair.'

Plan 'B' was deployed. I took hold of the violin, with all the grace I might employ in picking up an axe, and began to play. Ordinarily I would have introduced the piece of music I was about to perform. Indeed, such a formality should have been necessary, given that my appalling standard of musicianship meant that nobody in the room could have possibly recognised what it was. But an introduction was not possible—Plan 'B' relied upon the element of surprise.

With no conscious effort required on my part, the performance was truly unbearable. In a state of shock, my classmates looked to each other for some explanation. Dr Mantel's twitching brows were now in full flight, all but taking off. His face reddened. 'Stop, stop, stop!' he cried. 'What on earth are you playing, Lustig? That sounds nothing like *Heilige Nacht.*'

He was absolutely correct, of course. I was actually playing—or impersonating someone trying to play—*Eine Kleine Nachtmusik,* a considerably less technical piece of music.

'You are right, Herr Doktor,' I replied, attempting to sound hurt and bewildered by his observation. 'It is Mozart, just as you asked me to play.'

'No, Lustig,' he snorted, 'I asked you to play *Heilige Nacht*.'

'I am so sorry, Herr Doktor,' I began ruefully, 'but I understood that you wanted me to play Mozart, and I have spent *so* much time practising this piece. Had I known that you wanted me to play *Heilige Nacht*, I would have practised that. I did only what I thought you wanted.' Had I been adept at feigning a quiver of my lower lip, or at producing a small tear in the corner of my eye, I would have done so at this moment. Dr Mantel was not impressed, but my delaying tactics had borne fruit—they had carried us to the end of the lesson.

Given that most of my fellow students were wise to my antics, I assumed that this was also the case for Dr Mantel. Yet despite his stern warning that this behaviour would not be tolerated, I was never asked to play my violin again.

I continued to excel on the cymbals with the school orchestra, however, and my career as a percussionist soon flourished. At the age of fifteen I was accepted into 'Palma', an eight-piece jazz ensemble that had been established by Stanislau Wilder, the twenty-year-old son of our neighbour Dr Wilder.

Stanislau, better known as Staszek, was a student at the Polytechnic in L'vov and an exceptional musician. He played piano, saxophone, banjo, guitar and mandolin. Moreover, in order to finance his band, Staszek manufactured and sold short-wave radios. While most radios on the market at that time were able to reach the nearby European capitals—Vienna, Prague, Budapest, Rome—Staszek's radios were designed specifically to receive the jazz broadcasts from New York. Gifted with the most remarkable ear for music, he spent most of his nights in his father's stables, listening to the latest American standards and then writing out the orchestral scores. This 'home-made' sheet music business also contributed to his income.

The band's pianist Ziggy Binstock could not read a note, but did not need to because, like Staszek, he was a natural musician, blessed with the finest musical ear. Ziggy's father was a local Drohobycz photographer who won ten thousand dollars in an American lottery. His good fortune catapulted him into the Drohobycz aristocracy. One day he was photographing weddings and family portraits; the next he was specialising in model portraiture, distributing the photographs to various potentates and rulers. Perhaps his rise to fame came too quickly and easily, because soon after, he disappeared. He failed to return from a trip to Egypt where, he claimed, he was working as a photographer with a team of archaeologists. It soon became known around Drohobycz that he had actually eloped with one of his models.

I was enlisted to play drums and percusssion alongside Staszek and Ziggy, with Max Lambert on the trumpet and Gerry Galotti on the violin. We practised daily in the enormous living room of the Wilders' apartment.

Palma boasted an eclectic musical repertoire. We played a number of engagements in local restaurants and dance halls, which required us to produce two or three hours of quiet background music before switching to a number of more upbeat jazz sets after ten o'clock, when the younger set was out and about.

I had assumed that drumming and percussion would prove to be a fairly simple exercise, especially with my deft talent for the cymbals. However, playing with a professional outfit soon exposed my woeful inadequacies—never more than in our attempts to play 'La Cucaracha', which was an exceedingly popular standard during the 1930s. I could hardly hold the Latin beat in my head let alone reproduce it on the drum kit.

Despite the fact that Palma carried this ersatz drummer, we produced a good enough sound to secure an annual engagement at Truskawiec, an exclusive spa resort set in the foothills of the Carpathian Mountains. We worked through the summer holidays, earning only our food and board. These were perhaps the most enjoyable days of my youth.

Despite my role as the class entertainer, I took great pride in being a Class A student. I felt even more proud when I was approached by my Latin teacher, Professor Yedlinski, suggesting that I take up tutoring. He pointed me in the direction of two older boys at the back of the class, both seventeen years old and facing expulsion if they failed another year. He informed me that he had spoken to their parents, who were willing to pay me for my assistance. Each boy received seven hours of tutoring per week. I concentrated on teaching them subjects at which I excelled myself, rather than attempting to raise their scores across the board. At the end of the year, their moderate improvement managed to save them. In appreciation, these two strapping older boys willingly protected me against anyone who dared to intimidate me at school: a bonus payment.

This marked the beginning of my financial independence. I was fifteen, and I would continue to tutor students for the next three years. My father was pleased that I had earned the recognition of my teachers, but he was concerned that my ability to earn money would detract from my own academic performance.

This concern was further fuelled when he discovered that I had established a small but profitable business for myself trading in second-hand schoolbooks. What had begun as a tiny operation, involving only my classmates, had developed to the point where I was also buying books from the girls at the local Jewish private school—buying for a zloty, selling for two zlotys. Indeed, I had saved enough money to take a holiday in the mountains with my friend Abraham Lerner and our girlfriends, the four of us secretly squeezed into a single room. Within a short time, I was earning quite a considerable income—between 150 and 200 zlotys a month. This was perhaps even more than my own father was earning. I was never quite sure whether his outrage stemmed from, as he claimed, a fear that his own son might turn out to be a merchant rather than a professional, or from simple jealousy.

Being a Class A student, and a tutor at that, it came as a mortal blow to my ego when I was informed that I was to be transferred to Class B. The episode that triggered this action took place in my history class.

As usual, I was sitting beside my old friend Tauchner. The teacher turned to me. 'Lustig,' he said, 'who was the head of the Ukrainian government formed in L'vov in November of 1918?'

I should have been able to answer immediately, but as I paused, Tauchner leaned across and whispered the answer. Without thinking, I blurted out the name: 'Petlyura.' The entire class began to laugh—even the backbenchers recognised the stupidity of my reply. 'Petlyura?' queried the teacher in disgust. 'The War Minister? It was Petrushevych, you blockhead. Dr Petrushevych.'

I turned to Tauchner. Seeing the smirk on his face, I realised that he had set me up. We often played pranks on one another, but this dirty trick had left me seriously embarrassed before our teacher and the entire class. Dizzy with rage, I lost control and pushed him from his seat. It was that very day that I was informed of my impending transfer to Class B. Naturally, I thought that it was a punishment for my outburst.

My father was most disappointed in me, perhaps more so for not knowing the answer to the teacher's question than for attacking my friend. Yet he also felt that the punishment did not fit the crime, and he requested a meeting with the school principal, Professor Kanyousky.

The professor assured my father that the transfer had nothing to do with the incident in history class. In fact, the transfer was part of a change in school policy, a decision to mix the classes. The principal hoped that the 'brighter boys'—myself and our top Class A student, Chciuk, included—would encourage the other boys to try harder. 'We will see in a year if we have achieved any advantage,' he told my father. Subsequent years would prove that there was indeed a pedagogical benefit to mixing the classes, but from my perspective at that time, there was no benefit at all.

Regardless of what the principal had said, the move from Class A to Class B was a matter of considerable shame. It only strengthened my resolve to study even harder. For the next few months I read incessantly, which resulted in a severe case of eye strain and the need for prescribed reading glasses. Before too long, I realised that these glasses could contribute greatly to the enhancement of my intellectual persona. Ever the actor, I made sure I could be seen casually strolling the city streets with my hands folded neatly behind my back. 'Look at him, a real philosopher,' my mother would say, 'always thinking.' In reality, it had proved the perfect disguise in which to continually ponder the nature of the female form.

My matriculation examination took place in early 1935 and consisted of two parts: written and oral. My tutor, Stanislau Dubienski, was known as an *Eisenstudent*—'iron student'—because he was permanently at school. In fact, he refused to sit the final exams each year, for fear that he might pass and then be forced to do something with his life. He was a hideous fellow, with thin lips, sunken cheeks, a long hooked nose, and the eyes of a mouse. But I liked him. His great claim to fame was his mother's cooking. An invitation to dinner at Pani Dubienski's was considered one of the greatest honours in Drohobycz, and as a friend of Stanislau's I was blessed with an open invitation. Needless to say I took advantage of this, and I can attest to the fact that her food was undoubtedly the best in town. Even my own father agreed, much to my mother's vexation.

Stanislau's advice for the written part of my examination was most helpful. He instructed me to write whatever I wanted until I reached the last page, whereupon I was to conclude with something along the lines of 'Marshal Piłsudski, the hero and creator of Poland …' followed by a string of platitudes. 'The examiners will not have the patience to read all the bullshit, but they are certain to look at the last page,' he said. Oddly enough, this inspired me to write what I thought was quite a creditable essay. As instructed, I filled the last page with glowing references to Marshal Pilsudski. I received top marks.

I was accompanied into the oral examination by my Latin teacher and Class Coordinator, Professor Yedlinski. Before me sat three external examiners from the Ministry of Education. The firing squad.

'What would you consider the most romantic story in ancient Greek literature?' asked one of them.

'Orpheus and Eurydice,' I replied.

'So tell us what happened in that story.'

'Orpheus was permitted to enter the underworld to find his beloved Eurydice. And in order to save her from this land of death he wrote songs, accompanying himself on ...'

'Yes ... what instrument?'

Professor Yedlinski leant in close behind me and whispered, 'Lyre.'

I hesitated, as my mind flashed back to the incident with Tauchner. The hot flush that accompanied my disgrace that day returned, as did my memory of the far-reaching consequences of my mistake. Instinctively, I knew that my professor would not play such a joke, but almost involuntarily, I could not bring myself to speak.

'Well?' asked the examiner.

I felt beads of perspiration gather on my top lip. 'The lyre, sir.'

'Excellent,' said the examiner.

My nerves were in tatters.

'Gentlemen, I think this is enough.' In all, I had been there for less than five minutes. 'Congratulations, top marks,' he concluded. 'Send in the next boy.'

6 An Awakening

When she raises her eyelids it's as if she were taking off all her clothes.
COLETTE

LOOKING BACK, I am bemused by how quickly and seamlessly my preoccupations with boyhood games—cops and robbers, cowboys and Indians—dissolved to give way to a preoccupation with girls.

My first glimpse of the pain of infatuation came from observing Bruno Schulz, my art tutor. My mother had always harboured a somewhat deluded hope that I would develop into an artist, and my early failures to master the violin gave rise to an attempt to elicit my hidden talents with the pencil and paintbrush. While her cousin Bruno would have little more success than my violin teacher, he would nevertheless leave a lasting impression on me.

Bruno was a disciple of the ideal of love and beauty. He was the quintessential martyr, surrendering his soul to passion and nurtured by the angst of unrequited love. He worshipped the inaccessible in the form of my aunt Mila, a sensual, appealing woman who happened to be married to Moses Lustig, my father's brother. Bruno managed to impress Mila with his sketches, each depicting the bony figure of a man, wizened and bowed, beaten into submission by a world that overwhelmed him. In all of them, the downcast face was easily recognisable as his own. The only other subject for his sketches was the chamber pot, the most base of all utensils, the receptacle for human waste. These two-dimensional images of the chamber pot appeared so real that I recall experiencing the urge to piss in them myself.

The emotional longing I observed in Bruno Schulz was translated to the physical for the first time when I was about ten years of age, during my summer holidays, visiting the farm of my grandparents. It was here that I first learned about the birds and the bees.

From what I could gather, my mother's stepfather, Mr Elbaum, owned the entire village, which lay a few kilometres outside the small city of Sambor. He owned enormous areas of forest as well as the local sawmill. The trees were cut and the logs were transported along the river, channelled and sorted along the waterway which led directly into the mill. The freshly cut timber would emerge from the other side of the mill, ready for trucking. This was my first encounter with the production of building materials and watching this process would keep me absorbed for hours.

I was enthralled by country life: the squawking symphony of the animals as dawn broke, a veritable Noah's Ark; helping to tend the vegetable gardens and the orchards, collecting eggs in the morning, milking the cows.

There were so many cows, and yet only one bull. This made me wonder. One day a cow was placed in the paddock with the bull. The older boys amused themselves for a while by finding ways to annoy the bull, preventing it from mating with the cow. The mating finally ensued, providing an up-close demonstration of the facts of life.

My grandparents lived in an enormous farmhouse, which was filled with people during summer vacations. Elbaum's children from his first marriage would also spend their vacations there, and we all got along very well. Everything was so different from the city. There was a strong element of culture—the locals would arrive in the evenings to play music, accompanying the piano on guitars and mandolins.

I felt that something new and strange was happening to me in this environment. The milieu of new experiences, the fresh air, the hard work, the stuffiness of the city stripped away, and my brother's regular disappearing acts with a local girl in tow: all of this was affecting me. It was here that I began to notice the girls.

As is so often the case with young boys who suddenly become young men, my awareness of girls far preceded their awareness of me, and my hunger for the touch of their embrace remained unfed for years to come. Naturally, it was a frustrating period of my life, a time when constant rejection gave rise to a claustrophobic self-consciousness, an uncontrollable shyness, and an ever-present discomfort around young women.

With this change, this new-found appetite for romance, I began to view my friend Renata Himmel in a different light. We had been friends for as long as I could remember, and perhaps it was our casual intimacy that prompted me to imagine something more meaningful between us. Or perhaps it was simply her proximity. Whatever the case, my feelings were stirring, and in order to test the waters, at the age of fourteen I proposed marriage to her.

Our families were on holidays together in the mountains. We had an unspoken pact that we would always arrive last for lunch. It had already passed one o'clock—lunch was served at twelve-thirty and we still had the rickety old footbridge to cross before we could get there. We were running, and I suddenly stopped her. I said that I wanted to tell her something very important. When she protested that we were already late, I told her that it could not wait. I confessed my love for her, and I wanted her to remember that when we were old enough, I would marry her.

'This is what you stopped me for? This stupidity?' she said incredulously. She reminded me that we were too young to be thinking about it, and besides, since we were the same age, when we grew up I would be a boy and she would be an established woman. 'You will find *somebody*, don't worry about it,' she concluded, 'and if you do not find her, she will find you.' While I had no option but to accept her answer, I was hurt nonetheless.

My first attempts at physical contact with girls at that age were awkward and often disguised. During the winter in Drohobycz, the town's lake froze over, transforming it into a skating rink. Skating was a popular pastime among the local children, who gathered there each day after school. Cymberkiewicz, whose job was to keep the skating surface smooth, sold tea and chocolate biscuits to the skaters, as well as offering his services as a paid instructor.

Zosia Smyczek stood out from the crowd, not only because of the tight, suggestive sweater that she wore, but because each time she stood up and tried to skate, she would fall again. Clearly, she could not afford to pay for 'Cymber's' instruction. I observed her from a distance for a while before swooping down upon her like a falcon. Embarrassed and apologetic, she explained that she was trying to learn, by which time I had my hands firmly under her arms, subtly cupping her breasts while helping her up. I knew that she enjoyed this, and I would regularly offer to walk her home in the vain hope of taking this contact further. It would never eventuate.

The school for girls in Drohobycz was established by a Mr Blatt to serve the needs of parents who wanted their daughters to be raised in a Jewish environment. Ironically, while they paid considerable amounts of money for the privilege, Mr Blatt was a totally assimilated Jew who knew little about Jewish religious practice. For reasons known only to Mr Blatt, five boys—including Tauchner, Burstyn, Ziggy Binstock, Charles Wexelberg (a cousin of the Himmels), and myself—were invited to join the girls on their holiday at 'Tatra', a Jewish girls' holiday camp at Zakopane, set in the Carpathian Mountains on the Polish–Czech border. Mr Blatt's son Bob brought the number of boys to six.

Although the thought of going away to a girls' camp had excited us at first, we soon discovered that life at Tatra was inordinately dull. We could not go swimming because the lake was a day's walk away and the landscape was simply too dreary for hiking. Competitve sport among the boys was limited due to lack of numbers. Conditions were primitive and the food was largely inedible.

We were so desperate to amuse ourselves that we took to competing at the sport of drinking sour milk. We would leave about twenty glasses of milk overnight. By morning, the milk would have separated into three distinct by-products: off-white sour cream on top, which we would spoon off; a less dense, milky-white coagulated *leben* in the middle; and a misty water at the bottom. After drinking three or four glasses each, we would move on to the next stage of the competition— a race to the toilets.

Adding insult to injury, the girls wanted nothing to do with us. We were at an age where we were more than interested in a little horseplay with them, but they were at an age where they could think of nothing less appealing than pairing off with a pimply boy. And pimply adolescent boys we indeed were, resolute in our crude and awkward attempts to attract their attention. As they slept on the balcony below us, we lowered two volleyballs down to their eye level. Eliciting no response, we drew them back up, covered them with cow manure, and repeated the procedure. When one girl objected to our noisy disturbance with obvious disdain, we suggested that she cut them down herself. In the dark, she did so—and her hands were covered with manure as a result. She screamed, waking her friends and sending the group into a frenzy. It was an entirely unsophisticated and desperate stunt on our part, which served only to distance them further from us. I felt embarrassed and ashamed of my inability to come up with a more appropriate and mature approach to the girls.

I felt similarly awkward when I was invited to spend Saturday afternoons in various apartments and houses along Mickiewicza Street occupied by this or that doctor and his wife. My mother knew why I was invited: they had eligible daughters. My mother knew the system well. She was aware that she had two sons with a lot of value on the market. She had grown disillusioned with the elder son, but there was hope. Perhaps her younger son would contribute to her happiness by way of an aristocratic union.

There were three age groups present at these gatherings: fourteen to sixteen, eighteen to twenty, and girls over twenty. At fourteen, I was one of the youngest there (along with Milek Tauchner, who was not as eligible because his father was not a doctor). My job was to play the records so that the older boys and girls could dance. I noticed how they held each other. Various 'question and answer' games would be played. If somebody was not successful in the game, there was a penalty: he or she had to go into the other room. I was always being sent into the other room. Even if my question was a simple one, I was far too shy to find the words to answer. When I got there, I would remain silently self-conscious with the other exiles. I did not know what I was supposed to do or say.

After two of these parties, I promised myself that I would never go again. Two weeks later I was invited once more and my mother did not allow me to keep to my oath. Once again I was assigned the job of overseeing the music. I was too shy to dance myself. Eventually the dancing, and my job, came to an end. As usual, I was just sitting there quietly, watching the proceedings. Then a strange thing happened. Perhaps my sense of discomfort overcame me, but I suddenly felt compelled to talk. And what came out of my mouth was not just a passing comment, but an extended monologue. It concerned nothing in particular, just a story about young people in Drohobycz, fabricated as I went along. I soon sensed that I had acquired a most attentive audience, and with a kind of bootstrap effect, this encouraged me to continue. I managed to hold them captive for almost an hour and a half, and they were thoroughly entertained.

I had actually discovered my talent for storytelling many years earlier, though it had been temporarily disabled by the torments of adolescence. In fact it was Linda, the governess of the Himmel household, who first unearthed it when I was quite young. A large and broadly built German woman, Linda would tempt me over to their house with the promise of a chocolate or a biscuit. She had good reason. I would creep through a gap in the fence that stood between our properties and come into the house. I would then wind up the children's gramophone, choose a record for background music, and summon Ziggy and

Renata to hear one of my stories. They were fabricated as I went along, and I certainly could not have remembered them the following day. But they kept my audience amused for quite some time, allowing Linda to attend to other jobs around the house. She often referred to my talent as a God-sent gift.

My parents were unaware of this ability for quite some time. I was about thirteen before I had occasion to introduce it to them. It was one of many evenings when Dr Kaufman joined us for dinner. The conversation centred on politics, and for some reason, I started to participate—or to interfere with the discussion. This was most uncommon for me. My father turned to me with a smile and suggested that I should interject less because I was showing my immense lack of knowledge. He advised me that it would be more prudent to keep my ignorance to myself.

I cannot say whether it was a sense of embarrassment that prompted me. I do not recall being offended by my father's comments. Nevertheless, I went into my room and I picked up the violin. When I emerged, I began to tell them a somewhat cynical but humorous story about an old woman who found herself in a very grave political situation. To accentuate the mood of the tale, I found myself quite naturally plucking away at the violin.

Many years later I was reminded of that evening as I sat and watched the famous American comic Jack Benny perform one of his famous routines, which used the violin as a prop, much as mine had done.

The tale I wove that evening centred around the difficulties of growing old, and this woman's inability to improve her lot. My parents and Kaufman began to listen, and the moment I noticed that I had their attention, my performance improved. I felt proud that I had captured them as my audience. After about half an hour, my father stopped me.

'Why don't you tell us some more stories from time to time? But for tonight it is enough.'

I tried to interpret his use of the word 'enough'. Did I do something stupid? Was it that my father did not want me to reveal my stupidity even further? I was never sure. But I knew that the feeling of playing to an audience had excited me.

What I learned that day at the party (the one I had promised myself I would not attend) was that this talent could be used with astonishing effect in attracting the attentions of young women. It was indeed a kind of foreplay—Lustig style—and in the years to come I would sharpen the skill, augment it with intellectual knowledge and lace it with an ability to cite the scholars. I would develop it into a useful charm.

For the time being, however, there remained situations where the use of a soapbox was inappropriate, occasions when my introversion would once again come to the fore. There was the Debutantes' Ball, for example, where I was required to dance with the young women, not talk at them. My mother had worked diligently to instruct me in the 'salon dances'. At home, we would begin at the fireplace and move along the length of the lounge room. When it came to the Ball itself, however, I was bewildered. My mother urged me to invite a girl to dance, not understanding my reticence. In the absence of a fireplace, I had no idea where to start. And furthermore, the couples were dancing in circles, while I had been taught only to dance along a straight line.

With continued exposure to young women, my ongoing lack of success in their courtship became extremely frustrating, the more so because I had nobody to talk to about it, to advise me. My brother was far too old to take an interest in my social development. The only person who offered any advice at all was my tutor, Stanislau. Instinctively, I knew that his advice on how to woo a woman—to simply show 'it' to her, leave 'it' hanging proudly out of my pants—was ill-founded and highly inappropriate.

I was faced with my defeat not only in public, but in my own home as well. One afternoon, I innocently wandered into the kitchen to find my brother Anselm rolling around the floor with one of our maids. My first thought was that they were fighting, and I moved closer in order to intervene. When they screamed, in unison, ordering me to leave, I suddenly realised what I was seeing. Concern for their well-being was replaced by jealousy of my brother.

In an attempt to meet more girls, away from the influence of my mother, I agreed to accompany my friend Abraham Lerner to a meeting of a Jewish youth group in Drohobycz. Abraham had recently joined this movement of young Zionists, but he would not stay with them for long. Soon his sympathies would turn to communism. It was the presence of girls rather than any ideological sympathies that had prompted *my* decision to attend, and accordingly, I judged the merits of this group by the physical attributes of the gathered young women in the room. I was bitterly disappointed and disillusioned by this collection of thickset heifers, who sported legs that would have more suitably supported a piano. I glumly wondered if all Jewish girls were as unattractive.

It was with great and appreciative surprise, therefore, that I met my first girlfriend, Suza Brenner. I was sixteen. Abraham and I were playing chess at my house when he told me that he was late for a meeting with his girlfriend Tesha, and he could not keep her waiting any longer. It was already getting dark. Then he mentioned that she had a good friend with her, and that perhaps I should meet her.

We met them outside the Himmel place. As we approached, I was immediately struck by Suza's beauty. She was fine-featured with long, dark brown hair pinned to shoulder length, soft green eyes framed by long dark lashes, and a childlike smile that revealed her pearly white teeth. At fourteen, she was slim but mature in her figure, with long lean limbs. A Jewish girl with fantastic legs! I could not help wondering how it was possible that I had never seen her before.

I flushed as we were introduced. I was tense, though I always felt tense around girls. But she was completely relaxed and so easy to converse with. Abraham and Tesha soon took their leave and we started walking in the other direction.

Abraham had met Tesha through the Young Communist movement, and Suza also counted herself among its members. In fact, Abraham had instructed Suza to recruit me. Abraham's elder brother was being held in one of Marshal Piłsudski's labour camps. There was an assumption by many right-wing Polish nationalists that communism was a Jewish 'disease', and in fact many Jews *were* attracted to communism. The Polish communists were so persecuted at the time that they organised themselves into tiny secretive cells of ten to twelve people as part of an underground party apparatus.

Suza's appointed task in the party, upon Abraham's direction, was to recruit students like me from the middle class to build a front against Fascism. The Stalinists saw the likes of me as one of the patriotic bourgeoisie. Consequently, Suza and I spent much of our first date arguing about communism. Even at the age of fourteen, she was extremely erudite and persuasive, quoting long passages from Marx's *Das Kapital*. I was somewhat bewitched, for the first time a victim of someone else's volubility. Suza's various well-intentioned philosophies made me laugh, yet in her presence, I began to take an interest in the 'poor people'.

We continued to see each other and a solid friendship developed, one which would quickly turn to romance. While I developed some sympathy for her ideology, she began to enjoy the benefits of capitalism that came with being my girlfriend. She remained a devoted communist, but her lectures on class struggle and surplus value became less frequent. Her father, Chaim Brenner, was a mechanic, and the family struggled to eke out a living. When I brought Suza home to meet my family, she was amazed by the luxury of our lifestyle.

'Do you like this girl, Tedek?' asked Grandmother Kuhrmärker.

'Oh yes, Grandmother.'

'And have you seen her naked?'

'Why, Grandmother?'

She took my hand and cupped my fingers.

'If you can get your hands to fit over her breasts, just like this, that is how to tell if she is the right girl. If her breasts are not too small, and not too big, but fit nicely into your hand, then she is the girl for you.'

Decent advice was hard to find in Drohobycz.

Over the next three years, I would spend almost all my spare time with Suza. In summer we would go swimming at the local pool; take picnics in the fields outside town; pick berries and mushrooms in the forests. We even took holidays together in the mountains, at Karpate or Zakopane with Abraham and Tesha. It was a wonderful time, but it was not all clear sailing.

All of our friends were striving for social acceptance at this time; we all wanted to be popular. Sensing that I was the jealous type, and being young, Suza would play on my weakness. She had a very friendly and playful character and she would often flirt with other boys. I was extremely sensitive to this, and inevitably I would instruct her to 'behave, or else'. To my amazement, she behaved. But I felt that I had to assume the position of seniority within this relationship, to lead by example when it came to behaviour, to studiousness, to the rejection of frivolities. In this, my mother thought that Suza's influence on me was a positive one. In fact, my motives were not to better myself, but to set an example that might limit Suza's exuberance.

Despite my efforts, and despite our romance blossoming to a greater level of intimacy during the following winter, my feelings of suspicion and doubt would continue to overpower my trust for Suza. Perhaps these insecurities were born of my naïvety when it came to relationships with girls, or were simply a result of the intense hormonal activity of the teenage body. Whatever the cause, they imbued me, in an almost violent fashion, with a constant need to make love with Suza— anytime, anywhere. Perhaps it was a supreme effort to claim her, once and for all, as my own. Unable to grant her the benefit of the doubt, unable to allay my deepest fears, it was an effort that was bound to fail.

Suza and I were together until the time came for me to leave Drohobycz, to pursue my education further. I would return, but our relationship would not last the distance. Indeed, my two-year absence further exacerbated my suspicions. Perhaps I was mistaken about Suza, but this was my first intimate relationship with a woman. My awakening manhood generated feelings that were powerful, confused, and confusing. And mistakes are par for the rocky course of first love.

7 Hard Times

People don't ever seem to realise that doing what's right is no guarantee against misfortune.
WILLIAM MCFEE

AROUND 1930, WHEN I was thirteen years old, I began to notice that profound changes were occurring around me. A dark cloud had descended upon my family. In my perception, this seemed to coincide with the death of my mother's stepfather, Mr Elbaum.

As usual, we spent the summer holidays at the family farm in Sambor. However, on this occasion, with Grandfather Elbaum having fallen gravely ill, the harmony and good cheer that had once characterised these family gatherings seemed to have deteriorated, giving way to a profound discord. I was young and generally excluded from the adult conversations, but through my curiosity and my inclination for detective work, which often involved nothing more than simple eavesdropping techniques, I was able to ascertain that my grandfather's illness had given rise to a new set of family issues. Proposals concerning the future of the farm, the sawmill, the confectionary, and the rest of my grandfather's assets caused heated arguments and constant bickering.

A divide was emerging between those who were blood relatives and those who were not. While Grandfather Elbaum was deeply in love with my grandmother, she was not the biological mother of his children, and perhaps they resented the idea of her entering into the equation. As a thirteen-year-old, I took little interest in matters of the economy, but in hindsight, the collapse of Wall Street the previous October and the resulting world depression must have aggravated financial tensions as well as the passion with which these family arguments were being fought. Suffice it to say, following the old man's death, we had little to do with his family and we never visited the farm again. From my point of view, an idyllic world that had nurtured me from boyhood through to manhood was gone forever.

This episode ushered in a sad and difficult period for my family. At home, I began to notice small, subtle signs that my own parents were suffering from hardship. There was my father's frustration whenever my mother returned from the Rynek with yet another purchase, no matter how small; his increasing irritation when told of various business deals that provided his fellow lawyers with significant financial windfalls; his competition with Dr Hahn for Mrs Himmel's accounts. The fire in my mother's eyes was beginning to fade. Those smiling eyes that so endeared her to everyone were suddenly looking weary and tired.

There was such a difference between my parents in terms of their values, interests, education. I realised that my mother could not bear the thought that she had married a professor of law who had the potential to build a fortune, but chose not to do so. Over the course of the next few years, as these difficult times descended, this issue began to have an effect on their marriage.

On countless occasions I heard my mother complain. My uncle, Shimon Lustig, was my father's partner at the firm. Mother had taken the time to investigate the company books—the expenditure on Shimon, compared with the expenditure on my father—and had discovered that while my father was in the club playing chess, or bridge, Shimon was attending to the clients and eventually securing them for himself. My father had found the clients initially, but was not making the necessary effort to retain them.

Those clients my father did bother to retain were the very people who could not afford to pay him. It was not unusual for such a client to come knocking on the door of our home at seven o'clock in the morning, with tears rolling down his cheeks. 'I'm sorry, Dr Lustig, but they have come to my house and they are taking away all my furniture.'

My father would accompany the client to his house, hand the creditors some money, and then hand the client some money. Upon his return, my exasperated mother would ask, 'Did you lend them money?'

'Of course I lent them money,' he would reply, 'and they will pay me back when they can.'

There were times when I felt that my mother believed she had made a mistake marrying my father. Dr Samuel Lustig was an intellectual, a professor, a gentleman, a reader of Roman writers and historians.

He very much enjoyed conversations on this subject. His interests lay in the theoretical, not the practical world of wheeling and dealing for a dollar, or 'schmoozing' with colleagues and clients. Indeed, he would have been far better off with a very rich wife. But he was madly in love with my mother, and this made life even more difficult for her. She was aware of his unfailing devotion, but she also began to realise that this was hardly sufficient for her. She was saddened by his refusal to put more time and effort into the business, the only means of providing her with the kind of lifestyle she felt was her due.

Each year, Mrs Himmel would take her vacations travelling through Northern Italy or France. With our vacations on the farm now a thing of the past, I would spend school holidays with Mother. Father would visit us, usually on the weekends. Twice a year we would head to the same spot, often Karpate or another mountain resort close by. Occasionally we would travel as far as Rügen, an island off the north-eastern part of Germany, west of Gdansk. The summers on the Baltic Sea were rather wintry experiences. The sun rarely shone, but we sat on the beach every day anyway. We would eat schnitzels and potatoes day in, day out. I was extremely bored on these holidays, but I participated nonetheless. I had no money for entertainment. Each year I was told by my father, 'I have no money to give you to take on your vacation.'

I was concerned about my parents, to the extent that a boy of fifteen could take such an interest. I could sense that something was missing from their lives together. As a young boy with my life still before me, I was unable to identify what it was, but in time I would recognise that my parents' dreams, and their confidence in their abilities to achieve their goals, were gone. I did not have the courage for a direct conversation with them about these matters.

During the summer, I would collect my father each evening at six o'clock and we would take a walk. These were the most fantastic opportunities to exchange ideas and to learn something from him. Our conversations never broached the personal, however. They were restricted to theoretical matters. My father would extol the virtues of the Roman legal system, the strengths of German culture. I had always been impressed with the vast areas of the political map that were shaded pink, signifying the control of the British. So I would counter his arguments, drawing reference to the almighty British Empire, its imperial successes, the cleverness of its conquests, its parliamentary system, the *Magna Carta*.

'Thank God for the bloody British,' I would say, unaware of how my feelings towards the British had evolved into a loyalty.

'Have you ever heard any decent piece of music of English origin?' he would counter.

My father thoroughly enjoyed spending this time with me, and although he never mentioned it, I started to feel that he came to expect my arrival each afternoon and would wait for me at the office at this hour. While these carefree rendezvous with my father became less frequent as I grew older, as I began to spend more time with Suza and our friends, they represented something special to me. A mature and more substantial bond was established between us.

Two months after my matriculation, in late 1935, I received confirmation that I had been accepted into the University of Vienna to study medicine. This had been my ambition for as long as I could remember. On my twelfth birthday, my father had presented me with a book, *Hunters of Microbes,* by d'Krief. When I began to read it, I became fascinated, so absorbed that I could not put it down. I decided then that I wanted to study medicine. Later that year, my father purchased a microscope (not a child's toy, but a genuine model), and almost everything I could lay my hands on was prepared for observation on a glass slide. By the time I was seventeen, I had decided to become a surgeon. Like my father, I would be a highly respected 'Dr Lustig'.

Not only had I taken an intense interest in medicine, but I was also keen on the prospect of attending the University of Vienna. This was partly due to the famous work of Sigmund Freud, but also because of my mother's fond reminiscences of my birthplace. The university course would take six years, with two additional years of specialisation.

I would never make it to Vienna. Once again, forces far greater than myself would blow my life off course, sending me in a completely unexpected direction, to a destination for which I was hardly prepared. I would land in Palestine.

Hitler's Nazis had been in power in Germany for two years. Within two months of coming to power in January of 1933, on a platform of hatred that denounced Jews, bolsheviks, capitalists and the Versailles Peace Treaty, a Nazi campaign of terror against Jews was stepped up. Jewish-owned shops were closed down, Jewish professors were expelled from universities, and school textbooks were amended to include 'racial science'. In July of 1934, Austrian Nazis assassinated Chancellor Engelbert Dollfuss in an attempted *coup d'état*. While the coup proved unsuccessful, crushed by Dollfuss supporters, the domestic political situation remained highly volatile.

Throughout Europe, from France to Bulgaria, Fascist and anti-Semitic parties and movements were on the rise, becoming more brazen as each day passed. Poland was certainly not immune. The quasi-Fascist Rydz-Shmigly government, which came to power during 1935, had little regard for the Jews, other than in its collaboration with Zionist Revisionists to encourage mass Jewish emigration from Poland to Palestine.

Signs of this changing political mood were emerging all around me. There was a certain pointedness in the attitudes of many of my schoolteachers, and my peers seemed to be adopting a similar stance. I noticed this most profoundly on the soccer field. Perhaps this competitive environment elicited the worst of it. I played for a Jewish team at the time and it was soon obvious that our matches against the Catholic teams were becoming more aggressive, with anti-Semitic slurs flying ever thicker and faster.

As Jews, we knew only too well that such ugly developments had often waxed and waned through recent history. Nevertheless, my father had decided that the risk was too great to send me to Austria, the land of Hitler's birth, particularly since the medical course would commit me to staying there until 1941 at the very earliest. 'Anything could happen,' he explained. 'It would be madness for you to go. Europe is no place for Jews right now.'

There were few alternatives for me. While we knew of a number of local boys who had been sent to study at the University of London, this option was unavailable to us. The course fees and living costs were well beyond my family's means. Such was also the case for America. We discussed the matter, but it soon became apparent to me that my father had already found the solution. He had arranged for me to be sent to Haifa in Palestine, to study engineering. I was shattered.

All my life I had had this dream of being a doctor, a famous surgeon. Now suddenly I was to be a civil engineer—just a builder.

Palestine was not only out of Europe, but my brother was there. There was no medical faculty at the Hebrew University in Jerusalem, and my father felt that civil engineering and architecture were the next best options. And he could afford the three pounds a month that it would cost to live in Palestine.

Admission to the Haifa Technion was nowhere near as complex a process as admission to the medical school at the University of Vienna. My father had simply sent a letter stating his desire for me to study there, along with ten English pounds enclosed for the fees. Upon receiving news of my acceptance, he had arranged for a series of private tutors to help me improve my knowledge in the necessary subjects. Prior to my departure in September of 1936, I would take crash courses in drafting and English, along with refresher courses in mathematics and physics.

Mother burst into tears. Palestine was certainly not a part of the plans she harboured for her younger son. I discovered that this was not the first time that life in Palestine had loomed as an option for my family. A friend of my father's, a lawyer, had attempted to entice him to join him there during the early 1920s.

This lawyer had arrived in Jerusalem in 1921, where he proceeded to study Ottoman law. Within a year of passing his bar examination, he had become a judge, earning a considerable income. He wrote to my father, suggesting that a move to Palestine could help him to fulfil his professional ambitions. My father considered it seriously before raising the issue with my mother. She would not allow it. 'Never in my life,' she had exclaimed. 'If you want to go, you go. My sons and I will never go to that place.'

While my mother's concerns for me centred around the lack of culture and comfort that awaited me in my new home, the regional conflicts that were taking place in British Palestine lent some support to her reaction to my father's decision. Many young European Jews had chosen to migrate to Palestine since the end of the First World War, when the signing of the Balfour Declaration in 1917 committed Lloyd George's government to the establishment of a Jewish national homeland. The influx of Jews in subsequent years elicited a violent reaction from the Arab population, and by 1929 the British were forced to declare martial law in the face of clashes between the two populations. Throughout the 1920s and early 1930s, Arab political organisations lobbied successive British governments, with varying degrees of success, to limit the arrival of Jews into Palestine.

Between 1932 and 1935, the Jewish population of Palestine doubled. This was fuelled by European anti-Semitism, but was also encouraged by Palestine's High Commissioner, Sir Arthur Wauchope, a champion of the idea of a Jewish nation. The violence soon escalated. Jewish farms were raided at night, their crops and cattle destroyed, their occupants murdered. Many Zionist groups responded in kind. Over the next six months, hundreds of casualties were reported. Accompanying this spate of violence, a national strike of Arab workers and businesses was called.

My own emigration to Palestine was made easier because my brother Anselm was already living there. Shortly before my departure in 1936, I learned that tensions had soared once again with the outbreak of a short-lived but bloody uprising that became known as the Arab Revolt. It had begun with the murder of two Jews on a bus. The following night, two Arabs were killed in retaliation.

This was where I was going to escape the dangers of Nazism. I was moving from one part of the world where rulers and undecided borders changed with dizzying rapidity into another part of the world that seemed very much like it. My mother felt that I was in danger if I went to this unknown place. For her, it would have been better for me to stay at home in Drohobycz among the people with whom I was familiar. Better the devil I knew ...

Suza received the news of my departure quite well. For the past year she had been expecting me to go to Vienna, so from her perspective the sudden change in plans was hardly a change at all. Indeed, it was going to be easier for her to follow me to Haifa than to Vienna, and we agreed that when she finished her schooling, that is exactly what she would do.

In September of 1936, I bade my parents farewell and left Drohobycz for Palestine. There were no tears on my part. I had a return ticket in my pocket, and my father had told me that if six months in Palestine were unbearable, I had the option to return.

I felt for my parents, however. The last few years had been difficult, and I wondered how their marriage would fare now that both of their children were gone. I had learned to look after myself, having gained some level of financial independence through my tutoring and my book trading, and no longer saw my parents as the most powerful and influential forces in my life. My father's greatest pleasure was beating me at chess, and my mother ... well, there was a bright and energetic eighteen-year-old girl hiding somewhere behind her saddened eyes and her weary smile.

I knew that I would see them again, but I did not know precisely when.

8 Across the Seas, Another World Away

Le sort fait les parents, la choix fait les amis.
(Fate chooses your parents, you choose your friends.)
Abbé Jacques Delille

WHEN A YOUTH leaves his father's house, he returns a man. *If* he returns. And, I might add, if he leaves of his own volition. It would be the first time I had left home on my own, and I should have been excited about the prospect of embarking on a journey —liberated at last from the shackles of childhood and watchful eyes—into the unknown. Had it been my own choice to leave, perhaps an unbridled enthusiasm would have taken hold and propelled me headlong into a future ripe with possibilities. But somehow, the fact that I was being forced to go to Palestine dampened my sense of adventure and transformed a delicious rite of passage into a profound anxiety.

So, too, did the lack of fanfare surrounding my departure. There may have been other passengers waiting to depart Drohobycz station that day, but I certainly did not notice them. Under the gloomy cover of early morning, the four of us stood alone and forlorn on the station platform, which was desolate to the point of being surreal.

Father was weary, Mother distraught, Suza detached. I simply felt uncomfortable, painfully conscious of my ignorance of what to say or how to behave in such a situation. I soon sensed that I was not alone in my discomfort—everyone was searching for something appropriate to say. What ensued was an awkward display of politeness, more remarkable for what was not said than for the few meagre sentences we exchanged.

'I cannot believe you are really going,' Mother said finally, her bosom heaving dangerously, a lone tear rolling down her cheek. 'What if we never see you again?'

'Don't worry about Tedek,' Father emphatically assured her, and perhaps himself. 'I have *complete* confidence in him.'

My mother attempted another route. 'Make sure that you eat properly, and write to us every month,' she implored, her voice laced with that distinctive maternal supplication with which every youth is all too familiar.

It was the wrong choice. I felt the annoyance bubble up inside me. I was nineteen years old, about to leave my home and country, and did not appreciate being addressed like a child. I was also aware that unless I chose my words prudently, I too risked being overcome by the gravity of my fears. What to say in response?

'Don't cry,' I replied coolly, straining to maintain a façade of bravado, mostly for the benefit of Suza. 'After all, this is not a funeral. And I have got a return ticket, you know.'

The dreadful silence returned.

The train was late, prolonging this painfully arduous scene. I was suddenly overwhelmed with the feeling that I would look back on this moment as a decisive ending to a period of my life. I felt little sentimentality; rather, the conviction ushered in an acute anxiety, a rush of impatience. I desperately wanted this chapter to end, to move onto the next. When the train finally arrived, it took every inch of my resolve to force myself towards my seat. This was not because of any reluctance to leave my loved ones huddled together on the barren platform, but the acute embarrassment I felt boarding the carriage clearly marked 'Third Class'. I had always tried to maintain an air of affluence in Suza's presence, and she would surely notice this obvious demotion.

Slowly, almost excruciatingly so, the train pulled out of the station. A bend in the tracks immediately directed us to the left, allowing me no opportunity to look back. The train rattled on, and I sat silently by the window watching my familiar past fly by.

My father had expressed a confidence in my ability to survive on my own. I wished that I could have shared his conviction. Strangely, as the train moved forward and I sat on the cusp of this brand new life, I found myself recalling my first encounter with my own mortality.

I was ten years old and we were visiting Grandfather Elbaum's farm. As a rule, I awoke very early in the mornings during these sojourns in the countryside. I knew that I had two precious hours before I would be called for breakfast, and so I would make a beeline down to the river to play.

A channel approximately three metres wide veered away from the main waterway toward the sawmill. The trees that were logged from my grandfather's acres of forest were floated down this channel toward a line of vertical saws. A popular game among the children of the area was to pretend to be Admiral of the Navy, to gather small pieces of wood as an armada, and attempt to navigate them successfully through the line of saws without them being sunk. The admiral with the fewest casualties was the winner.

One morning, I headed down toward the channel to organise my fleet. Another local boy had seen me leave the farmhouse and had followed me there. It was a declaration of war. The contest was on. This other young admiral began floating his armada toward the saws from the opposite bank of the channel. I was suddenly struck by a tremendous idea. A number of logs were heading down the channel, and I reasoned that it would be to my tactical advantage if I could divert the monstrous logs across the strait to intercept his ships. It was a risky strategy, but one which, if successful, would prove me to be a fearless conqueror. I found a long stick and made my way onto the narrow footbridge that crossed over the channel. I leaned over the bridge to improve my leverage and began poking vigorously at the logs.

Before I knew it I was in the water. I was swept past the bridge and the currents were drawing me ever closer to the line of saws. For the first time in my life, I felt complete terror. The saws were wild animals before me, their razor-sharp teeth ready and waiting to devour my hapless form and spit my remains out the other side. Panic-stricken, I thrashed through the water, my arms and legs flailing uncontrollably as I tried to reach the bank or find something to buffer myself against the current. All other sound was drowned out by the ceaseless gnashing of the saw teeth, intermingled with the hysterical laughter of my not-so-worthy adversary.

Within just a few metres of the saws and my certain doom, I spied a lifeline. A small branch protruded from the bank within arm's reach. I made a desperate lunge and managed to grasp hold of the slender limb. Praying it would not snap, I dragged myself out of the perilous waters. My heart pounded wildly as I lay on the bank, terrified, not daring to move. I don't know how long I lay there, wet, bedraggled but alive.

A shadow fell over me. I looked up at the hulking form above.

'Why are you wet? What on earth have you been doing?'

demanded the very large woman who was now standing over me blocking out the sunlight.

My mother had sent one of the village women to find me. I lay in the grass, silent and unresponsive. I was not at all inclined to explain the situation to her. Besides my obvious shame, what could she know about armadas, the dangers of warfare, or death on the high seas? She lifted me roughly to my feet and dragged me by the scruff of the neck back to the house.

When Mother asked me what happened, I was more forthcoming. But my bravery in the face of such terrible adversity seemed to escape her. At that moment, she behaved less like the mother of an admiral and more like a mere mother. I was very disappointed.

'You're not going out today,' was her all too facile response. 'Do you realise what could have happened to you?'

Well, of course I knew, I knew even better than she did. But I had also learned that I had the inner fortitude and the agility to escape desperate situations. I had saved myself.

That knowledge returned to me as I sat on the train, heading for a foreign land on my own, the perils of which I knew nothing. As a child, I understood the sawmill experience to be about survival and the acceptance that there were things in the world that would have to be survived. As a man, the greater realisation was that it was all too easy to be swept aside by forces greater than myself.

In L'vov, I changed trains for Constanta, the Black Sea port in Romania from which my boat would depart for Palestine. On the locomotive, in bold letters, was written *Policja Polska*, alerting us all to the fact that this train was Polish property—a final reminder of my provenance.

I was joined by a number of boys who were also heading to Haifa to study at the Technion. Koch was my age, a diminutive fellow with a decidedly hostile manner. His father was an accountant in L'vov. I learned that he had already spent a year in Haifa, and had returned to L'vov for his holidays to see his family. Naturally, I was curious to know about my new home and I set about interrogating him about our destination.

'So, what's Haifa like?' I asked him.

'It's all right,' came the offhand reply.

'And the Technion? What do you think of it?'

'It's all right.'

Clearly, Koch was not one for small-talk.

'Is it a good school?' I persisted.

'You are new? Well, you'll just have to see for yourself, won't you?'

I was stunned by his bad manners. I decided immediately that I did not like him. I sat back in my seat and observed this oaf in action. As he spoke with his friends, I quickly discovered his Achilles heel. Koch felt painfully inferior. He would recount a story and then burst into an hysterical laugh that loudly demonstrated the required audience response, but in the process all but killed the punchline. So there was Koch, laughing like a madman at some joke to which only Koch was privy. It was a disturbing sight.

His friend Leder was a perfect snob, even less approachable than Koch. But unlike his insecure friend, Leder was blessed with a superiority complex so complete that it permeated his every action. He was a horribly opinionated young man who compensated for his own less-than-average height by holding his head unnaturally high and looking down his substantial nose at others as a matter of course. His father was a prominent lawyer in L'vov, and he made sure this was a well-known and deeply appreciated fact. When I dared to speak with him, I had the distinct impression that at best, he was merely tolerating my presence.

There was another boy with them, who afforded me no opportunity at all to converse with him. He simply ignored me. It took little time for me to realise that this group of Jewish boys on the train were all from wealthy, bourgeois families, and they openly exuded a self-indulgent, exclusionist attitude. I supposed that they considered me a small-town boy from Drohobycz. While I apparently had little to offer them, they certainly had little to offer me. Consequently, I treated them all with an air of indifference—except for Leder, who I felt at least had some substance, and for whom I developed an active distaste.

The train to Constanta travelled an almost ramrod-straight route through the endless cornfields of Romania. As far as the eye could see, there was nothing but one continuous golden carpet. I saw tall stems, each one rooted to the spot, at the mercy of Mother Nature to ensure reproduction. The words of Stanislau Dubiensky, my matriculation tutor, suddenly came back to me: 'Everything revolves around the female reproductive organ. People kill each other for it.' Would I be at the mercy of Mother Nature? I thought of Suza, and wondered how I would fare without her.

Suza had been quiet and reserved at the station, where her behaviour was undoubtedly influenced by my parents' presence. What concerned me, however, was the nature of our exchange the previous evening. From my perspective, our farewell should have been somewhat melodramatic, but Suza seemed not at all emotional about my departure. Being young and egotistical, I had wanted to see weeping, a demonstration of distress with an appropriate level of lament. Reasoning that such an ardent response from Suza would be evidence of her true feelings, I had prepared for such a concentrated display. But my expectations had turned out to be the work of an extravagant imagination, and totally unjustified. She appeared coolly indifferent, almost detached. I was disappointed, and her lacklustre performance fed my suspicions about the sincerity of her feelings for me.

The train arrived at the port of Costanta, where we stayed overnight in very ordinary accommodation. The ocean voyage took two days and two nights, during which I learned unequivocally that I did not have the stomach to be a sailor. The shared cabin that my fare allowed was on the lowest deck, indeed in the very bowels of the vessel, and was far too grim to occupy. A bucket was my best friend during the first dreadful night. I would vomit each and every time I tried to lie back on my bunk. By the second night I had discovered a more sanitary method of travelling the seas. Despite the crisp night air, I slept outside on deck. It did little to allay my illness, but I stayed close to the railings so that I could simply lean over as the urge took me and surrender the regurgitated second-rate galley fare to the sea where it belonged.

At five o'clock the following morning, the boat docked at Haifa's port. In a semiconscious state, suffering from a not-so-half-hearted nausea, I opened my eyes and glanced past the ship's railing toward the wharf. In the dark just before the dawn I thought I saw a dozen or more people on the wharf, with dark brown faces, their bodies wrapped in unshapely garb, carrying what seemed to be oversized bundles on their heads. It was a scene from the Bible—Slaves in Egypt. As I sank, exhausted, back into my slumber, I wondered whether this textbook image of the ancient Middle East was real, or simply a trick of my feverish imagination, a dream born of seasickness and my apprehensions about arriving in such a foreign land.

I woke, this time to a glorious sunrise. Before me stood the city of Haifa, its simple sandstone structures suddenly and brilliantly illuminated as the first rays emerged from the confinement of majestic Mount Carmel, which loomed large over the city and surrounds. A watchful sentinel, the mountain served as an awesome backdrop for Haifa's transformation in the early light into an artist's rendering of breathtaking beauty.

I looked back to the wharf below. There, in the clear light of day, were the people of my dream made real, and seeing their predicament shook me roughly awake from my reverie. They were Bedouins clothed in traditional robes, packages perched precariously on their heads, plodding in step with each other like some ancient chain gang. Beside them, unencumbered by such perilous headwear, stood their master, cocky and sure, wielding a whip. A sickening *crack* periodically split the peace of the dawn air, the auditory accompaniment to my first vision of Haifa.

My senses were assailed by the beauty of a Holy Land dawn, which quickly dissolved into the sheer horror of this biblical pageant in which slavery appeared alive and well. This was the reality of life in Haifa and it was hauntingly cruel.

'Oh my God,' I silently panicked, 'what have I done?' I quickly reached across my chest to the breast pocket in which my return ticket was safely nestled. I patted it to reassure myself.

Part II

ISRAEL

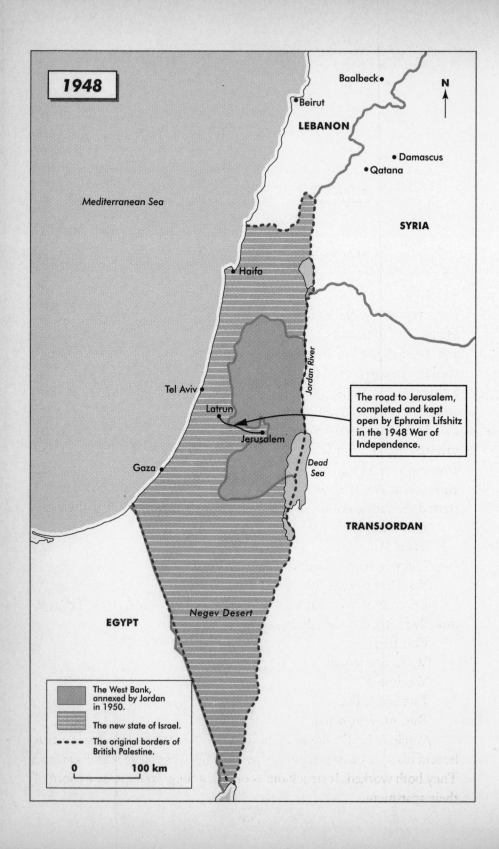

9 Life in the Holy Land

I have not found so great faith, no not in Israel.
St Matthew 8:10

I WAITED FOUR hours before my number was called to disembark at Haifa. The immigration post was enclosed with a barbed wire fence, and I spied my brother on the other side. Anselm waved to me. I couldn't take my eyes off him—he looked so odd, dressed in shorts and a singlet, with flimsy sandals on his feet. In Europe we had all been attired in crisp suits, as I was dressed now.

The paperwork finally dispensed with, I made my way gingerly towards the familiar face. Anselm greeted me in Polish. It was not an emotional reunion. I was exhausted, and my talkative brother chatted enthusiastically as if we were resuming a conversation that we had started yesterday, not the three years for which we had been separated.

'How are you, Tedek?' he asked me.

'Tired.'

'Did you see the Bedouins?'

'Yes. Very strange. It's so hot here, Anselm.'

'Of course it is. Palestine is hot. You'll get used to it. Let's go directly to my flat. Or rather, our flat.'

'Our flat?'

'We have a tenant.'

'You lease?'

'Part of the flat.'

'But, Anselm, why?'

Anselm's letters home had given my parents the impression that he and his wife Lusia were enjoying a comfortable lifestyle in Palestine. They both worked. It struck me as odd that they would lease a room of their apartment.

'Don't ask questions,' he replied curtly. 'When you have been here for a while, you will understand. You'll understand everything. Nothing is complicated, just a little unusual—the way people live here.'

He led me away from the port and onto the street, where we boarded an overcrowded bus. The vehicle was old and decrepit, its chassis eaten away by the salty sea air. The intrusively loud conversations between the passengers who sat, stood and leaned wherever they could blended into a cacophony of foreign sounds as the bus began to weave its way up the slopes of Mount Carmel. I wondered how well I would fit into this alien world as my mother's words returned unbidden to me: 'an uncivilised place, home to the Philistines'.

Anselm turned to me. 'Here we are,' he said, 'home.'

I picked up my bag and dutifully followed my brother home.

Anselm's small, shabby two-bedroom apartment was situated in an area known as *Hadar Carmel*. I would soon learn that one's address on Mount Carmel reflected social standing. The wealthiest people in Haifa lived on top of the hill, in the suburb of *Har HaCarmel*. Anselm lived in the area directly below this.

'You see,' he remarked as we entered the apartment, 'we have a common kitchen. We share it with the tenant. The amount of water we each use has to be equal.'

'Why?'

'Tedek, you will soon find out that we have everything here in Haifa … everything, that is, except water.'

'I did not see any trees here either, or grass,' I remarked, rather belligerently.

'Of course not. But that is because of the water. This is where you are going to sleep,' he said, pointing to the kitchen floor. There was no mattress, no pillows, no blankets. Just the hard floor.

'The tiles are laid on a mixture of sand and cement, which is very expensive because of the price of the sand,' Anselm continued.

'But this whole country is sand.'

'Ah, yes, but they use a *special* kind of sand.'

I sensed that my brother was going to keep chatting away about the special sand and anything else that came to mind unless I stopped him. I was exhausted, my mind whirling, and I felt the urgent need to cut our conversation short. 'Anselm, I have to lie down.'

I slept as soon as my head hit the floor. When I awoke several hours later, my entire body was trembling violently. I was covered in perspiration, and when Anselm took my temperature, the thermometer read forty degrees.

'Anselm, I think I am dying.'

'No, no, Tedek. Don't worry, you're not dying. This is just a kind of welcome. You have been attacked by the bug, and it has laid you out cold on the floor. An invisible bug that we call the Palestine bug.'

An invisible bug? This did nothing to allay either my terror or my symptoms, a fact not lost on Anselm. He could see that I was frightened, and softened his bedside manner a little.

'Look, in the worst case—and I cannot see why you should be subjected to the worst case—when you reach a temperature of forty-one, you are finished. Frankly, Tedek, I suffered the same condition when I arrived. So did Lusia. Don't worry about it, just go to sleep.'

'Should I eat something?' I meekly enquired.

'No. You will just throw it up, so why should I waste the food?'

I spent the next forty-eight hours on the kitchen floor, completely immobile. I remember little through this stupor, except for my sister-in-law Lusia's greeting. 'Oh, hello,' she said, looking down on my supine form. 'You must be Tedek. I remember you from about two years ago.'

My only other encounter during those awful days was with the tenant, a heavyset fellow with glasses, and with a sea of perspiration flowing down his legs. I remember the sweaty limbs quite clearly because I was viewing him from a prone position on the floor. It was night, and I was worried that he would not see me there. Had he stepped on me I had no doubts that I would have been crushed under his formidable bulk. Unable to muster the strength to speak, I simply groaned, and hoped that this would alert him to my presence.

After two days in this condition I comforted myself with the thought: 'I have a return ticket. I am going home. This is a crazy country.'

By the end of the second day, my fever had broken, giving way to a fit of temper I thought quite justifiable. I hadn't been prepared for this, and now I was angry that my brother hadn't been prepared for me either, even though he knew well in advance that I was coming. It was hot and uncomfortable and he had not obtained anything else for me to sleep on.

I wanted to get up and tell him so but there was no chance of that.

I couldn't even drag myself up on all fours. Anselm laughed. I was too weak to speak my mind.

'I expected that you would not be able to move,' he said knowledgeably. 'You were in a coma for a half a day longer than described by the books.'

As soon as I had regained my strength, I set about exploring my new home. A thirty-minute walk down the hill from Anselm's flat took me downtown. It was soon clear to me that Haifa was first and foremost an industrial city, built primarily on the export of oranges and grapefruit grown in the orchards that surrounded the city. The other major industry involved the oil refinery on Haifa harbour. Crude oil from Kirkuk in Northern Iraq was transported along pipelines to the British in Palestine—to Haifa, where it was refined.

The 1920s had witnessed the beginnings of Jewish industry in Palestine. Between 1924 and 1928, large numbers of middle-class Polish Jews migrated to Palestine as economic refugees after the creation of Poland following the First World War. The Jews were uniquely vulnerable to successor-state xenophobia. During the 1920s, those branches of industry and commerce which were heavily represented by Jewish concerns were nationalised. One-third of the nation's Jewish merchants were driven to bankruptcy. This influx, often referred to as 'the Fourth *Aliyah*' (wave of Jewish migration to The Holy Land), resulted in the urbanisation of Palestine's major centres. The population of Tel Aviv trebled during this time. Jewish industry developed. In Haifa, a power station, salt works, a flour mill, an oil and soap factory, the Nesher cement factory, and a number of textile plants were established.

I was considered part of the the Fifth *Aliyah*, which spanned the 1930s. It also involved large numbers of eastern European Jews, but now included central Europeans—Germans, Austrians, Czechs—fleeing the rumblings of Nazi anti-Semitism. Many of these immigrants had been active Zionists in their old countries and a great many of these settled on the land—on *kibbutzim* and *moshavim*, where they could maintain their ties with political parties and national federations. Others chose to settle in the urban centres, which, like Haifa, soon began to resemble large cities. With their arrival, there was an enormous rise in capitalist enterprise.

Despite this economic growth, the general standard of living in Haifa was poor. Water was strictly controlled and extremely expensive. If you showered once or twice a week you were considered bourgeois.

Only a select few—those with thriving export businesses—were able to afford simple luxuries such as a telephone. Imported goods were almost non-existent, and only those who could afford to live in the chic new houses being built in the tree-lined streets of *Har HaCarmel* atop the mountain were able to buy items such as cars, which were all imported.

On my way back from the city, I stopped to look at the Technion, my scholastic home for the next four years. It was located on the hill below Anselm's flat and occupied an entire block, contained within four streets. The original building was designed in the Ottoman style, reflecting an appreciation of the permission granted by Constantinople for the construction of the Technion in 1913. It was not overly ornate, however, since funding had always been scarce.

While there, I decided to enrol in my engineering course. And it was here that I first encountered my nemesis in Palestine: the Hebrew language. I was extremely thankful for the language classes my father had organised prior to my departure from Poland. But even coupled with the basics I had acquired in order to perform my bar mitzvah, I had scarcely enough knowledge of the language to complete my enrolment forms. Naturally, I also enrolled in a Hebrew class. Since the entire course would be taught in this strange and guttural language, I had little choice.

Before commencing my course at the Technion, I enquired at the Hebrew University in Jerusalem about the possibility of studying medicine. Unfortunately, without a medical faculty, the closest I could get to a medical degree would be to study biology in their Faculty of Science. I was resigned to becoming an engineer.

After two nights sleeping on the kitchen floor, I was banished to the small balcony of Anselm's apartment. Since their tenant found no good reason to allow me to share his sleeping quarters, I had no alternative. Even after I had grown accustomed to the fact that I was nightly fodder for the mosquitoes and sandflies, it was a short-term housing solution at best.

After a few days in his house, it dawned on me that my brother was not working. Nothing had been said, but it soon became obvious. When I asked him about it, he said his temperament had got him fired from his factory job.

Unemployment was high, and although Anselm walked to the employment office each morning to seek casual work, none was forthcoming. He received a nominal benefit from his labour union, but for the most part he was surviving on his wife's wage. Lusia was holding down a clerical job that paid a meagre four pounds per month. It did not take a genius to calculate that they were living on a shoestring, so I decided to contribute half of my allowance of six pounds each month to my brother.

Contrary to the sunny existence depicted in his letters, Anselm and Lusia's life in Palestine was difficult and drab. Returning home empty-handed from the employment office each day, he had an air of fatalism, but also a sort of quiet relief. 'Oh well,' he would say, 'tomorrow is another day.' He would then settle himself onto the sofa and open a book. He read German books only, and more often than not they were novels by Karl May, the most famous exponent of that quixotic yet powerful genre, the German western. This would occupy him completely until four o'clock, when he would start to prepare dinner for Lusia's return.

My brother had no skill in the kitchen and, to make matters worse, he didn't have the budget to buy any decent ingredients. Furthermore, after starting the preparations he would return to his book in earnest, become absorbed, and invariably overcook the meal. Without fail, the result would prove totally inedible. What should have been slices of liver with macaroni looked and tasted like leather shoes with rubber laces.

Routinely, Lusia would return home from work, take one look in the frying pan, and immediately throw its contents in the bin, or at the wall, or at Anselm.

'Have you got something else?' she would screech.

Having anticipated this question, he would victoriously present a fresh piece of meat that he had saved just for her. But Anselm and I were not so lucky. We survived on an inordinate amount of bread—sometimes fresh, sometimes not—supplemented with some dates and a few grapes. By the time Anselm had ruined the dinner and we had chewed and digested our own humble meal, it was time for bed.

This constituted my staple diet for quite some time, until one day, while out strolling around the area, I noticed a small zoo. Beside a cage of monkeys stood a portable kiosk, manned by a man selling bags of peanuts. For a few *piastas* I could purchase quite a large quantity of nuts. I had no intention of feeding them to the monkey. While they remained with me for three or four days blocking up my system, they were a more than reasonable substitute for stale bread.

With sadness, I came to understand that, despite his bravado, Anselm was clearly unable to support himself. His wife was frustrated with him and reacted violently, and I felt pity for my older brother. Yet he was doing little to improve his lot. Neither he nor Lusia was making any attempt to learn Hebrew. Nor did they feel that there was any reason to. They had remained members of *Hashomer Hatzair*, the collectivist, socialist group, but Anselm had lost all enthusiasm for things ideological or political. Indeed, Anselm had lost his passion for most things.

Hashomer was at the leading edge of the radical kibbutz movement, with communal dining, collective education, and group confessionals. But this lifestyle was not an option for Anselm and Lusia. After all, Anselm was of the opinion that, as the son of Dr Lustig, he was superior to others. As with many bourgeois leftists who tried to make it on their own, Anselm and Lusia's radicalism was hollow and contradictory. Their idea of practical revolutionary activity was to 'collect' cutlery from cafés to supplement their provisions at home.

Before long, my sleeping on the balcony became intolerable. The plan was to move into another two-bedroom apartment, with Anselm and Lusia taking one room and leaving the other room for me. When I began my course at the Technion, I would seek out two fellow students to share my room. We would each pay Anselm one pound per month in rent.

Josef Oberlander was from Sambor, the small town near Drohobycz. Although three years my senior, he too was commencing his first year of the course and consequently was in my class. He had been on the train from L'vov and the further we had travelled, the more boisterous he had become. There had been no mistaking this boy's personality: his bullock-like build, his squarely set jaw and low brow reflected his obstinacy. He was combative and stubborn and not overly intelligent, but I sensed that underneath the bluster, he meant well. In time, we developed a dynamic that picked up where my friendship with Chiuk and Tauchner left off. We would constantly pit our knowledge against one another in a battle of quotes and citations.

Our room-mate was Igor. Polite and sensitive, and at a towering six foot two, he was truly a gentle giant. But Igor had a problem. Preoccupied with the girl he had left behind in Poland, he was unable to concentrate on his studies. Nor was he able to accept life in Palestine without her. When I asked him to show me her photograph, his protective jealousy prevented him from doing so. I was also from Drohobycz, and this was a little too close for comfort. Igor would sit quietly on the balcony pensively contemplating the vast sea that separated him from his girlfriend, writing one letter after another.

Such blind devotion and intense pining would only serve to harden the inevitable blow. Six months later, I came home to find Igor in tears. In his hand was the classic 'Dear John' letter, and to make matters worse, the bad news had been conveyed via his father, a medical practitioner. At the end of the letter, his father had penned his own homily:

'Don't worry, son. It is better this way. It is a well-established medical fact that when blood is contained within the penis, the brain is deprived.'

'This is all that my father can offer me?' Igor cried incredulously.

My mind turned to Suza. Igor's pathetic display strengthened my resolve to concentrate on the future rather than dwell in the past. In truth, I had already been in two minds about my own girlfriend when I left Drohobycz. But my lack of contact with girls since arriving in Palestine had, at times, sent me into sporadic bouts of melancholia. Suza and I had exchanged a few letters, but gradually I had adopted a formal tone in my writing. I knew now that I had to protect myself from the ailment that afflicted my maudlin room-mate.

At the conclusion of our first year at the Technion, Igor returned to Poland. Another student from the Technion took his place in our room, another Polish boy, who enjoyed the distinction of having an uncle who was a professor of surveying in London.

At some point during our second year in this flat, Oberlander started to spend less time at home. I surmised that there must have been a girl involved. I soon discovered that he had become romantically attached to the woman who cleaned the stairwell in our block of flats each afternoon. It had never crossed my mind that this woman might appeal to him. She was older than he—indeed, she looked considerably older—and she had two children of her own. Eventually, he moved out to live with her. He completed his course, but I lost contact with him. He transferred into electrical engineering while I elected to study civil and structural engineering.

I lived with Anselm and Lusia for two years until I returned to Drohobycz during the 1938 summer holidays, after completing my second year of engineering. Anselm did not work at all during this time. Indeed, he would not find another job until I managed to organise work for him at the oil refinery in 1940. When he was not reading his German westerns, he played chess. But since there was nobody around during the day, he would play against himself. I found these solitary occupations to be no basis for a life at all. At least his cooking had improved with the help of Oberlander, who was quite a competent chef in his own right. Still, my concern for my brother grew.

I resolved that Anselm needed to get out of the house, to be involved in something, anything at all. There was a broken gate in the block of flats. Anselm was a natural handyman and I suggested that he fix it. We finally managed to convince the landlord that the job needed doing, and that perhaps he should pay for it. Anselm calculated that it would cost two pounds for materials and labour.

'Don't worry about the labour cost, Anselm—you've got nothing else to do anyway,' I counselled, fearing he would lose even this meagre employment.

We quoted one pound for the timber, but the landlord decided that it was still too expensive.

'Let's fix it anyway,' I said. 'Instead of buying timber we can rebuild the old gate. It will only cost us the time. And then we will have something to show others. Perhaps we could start a maintenance business that way.'

We started the job at eleven in the morning. We worked all day and before we knew it, Lusia was standing on the staircase above us.

'Anselm, is everything ready for dinner?' she yelled.

'What?' he answered in disbelief. 'You couldn't possibly expect me to prepare the food *and* fix the gate.'

Lusia was furious. She ordered him upstairs to help her with the meal.

Anselm never finished fixing the gate. Recycling the timber did not result in a satisfactory construction, and rather than persevere with an alternative solution, once again Anselm went back to his book.

His marriage was deteriorating, as Lusia became ever more frustrated with his lack of motivation. As her impatience grew and her volatility increased, his self-esteem withered away. At the dinner table, he would desperately start arguments in order to prove that he was right and everybody else at the table was not. He was trying too hard, often struggling to express himself as an intellectual in a vain attempt to demonstrate self-worth.

'For God's sake, stop talking!' Lusia would shriek.

'Please, let him continue,' I would reply more often than not.

I became the empathetic brother, and often the go-between, since I felt both pity for my brother and a grudging sympathy for my sister-in-law's situation.

On my return from Drohobycz in 1938, I urged my brother to consider moving onto a kibbutz. At least he would have work, and the necessities of life would be provided. But I approached the issue on another level completely. He had often complained that in her frustration with him, Lusia refused to allow him to touch her.

'So, go to a kibbutz,' I urged him. 'With their philosophy of sharing, you might find that you can have any woman you like.'

This sparked his interest. Lusia was completely opposed to the idea of taking up the kibbutz lifestyle, however. When she heard that I had approached Anselm with the idea, her attitude toward me changed dramatically. From being someone in whom she could confide, I became a threat, a traitor, an interferer in her personal affairs.

I realised then that I needed to stand on my own, and create a life for myself in Palestine. This meant leaving Anselm and Lusia to their own devices.

10 Student of Life in Haifa

I have never understood why one's affections must be confined, as once with women, to a single country.
JOHN KENNETH GALBRAITH

I FOUND IT ironic that the engineering course would be taught in Hebrew. The Technion was established along the lines of a German gymnasium, and while German was generally regarded as the *lingua franca* of science, the archaic language of Hebrew was woefully deficient in technical vocabulary.

Indeed, historically, the Haifa Technion lay at the centre of what was almost a war between Hebraism and Germanism in Palestine. Prior to the twentieth century, the Jews of Palestine spoke a mixture of Yiddish and Aramaic. Only prayers and synagogue services were conducted in Hebrew. Around the turn of the century, however, this would change. Eliezer Perlman, an orthodox Jew and Zionist, studied at the Sorbonne where he learned of the role of literature in the growth of French nationalism. By 1880, he wrote that he had 'decided that in order to have our own land and political life, it is also necessary that we have a language to hold us together. That language is Hebrew. But not the Hebrew of the rabbis and scholars. We must have a Hebrew language in which we can conduct the business of life.'

He migrated with his wife to Palestine and thereafter vowed never to speak any language but Hebrew. He taught the language at an Alliance school—a school sponsored by *Alliance Israélite Universelle*, where French remained the principal language of instruction. He also founded a number of Hebrew language newspapers, the circulation of which rarely exceeded two hundred. When he attacked the orthodox community for their opposition to the use of Hebrew, they attacked his office and denounced him to the Ottoman authorities for treason. At one stage, he was briefly jailed.

In time, however, Perlman's ideas began to take hold. He wrote textbooks and started newspapers to which the agricultural communities began to subscribe. He researched Semitic roots of words that he could incorporate into a contemporary vernacular. By 1904, with modest grants from the Zionist organisation, from Baron Edmond von Rothschild, and from other Jewish sources, he published the first volume of his modern Hebrew dictionary.

Over time, he secured the support of a number of teachers, including those who taught at the Alliance schools and within Zionist agricultural colonies. In addition, he gained the sympathy of a number of teachers at the *Hilfsverein der Deutschen Juden*, which operated a network of fifty schools based on the German system of education. By 1903, a Hebrew Teachers Association had been formed.

Ironically, it was the German *Drang Nach Osten*, an imperialist expansion into the Middle East in the last years before the First World War, that threatened the impressive progress of Hebraisation. The directors of the *Hilfsverein* schools began offering courses taught exclusively in German. The issue of Hebraism versus Germanism came to a head when plans were laid in 1913 to establish the Haifa Technical Institution. As the administering agency, the *Hilfsverein* was determined that the Technion should be the very foundation stone of the Jewish community's educational structure—and a spectacular example of *Deutsche Kultur*. The German Jewish members of the Technion's Board of Governors proposed that all technical subjects be taught exclusively in the German language.

In October 1913, the Hebrew Teachers Association proclaimed a strike in all *Hilfsverein* schools, and students demonstrated outside the German consulate in Jerusalem. The Technion crisis seemingly threatened the entire Hebraic nature of the Zionist renaissance. The Zionist organisation set about establishing more than a dozen new Hebrew language schools and campaigned worldwide for funds.

By February 1914, the language controversy ended when the Board of Governors agreed that all Technion courses would be taught in Hebrew. The Hebrew Teachers Association, subsidised by the Zionist Organisation, founded a board of education to administer the curriculum and establish teaching guidelines for all non-orthodox Jewish schools in Palestine, including the *Hilfsverein* schools.

By 1916, forty per cent of the Jews of Palestine (excluding the old orthodox community) spoke Hebrew as their first language. However, I would soon discover that in the twenty years since, very little progress had been made in creating Hebrew terms for the engineering jargon I would be learning at the Technion.

To make matters worse, a large number of my professors were also part of the Fifth *Aliyah*. Many of them were Germans who had been recruited to the Technion for their expertise. But now they had to teach in Hebrew, a task they found just as difficult as the students found trying to understand them.

For many of the lectures, the professors read from printed notes that were written phonetically using the English alphabet, so they were speaking in Hebrew but had no inkling of what they were reading. Question time was even more ridiculous. While many of the students could only express their questions in Polish or Yiddish, often the professor spoke only German or English. Even assuming that he understood the query, he could not necessarily answer it in their own tongue, let alone Hebrew. The only solution was an eclectic approach: to use whichever language best suited the individual situation.

I had a slight advantage in that I spoke a little English. Indeed, my English was somewhat more advanced than my Hebrew, thanks once again to my father, who organised a tutor for me for the year prior to my departure. Mrs Bachanrott had suddenly appeared among the Drohobycz social set, after having migrated with her husband from London. She was in her early twenties, and considerably younger than her husband. She was stunningly beautiful, with long blonde hair and the face of an angel. I would go weak at the knees whenever she smiled and unfortunately for me, she was a particularly happy person. My lessons took place through the winter, but it did not take too much imagination to realise that her figure, beneath the heavy clothing, matched her face as one of God's true works of art. Of course I found it difficult to concentrate on learning the language, but despite it all, I progressed quite well. Perhaps I had made the extra effort in order to impress her.

I began taking Hebrew classes before commencing the engineering course proper. My professor, an elderly gentleman with the appearance and stoic demeanour more commonly associated with a rabbi, was one of seven teachers officially selected to carry on the work of Eliezer Perlman—to revive the ancient language and create new terms appropriate to the modern world. I enjoyed these sessions immensely, though I was more interested in examining the logic and syntax of the language than in actually learning to speak it. Furthermore, what I was learning was not the language commonly spoken at the time. On the streets of Haifa, conversational Hebrew remained unrefined, still intermingled in a patois with Arabic, Yiddish or Polish.

My inability to converse in Hebrew on the streets of Haifa was further exacerbated by the fact that I had nobody at home or at school with whom to practise the language. Anselm and Lusia were still speaking Polish and had no desire to speak Hebrew, and nearly all of the students at the Technion were Europeans who struggled as I did to learn the tongue.

Language was not the only problem I encountered trying to fit into life in Palestine. Having come from the cold, wet and dreary conditions of north-eastern Europe, the Middle Eastern climate was just as foreign to me as the language, and in many ways even more of a shock to my system. And I had arrived at the end of a long, hot summer. There were times when, in the intense heat of the day, I forced myself to hike to the top of Mount Carmel in order to breathe the clean, fresh air up there, closer to the sky. My only respite came each evening, from six o'clock until ten, when a slight breeze sprang up from the west, rippling over the city from the Mediterranean Sea.

The only other hint of a draft to pass through Haifa arrived each morning at about 7.30 and lasted for an hour. After a restless night and waking in a pool of perspiration, I found that this temporary relief provided the only opportunity to catch up on some decent sleep. It struck me as ludicrous, therefore, that the Technion expected us to be in the lecture theatre and ready for work at seven o'clock each morning. Even more so given that there was no water with which to refresh ourselves after tossing and turning in a sweat all night long. Naturally, the early morning lectures were rarely more than half full.

But there was another reason that lectures were not attended by all the students. It had less to do with the climate, and more to do with the politics.

Like most higher educational institutions, the Haifa Technion was a breeding ground and recruiting area for political factions, but perhaps more so at this stage because of the burgeoning movement of Jewish nationalism in British Palestine. For many of the students, who had some Zionist affiliation dating back to their respective homelands, it was quickly becoming the issue of the day. Membership in the various student groups was strong, but I soon realised that this membership was grounded in more than simply ideology. There was the matter of peer pressure. I felt compelled to join in order to fit in. An even greater motivation than this, however, was the more mundane issue of job prospects. And for the Jews of Palestine, politics and job prospects were practically inseparable. After all, the Jewish Labour Federation—the union—was inextricably tied to the most powerful Labour Zionist party, *Mapai*.

The two main political factions of the Labour Zionist movement—*Achdut HaAvodah* and *HaPoel HaZair*—had combined their efforts to create a supposedly non-partisan, purely labour federation. The *Histadrut*, the Jewish Labour Federation of Palestine, was founded in Haifa in December 1920.

Initially the *Histadrut* concentrated on securing work for immigrants on the land, primarily in the citrus groves of the coastal belt. With the bulk of the Jewish workforce pouring into the cities during the 1920s, *Histadrut* turned its attentions to the urban areas. It organised unions not only among manual labourers, but also clerks, technicians, and even doctors and lawyers. Labour exchanges were set up for job applicants, and collective bargaining was undertaken on their behalf.

Histadrut's function was by no means limited to that of a bargaining agent for workers. It served both the Zionist ideal of rebuilding the country and the socialist aim of establishing a Jewish workers' society in Palestine. It established a central economic corporation, the *Chevrat Ovdim*, to serve as a holding company for a wide variety of independent undertakings. *HaMashbir HaMerkazi* served as a cooperative wholesale society to buy the products of the *kibbutzim* and *moshavim* and in turn, sell them through its chain of retail outlets. *Tnuva* was established as a marketing outlet for *kibbutz* and *moshav* dairy produce. A workers' bank (Bank *HaPoalim*) served as its major credit instrument for the farm settlements and labour enterprises in the cities. Its housing company, *Shikum*, provided workers with apartments at the lowest non-profit rentals. Cooperative ventures ranging from bus transportation to hotels and restaurants were also established. In 1925, *Histadrut* began publishing its own newspaper, *Davar*.

To broaden the employment market, the workers' federation launched a number of its own industrial companies. The largest of these, *Solel Boneh* (Paving and Building), was established as a semi-independent contracting agency for road building, and later, for public construction. Within two years, *Solel Boneh* was handling contracts from private investors, the Zionist Executive, and even the mandatory government. It drained swamps, built roads, erected housing and office buildings; and in the process, it opened up thousands of new job opportunities. As early as 1930, *Histadrut* was employing 75% of the Jewish working population of Palestine. By the late 1930s, the *Histadrut* had become much more than a powerful institution in Jewish Palestine. For a majority of the Jewish settlement, it was all but synonymous with Jewish Palestine itself.

A new series of Arab riots in 1929 had revealed the urgent need for Jewish political consolidation. The leaders of *Achdut HaAvodah* and *HaPoel HaZair*, the two factions that had founded the *Histadrut*, sensed that the issues uniting the two labour factions were more important than those which divided them. In January 1930, the membership of both groups voted approval for a merger. The ensuing united party became known as 'Mapai' (*Mifleget Polai Eretz Israel*), the Land of Israel Workers Party.

Mapai steered away from the traditional issues of Zionist politics and concentrated instead on pragmatic gains for Jewish workers and the Jewish national home. A judicious blend of nationalist idealism and social gradualism ensured *Mapai* control of the *Histadrut* as well as the Jewish National Congress and the Jewish Agency's political department. From then on, *Mapai* led the Jewish settlement through the mandatory period, and would eventually become the largest single party in Zionist Congresses.

Haifa Shelanu Adomah—'Our Haifa is Red'—was the catchcry of the powerful Labour Zionist *Mapai* movement in Haifa, led by Abba Choushi, who would later become mayor of the city. Arieh Stern, a student in my year at the Technion, served as Abba Choushi's *Schickyingle*, or 'messenger boy'. An unkempt fellow with a straggly beard, who obviously could not afford a bath, Arieh's job was to 'spread the word' among his fellow students and take charge of recruitment to the party.

I avoided him, for hygienic reasons, and he tended to see me as an example of decadence and bourgeois class. Many years later, after the War of Independence, I met him again. He had progressed steadily through the ranks of *Mapai*.

'What have you been doing all these years?' I enquired.

'You may not believe it, but I am Israel's ambassador to Italy. I am living in Rome now.'

He was right. I couldn't believe it. The slovenly *Schickyingle* was now an international diplomat.

'Well, I have enough of a sense of humour to believe you, no matter how fantastic it sounds', I replied. 'Looking at you now, I can't help but believe you. After all, you are washed and look quite presentable.'

'Lustig,' he pronounced, his tone confiding and conciliatory, 'it is important to be in the right place at the right time, and to know how to count.'

It was simple but good advice.

'If you need a messenger boy in Rome, Stern, I am available,' I offered.

Libertowsky was also a messenger boy for the party, another *Schickyingle* for *Mapai*. He was responsible for organising jobs for the students through the *Mapai* student group, which served as a kind of student *Histadrut*.

Mapai dominated student politics at the Technion. Anyone who needed a job to supplement his student income joined the party. And there were very few who could afford to study and live in Haifa without the help of a part-time or holiday job. There were only three in my year—Weidenfeld, Brauder and Reichert—who not only had enough money to avoid working, but were able to afford to travel into Lebanon for skiing vacations on a regular basis.

Weidenfeld and Brauder were constant companions who nonetheless would have been happy to execute one another. Weidenfeld was solidly built, dynamic, and highly intelligent. But he was also arrogant and dogmatic, never allowing another to have the last word, and unfailing in his belief that he was always, undeniably right. In contrast, his friend Brauder (whose claim to fame was his grandfather, the well-known and highly respected Chief Rabbi of Lodz), was a skinny boy with a long, angular face and a prominent nose, who in no way projected any strength of character. But the two boys shared one trait: a devoted bourgeois self-indulgence that they had carried with them from Poland. I always felt that Palestine was the great 'leveller', and I learned early on that it lacked an audience for my own attempts at snobbery. The fact that my father was a respected lawyer in Drohobycz carried no weight here, but the irrelevance of invoking such ancestral status symbols seemed to be lost on Weidenfeld and Brauder.

Weidenfeld was one of the few students who actively avoided participation in the student union. He had no need of a job, and he considered himself above taking any interest in the Zionist movement. Indeed, it could be argued that he was in fact a rabid anti-Semite.

In a typical confrontation, he approached Brauder, who was busy cleaning out some glassware after a chemistry experiment. Brauder was a placid boy and no match for Weidenfeld's brute strength. But Weidenfeld constantly picked on him anyway, no doubt seeing him as an easy target.

'Look,' barked Weidenfeld, 'how long is it going to take you to finish this?'

'What does it matter?' Brauder replied, clearly resigned to yet another confrontation. 'I'm not cleaning them for *you* anyway.'

'Don't be arrogant,' warned Weidenfeld, who looked for any excuse to harass him. 'You know that I can fix your fat, Jewish nose any time I want. It makes me sick to look at it.'

And on it went. The vicious tongue-lashing escalated into hysterical rantings. The rabbi's grandson was in no position to respond—he would have been crushed by Weidenfeld. He had to sit there and take the abuse.

There were a number of students who joined *Mapai* simply for the work, even though they were ideologically opposed to the Labour Zionist movement. Ephraim Lifshitz was a tall, lanky boy renowned for a physical prowess belied by his physique. It was a power born of his choleric temperament that generated quick, aggressive responses. It was a well-known fact that if you valued your life, you did not mess with Lifshitz.

His best friend Reichert was short but solid and unbelievably strong. He, however, did not use his impressive physical presence to intimidate. An honourable fellow, he was always well mannered and very pleasant. Lifshitz often joined Weidenfeld and Reichert on their sojourns in Lebanon, but unlike his fellow travellers, he did not have the support of a wealthy family. If Lifshitz needed cash, he would simply call for a card game. After an hour of blackjack or baccarat, he would leave the table with his considerable winnings. 'Thank you very much for playing, gentlemen,' and he'd be off.

Lifshitz and Reichert stood in direct opposition to the left-wing *Mapai* party. They were Zionists, but were among the minority right wing Revisionists, followers of Vladimir Jabotinsky.

Dr Samuel Lustig, in the Austrian Army during World War I

Mrs Lucia Lustig

Ted, Samuel and Lucia Lustig, with a cousin, Anselm Lustig (not to be confused with Ted's brother, Anselm)

Lucia and Samuel Lustig

Himmel house, then and now *(See pp. 5, 20)*

Ted Lustig, aged about 20

Renata Himmel *(See pp. 5 ff., 20–21, 44–45)*

Drohobycz street scenes, then and now

Left to right: Joseph Kuhrmärker, Matila Kuhrmärker (Ted's paternal grandparents); Dr Samuel Lustig; Anne Elbaum (Ted's maternal grandmother); Lucia Lustig; Moritz Grossman, Munia Grossman

At 'Tatra', summer camp for girls. The boys pictured in top row are (l. to r.) Ziggy Binstock, Ted Lustig, Milek Tauchner, and Charles Wexelberg. *(See p. 46)*

Ted's friend Abraham Lerner, who introduced him to Sophie 'Suza' Brenner. *(See pp. 45 ff.)*

Jazz band Palma. Pictured left to right: Max Lambert, Ted Lustig, Gerry Galotti, Steven Wilner, Joseph Friedman, unknown, unknown, and Stanislau Wilder, the band leader. *(See pp. 38–39)*

Sophie 'Suza' Brenner, aged 14. *(See pp. 50 ff.)*

Ted, aged 18, with Ziggy Binstock and another friend, Goldberg

Dr Samuel Lustig (right), with his brother, Dr Moses Lustig, c. 1936 *(See p. 43)*

Suza and Ted, strolling in Mickiewicza Street

Ted's aunt, Lonia Lustig (Yaron), and her son Alex Yaron
(See pp. 104 ff.; 184–185)

Suza

The town and harbour of Haifa *(See pp. 55 ff.)*

Above: Ephraim Lifshitz, a close friend of Ted's
(See pp. 86, 114–116; 216–217)

Above right: Anselm and Lusia Lustig
(See pp. 31–32, 69 ff.)

Right: Anselm Lustig, aged about 73

Left: Sarah *(See pp. 145 ff.)*

Below: Abraham Meiri (centre), Ted's closest friend in Palestine, pictured with Sarah, Ted and Iris in 1947 *(See pp. 114, 116)*

Below: Ted, Sarah and Iris on holiday, c. 1954–55

During the First World War, persecution of the Jews of Palestine by the Ottomans, particularly Beha-a-Din, the Turkish governor of Jaffa, sent many thousands into exile to refugee camps in Egypt. It was here that Jabotinsky founded the Zion Mule Corps, a Jewish legion that fought beside the British against the Ottomans. By 1920, he had founded and became first leader of the *Haganah*, the first Jewish armed force. They single-handedly led the resistance to the Nebi Musa riots in 1920. To many young Jews, Jabotinsky became the very symbol of militant Zionism.

Reacting to Chaim Weizmann, who believed that a Jewish majority in Palestine was neither necessary nor sufficient for the development of Jewish civilisation and culture, Jabotinsky founded the Revisionist Zionist movement, which espoused the radical idea of creating a Jewish majority in Palestine via a program of mass immigration. It was denounced as 'treason' by the mainstream Zionist Organisation, but the idea gained momentum and by 1931, fifty-two Revisionist delegates had been elected to the Zionist Congress. Jabotinsky's group then officially split from the Zionist Organisation to become the 'New Zionist Organisation'.

By the late 1930s, a new group of younger leaders radicalised the Revisionist movement. The source of the new orientation was the *Betar* youth movement, an intense, militant group that shared Jabotinsky's ideas. He had met representatives of the movement while travelling in Lithuania and Latvia in the early 1920s. Their leadership veered further right than Jabotinsky himself would have liked. At times they came dangerously close to emulating the *Giovanni Fascisti* of Italy. Jabotinsky had no objection to militarism *per se*, but his model was Garibaldi rather than Mussolini. Although a devoted socialist in his youth in Russia, he was shaken by the effects of the Bolshevik revolution. Now he had little patience for a socialist egalitarianism; rather, he pinned his hopes on the emergent Jewish middle class of Palestine.

The hostility between the Zionist Left and Jabotinsky's right-wing followers reached its apex in June of 1933, when Chaim Arlosoroff, director of The Jewish Agency's political department and youngest of the *Mapai* leaders in Palestine, was shot and killed by a Revisionist worker. This hostility continued for many years to come.

Religious Zionism, represented by the *Mizrahi* political movement, was poorly represented at the Technion. After all, the vast majority of students were middle-class, liberal Polish Jews, who did not practise orthodox Judaism. This was true of Haifa generally: the orthodox immigrants tended to settle in Jerusalem rather than the industrial town of Haifa.

For the first two years of my course, I did not have to work to supplement my income. Despite contributing half of my allowance to Anselm and Lusia, I had enough money to survive—though only just. So while I was an enrolled member of the student Zionist movement, ideologically I had little interest in Zionism. As a rule, most Zionist movements were inherently anti-British, and I had a most unusual trait for a Jew in Palestine—I was ardently pro-British. Over and above this, however, I believed student politics to be a complete waste of time and energy—a culture of nit-picking and arguing while ignoring the more important issues of the day, such as human sickness and poverty. As a student engineer I was more concerned with issues of town planning—hygiene, sewerage—how the standard of living in Haifa could be improved. I was wary of losing sight of the trees for the forest. I believed in addressing one issue at a time, on its individual merits.

I was angered by the attitudes of so many of the students who joined *Mapai*. Their priority was to the party, so much so that they treated the engineering course with an air of nonchalance, attending classes if and when they wanted and behaving as though they were immune to failure. They took no interest in what they could do as engineers; rather, they were becoming obsessed with what they could achieve as Zionists and freedom fighters. Ultimately, this strengthened my resolve to achieve scholastic excellence, to make something of myself as an engineer in Palestine without the backing of a collective, or the distraction of political grandstanding.

My goal suffered a setback when, at the end of first year, I failed two subjects. While I was allowed to answer the exam questions in Polish, I knew that my inability to speak Hebrew, the language in which we had been taught all year, was largely responsible for the fall from academic grace. During the summer vacation, I made a concerted effort to improve my Hebrew and prepare once again for the exams with renewed vigour and language skills. I enlisted the help of Oberlander, whose Hebrew was slightly more accomplished than mine, but more often than not his determination to bamboozle me in our ongoing battle of general knowledge left me more confused than when we started. I was re-examined at the end of summer and this time, I passed with flying colours.

While I did my utmost to avoid any active participation in Zionist politics and the student union, I had been unable to ignore it completely. Soon after commencing my engineering course, I was visited at home by a fellow Technion student, whom I did not know. It was seven o'clock on a Saturday morning. He was wearing a military-style uniform and brandishing a gun.

'Are you Lustig?' he bellowed.

'Yeah,' I answered, still exhausted from a sleepless night in the heat.

'*Fahrshtast Yiddish?*' he asked, slipping into the language of the Polish villages, the better to make my acquaintance.

'No,' I replied. 'English.'

'You will be picked up by your tender tonight after *Shabbos*,' he ordered.

'What do you mean?'

'Don't ask questions. You will be collected tonight and will go through training.'

Now I knew who he was, where he was from and what he was ordering me to do.

'Look,' I tried to explain. ' I have absolutely nothing against Jews or Arabs or whomever. I just don't want to shoot people.'

'You don't know what you're talking about,' he growled, dismissing my objections. 'And I am telling you that they will come to pick you up and you will go!'

With that, he was gone. I realised that this was the *Haganah*, which was now being sponsored by the *Histadrut*. Indeed, its somewhat covert activities had grown considerably as a result of the latest spate of Arab riots.

Later that day I was collected by another uniformed youth. He was a *Sabra*, Palestinian-born, and from his appearance I could tell that he was a *Sephardic* Jew, of eastern rather than European extraction. He did not address me, but simply gestured to me to move outside and then escorted me to his jeep. I began protesting, as I had done earlier that morning, but he ignored me, concentrating instead on starting the motor of his vehicle.

I lost my temper.

'I am not to be treated this way. I need to know about these things in advance.'

His reply, in Hebrew, was simple.

'Speak Hebrew. I don't understand what you are saying.'

Of course I could not, effectively ending my protests. We drove in silence.

I was taken to Ahuza, a settlement on the top of Mount Carmel. There we were met by my 'tender'—my immediate superior—who handed me a revolver and pointed to a large water tank.

'You sit there. If you see some Arabs approaching, hold the gun and point it at them. By the way, don't shoot, because you have no bullets.'

This struck me as absurd. 'I'd rather have a stick,' I remarked.

'There are plenty of sticks on the ground. Take one.'

He left me on my own. I was to guard the water tank all night.

I realised that my most vicious enemies on this watch were not Arabs, but mosquitoes. Large, bloodthirsty, merciless winged squadrons of them attacked me in formation throughout the night, stabbing through the thin fabric of my unsuitable sweater. By morning I was covered in bites. For most of the night I sat there, vainly swatting at the insects and seething. 'I don't owe these people anything, and they don't owe me anything,' I thought to myself. 'Never again, never.'

Until the next time. The following week, when my tender came to collect me, he informed me that this post was now my new and sole responsibility. That second week, I decided to refuse the revolver. It was safer. After all, if an Arab intruder were to realise that the gun was an empty prop, I would be in real trouble. After the third week, I finally managed to weasel out of the detail.

'Look,' I pleaded, 'I came here to study. I have never suffered from heroism; in fact I have always tried to avoid it in any and every possible way. So leave me in peace.'

'You'll beg to come back,' replied the tender.

Despite my active lack of interest in Zionism and my decidedly unpopular pro-British leanings, I learned that it was prudent not to openly portray myself as someone who was not a patriot. So I often made sure I was seen at various meetings and demonstrations before quietly disappearing from the scene. All this would change, however, upon my return from Drohobycz in 1938. With war in Europe imminent, I knew that my ties with Poland would be cut on every level. I would need to find work, and consequently, I would need to demonstrate some degree of interest in the student union, purely as a matter of survival.

My first two years in Palestine were anything but comfortable. I struggled with the language and the climate, felt nothing but pity for my brother and his plight, and had absolutely no contact with girls. Most of all, I was lonely. While I was not unpopular at school, I cannot say that I made any close friends. Certainly, there was no one with whom I could speak my mind openly, to whom I could entrust my hopes and fears, or from whom I could seek advice about matters that were important to me. I had no confidant, and it occurred to me how much I missed my father and our evening walks through the park.

11 The Storm Clouds Gather

Half of the harm that is done in this world
Is due to people who want to feel important.
They don't mean to do harm—but the harm does not interest them.
T. S. Eliot

In August of 1938, having completed the second year of my engineering degree at the Technion in Haifa, I returned home to Drohobycz to spend the summer break with my parents, at their insistence. I was to have spent three months in Poland, but ultimately, my holiday would last just four weeks. What I saw, and what I sensed, would drive me from Drohobycz for the very last time.

I loved my home town, the small Galician city where I was raised. All of my most potent childhood memories were inextricably bound to this place—family, friends, school, my mother's kitchen. The outlying forests and fields, a glorious setting for my youthful adventures and imaginary games. The lake, where we gathered to swim in the summer and skate in the winter. The park on Mickiewicza Street, where I spent so many hours with my father, strolling and discussing matters of philosophical importance. The giant tree standing outside my window, that had served me so well as a target for my knife-throwing practice, and later as a support for my lovemaking sessions with Suza. Drohobycz was where I first tasted love, and lovemaking; where my character was fashioned, and where the values were forged that would carry me through life.

But something had changed. And it wasn't just me.

What had not changed was the lives of the Jewish people of Drohobycz. My parents remained as I had left them two years earlier. On my first night home, I was promptly sent to bed with a glass of hot milk. My mother's culinary laws were intact and inflexible. I did not dare to reveal the deficiencies in my own nutrition since my move to Palestine: three meals a day was considered two too many and I had become positively anti-vegetable. To me, the tomato was now and would always be a communist plot to destroy a person's will through his diet. And I certainly was not going to tell her the sort of foods I had been eating. My mother would have neither understood nor approved.

She remained blithely ignorant of my adulthood. At breakfast each morning, as she had always done, my mother presented me with two soft-boiled eggs, cooked just the way I liked them. As a child, I had been very particular about the consistency of the egg white—not too hard, so I could quickly swallow them down. Furthermore, I would only eat them if paid. Two zlotys: one zloty per egg. Although I was now too old to charge a fee, she loudly cajoled me into eating them anyway, as was her habit. My father's characteristic response—'Lucia, don't harass the boy!'—preceded their usual bout of playful bickering. I sat between them at the table reading the newspaper, quietly absorbing the good-natured banter of my revisited past.

As the days passed, I became acutely aware that while it was 'business as usual' for the Jews of Drohobycz, there was serious political movement afoot. The previous two years had seen Nazi Germany's remilitarisation of the Rhineland, annexation of Austria, and partition of Czechoslovakia in swift succession. Hitler had progressively disenfranchised the Jews and his anti-Semitic sentiment was beginning to take a strong hold in neighbouring Poland.

During my visit I travelled to nearby L'vov, where I stayed for three days with my Uncle Moses, my father's brother. He worked as a journalist for *Chwila*, the local Jewish newspaper, the same paper that had employed my father's late brother Abraham so many years earlier.

While there, I took the opportunity to meet with some old school friends, who were now attending the University of L'vov. The setting was the local bakery, *Justca Zalskego*, famous for serving the finest pastries in the area and perhaps the whole of Poland. Zakszewski and Chciuk were Poles and Initski was Ukrainian. I met with them to reminisce about our school days, but more importantly, I organised this gathering because I sought to understand the extent of these recent political developments from a gentile perspective.

For a while, we filled this otherwise sedate and conservative shop with our boyish laughter. We recalled the easy camaraderie of our shared school days: Professor Mantel and the infamous 'Dr Schmuck' episode; the violin concert that wasn't ... Convulsing with glee, they jovially ascribed to me, Tedek, the title of 'class clown'. It was true; I had always been an entertainer. Then, as our laughter subsided, one of them added good-naturedly, 'You know, Tedek, if all the Jews were more like you, we wouldn't have the problems we have now.' To my concealed horror, the other two agreed wholeheartedly.

We moved on to other topics. Peter ('Sasha') Zakszewski had become editor-in-chief of the university newspaper. Supported by the *Poznan* movement, to which only 'pure' Poles were granted admission, its ideology was virulently anti-Semitic. Sasha's editorial appointment surprised me, given that he had always encountered difficulties when it came to spelling his own name. He had failed his matriculation exams, but had repeated the following year, while I was in Palestine, and this time he had managed to pass. He was certainly no intellectual wizard, but his outspoken manner had made him popular among the boys. In the current political climate, it appeared that when it came to the selection of senior staff, intelligence held less weight than the charismatic ability to voice the *zeitgeist* of the moment.

Zakszewski confirmed my suspicions, emphasising that he was not required to write the articles himself. Rather, he was appointed simply to oversee the ideological content of the journal. He must have detected a look of disdain on my face, because he concluded by addressing us all with an apologia. 'Tedek knows that I am not anti-Semitic towards *him*. We are best friends,' he added, 'but others don't share this sophisticated attitude. And beyond all that, we have to make a living.'

Peter Zakszewski was driven by a combination of bigotry and resentment, which I knew he had inherited from his father. Pan Zakszewski was a lawyer, like my father, but did not reside in Mickiewicza Street as many of the city's lawyers did. He lived with his wife and three sons in a small, shabby apartment behind the Rynek, his office occupying one room of the dwelling. It was well known that he attributed his relative lack of financial success to the Jewish lawyers of Drohobycz, with whom he was forced to compete.

Tadek Chciuk was one of my oldest and dearest friends. We had met at Pani Fichmanowna's pre-school and had been together in the same class throughout our schooling. He was a highly intelligent but humourless boy, an entirely reliable and loyal friend. He had always been a devout Polish nationalist, and while Zakszewski was now concerned with the practicalities of materialism, Chciuk had his mind on ideological issues. Quietly, but knowingly, he leaned across the table to address me. 'Tedek,' he said, 'we go back a long way. *Please* take my advice. Pack up and go back to Palestine. I am not telling you this because *I* am anti-Semitic, but because we are *all* anti-Semitic.'

I trusted Chciuk at his word, and I realised at that moment that the sooner I left Poland, the better. I felt terribly downhearted after this encounter. These boys were some of my oldest friends, and until that moment, I had still looked upon them as such. I was deeply saddened by the thought of what might have been possible between us if Europe had not been so intent on destroying itself.

Ominous black clouds were gathering, and I knew that when the storm finally broke, it would destroy everything in its path. Why couldn't the Jews of Drohobycz see what I was seeing? I confronted my Uncle Moses with my fears. Although he was a devoted Revisionist Zionist, he would refuse to leave Poland for Palestine. 'If I left this post, who would be left behind to advise all the other Jews?' he asked rhetorically, answering a question with a question as was his habit. Ironically, that same year, the leader of the Revisionist Zionist movement, Vladimir Jabotinsky, would call for the mass evacuation of European Jewry. His warning did not refer specifically to the dangers represented by the Nazis, but also the eastern Europeans, and especially the Polish.

Two years in Palestine had changed me profoundly. I had discovered that a young man of my age was supposed to have ideals. My Jewish friends in Drohobycz had noticed these changes. 'What the hell's wrong with you, Tedek?' demanded Ziggy Binstock. 'The future this and the future that … Who talks about the future?'

I had seen the young Jews in Palestine striving for their principles, working eighteen-hour days to build a nation. In stark contrast, my visit home had revealed the young Jews of Drohobycz as a decadent, lazy people. So secure in their way of life, so complacent, so seemingly indifferent to the political rumblings, they carried on as usual, and I sensed that they would be easy prey for the impending catastrophe.

Despite the overwhelming revulsion I felt for the news conveyed by my three old school friends, I knew that they were telling me the truth as they understood it to be. It had become obvious to me that my parents were in grave danger.

I spoke to my father and warned him that the Jews of Poland would inevitably feel the violent force of anti-Semitism. I implored him to consider leaving Drohobycz, to resettle in Palestine. But even as I spoke, I knew that this would not happen. My parents were too old to travel across the world and start again in such a foreign land. Their lives had already passed them by, and I had long been aware of their weariness. They were beyond the pursuit of their ambitions here in Drohobycz, let alone in Palestine. And even if my father had wanted to leave, my mother would never have followed. Indeed, she still hoped that I would choose to stay in Poland, in the safety and security of their home, under her watchful, protective eye.

My mother had early disclaimed her heritage and actively discouraged my own. That she could be persecuted for being Jewish was to her unthinkable. After all, she did not think of herself as Jewish. And furthermore, to a devoted Europhile, Palestine would never represent anything but a primitive backwater, devoid of all things cultural and comfortable, and home to nothing more than a bunch of Philistines and an intolerable climate.

Nevertheless, I persisted. Over the coming days, I pleaded with my father repeatedly. I even spoke with our longtime neighbour, Mrs Himmel. As one of Europe's wealthiest women, she would certainly have the resources to move the whole neighbourhood to Palestine. She had already decided against sending her son Ziggy to Vienna to study. And, as her lawyer, my father had seen to her arrangement of susbtantial provisions for both Ziggy and Renata in the form of a Swiss bank account, 'in the event that something should happen to her'.

Despite my efforts, my parents were not going to move. Neither would Mrs Himmel.

Returning to Drohobycz was like a bad dream. I had to escape it as soon as I could. So much appeared to remain unchanged, but with every old friend I met and in every street I walked, I felt my past evaporating. The sweet innocence of what I had left behind was gone. In its stead was a changeling town, tinged with the slight but unmistakable scent of decay. I dreaded to think what the approaching cowboys had in store for the Indians.

Betrayal was thick in the air. And there was Suza.

Hardly a day had passed in Haifa when I did not imagine myself in my girlfriend's arms. But time and distance had been the enemies of love. We had parted with an understanding that she would join me in Haifa at the earliest possible opportunity, but I must admit that I had cooled to the proposition. We had corresponded, although not regularly, and my letters conveyed a tone of formality in order that I would not be misunderstood. Now that I was back in Drohobycz, I felt confusion and little else, save for a reluctance to face the inevitable reunion.

Suza had telephoned the house several times upon my arrival home but I refused to take the calls, hoping to postpone our reunion for as long as possible. The following day, when she arrived at the house in tears, I could delay it no longer. We greeted each other formally with a handshake, before I offered a comment to break the tension. 'You look very nice,' I said, 'even nicer than you look in my dreams.'

It was true, she was beautiful.

The flame rekindled, I invited her inside. Before I knew it we were in each other's arms again.

Perhaps the wave of emotions that had surfaced during my first days back in Drohobycz had got the better of me. While Suza appeared to have remained loyal to me, I began to suspect that in my absence the young men of Drohobycz had tested this loyalty to its limits. Too many young men, many with whom I was acquainted, greeted her and were greeted by her as we walked in the town. The winks, the nods, the subtle hand gestures, the knowing smiles, all played on my growing jealousy. Adding fuel to the fire, a number of my friends had taken it upon themselves to make suggestive inferences concerning Suza's fidelity.

I did not confront Suza with these suspicions. I neither sought nor obtained confirmation either way. I did, however, actively discourage her plans of meeting me in Haifa and subsequently becoming my wife.

I saw very little of Suza during my stay in Drohobycz. This came as a surprise to my parents, who understood us to be an established couple despite my two-year absence. My explanation that my priority was to finish my studies served both to cut short my mother's relentless interrogations and to reinforce her view that I was truly a gentleman of character.

Between the betrayal of my heart and the imminent betrayal of my people, it was time to farewell Poland for good.

I was awakened from a deep slumber at five o'clock in the morning. It was time to leave. I would be travelling by train to the Romanian port of Costanta before embarking on a boat bound for Haifa. Why on earth I had to catch a train at this ungodly hour was beyond me—I was never an early riser. Still half asleep, I gathered my belongings and left for the station with my parents.

In this dream within a dream, I had to bid farewell to my home and my family once again. This time, I was struck by an overwhelming sense of loss. Would this be the last I ever saw of them? Would I be saying goodbye to my loved ones for the last time? I knew it would be. There were no tears; I was going to be strong.

Instead, a question was repeated over and over in my mind. How is somebody supposed to behave in this situation? I was only twenty-one, and in so many ways still just a child. What more could I have done? I felt so powerless. What was I going to do now? I was certain of one thing. I was going to learn how to look after myself. I was going to survive.

Some months after returning to Haifa I received a letter from Suza's sister. Suza had been pregnant. She was just a schoolgirl. And with the entire school aware of her predicament, she had aborted the child. A photograph of Suza was attached to the letter. When I looked at the photo, I could not help noticing that she looked substantially older than her years.

I began to weep. What had I done?

I promised myself that as soon as the troubles in Europe were over, I would return to Poland and find her. I swore to myself that I would look after her, provide her with a university education, feed her, clothe her.

The next time I saw Suza was thirty-five years later. She was married and living in Baden. I had gone there specifically to apologise to her. She denied any knowledge of what I was talking about before dismissing the issue completely.

In September of 1939, following the German invasion of Poland, the mail from home suddenly stopped. I received a note from my father. Its message was brief and unmistakable: 'Don't contact us.'

I would never see or hear from my parents again.

Between 1939 and 1941, Eastern Galicia was occupied by the Russians. The German–Soviet Boundary and Frienship Treaty, signed at 5.00 a.m. on 29 September, saw Poland and Lithuania disappear from the map. In return for including L'vov, with the nearby oil wells of Drohobycz, on the Soviet side of the line, Stalin promised to provide Germany with 300,000 tonnes of oil a year. It was an agreement which, by all accounts, spared the lives of my parents and the rest of the Galician Jews for two years.

On the night of 29 June 1941, the city of L'vov fell to the Germans in what has been referred to as 'a nightmare of carnage and chaos', beginning with the massacre of three thousand Ukrainian political prisoners. No sooner had the Russian troops withdrawn, some having to break out of an encircled city under siege, than Ukrainian nationalists began slaughtering Jews in the streets.

In Drohobycz, SS Sergeant Felix Landau, one of the instigators of the murder of Austrian Chancellor Dollfuss in 1934, described in his diary the final moments before a massacre of Jews in a nearby wood: 'We order the prisoners to dig their graves. Only two of them are crying, the others show courage. What can they all be thinking? I believe each still has the hope of not being shot. I don't feel the slightest stir of pity. That's how it is, and has got to be.'

Two weeks after the first massacre of Jews in Drohobycz, Landau wrote: 'In a side turning we notice some Jewish corpses covered with sand. We look at each other in surprise. One living Jew rises up from among the corpses. We despatch him with a few shots. Eight hundred Jews have been herded together; they are to be shot tomorrow.'

12 LEAVING THE PAST BEHIND

Maturity is the capacity to endure uncertainty.
JOHN FINLAY

Pride, avarice, and envy are in every home.
THORNTON WILDER

I LEFT DROHOBYCZ for the last time with a new enthusiasm for Palestine. My father had been right. Europe was no place for Jews, and now I was determined to build a future for myself in my new home, despite its difficulties. I had come to terms with the fact that little remained for me in Poland. My time with Suza was over, that much I now knew for sure. I had other ambitions: I would complete my studies and forge a career in Palestine. I would devote myself to the pursuit of Hebrew and I would strive to fit in—I would not make the same mistakes my brother had made. *Har HaCarmel*, the very top of the mountain, was now in my sights. I would wed and raise a family there too. I imagined myself marrying the daughter of a wealthy *pardesan*—an orchard owner.

My second journey from Poland to Palestine bore little resemblance to the first. Two years earlier I had left Drohobycz with an acute sense of anxiety, trepidation, and a profound anger that my fate had been chosen for me. Now, a calm had descended upon me as resolution replaced indecision, and uncertainty gave way to a certain knowledge of what had to be done. Even my seasickness had subsided. I had suffered terribly on the return leg to Poland, but now the state of my stomach seemed to reflect my new resolve, tolerating the twists and turns that my life was taking.

My recently discovered interest in architecture was further stimulated by an overnight stay in Alexandria. I was awestruck by the massive scale of the buildings, by the arrangement and texture of the columns and obelisks, colonnades that were at once functional and aesthetic, bearing the weight of these giant edifices. As the early morning sun rose over the horizon, I marvelled at the harnessing of light in these man-made spaces. The masterly use of the earth's axis and precession, a delicate interplay between man and nature, revealed much about this civilisation—a people who clearly had the knowledge to conquer the elements in their architecture, but chose instead to integrate them into a bold statement of their world view.

Before reaching Haifa, the ship also stopped in Beirut, affording me the opportunity to assess for myself the glowing reports of my fellow students at the Technion. While Alexandria had whetted my appetite for architecture, Beirut appealed to my hunger for personal success and the material riches I hoped would accompany it. It was truly a beautiful city then, the 'Riviera' of the Middle East, and it proudly boasted the riches of international culture and business. I had heard that the way of life was different from that of Palestine, but I had never imagined such a contrast. Compared with the arid, industrial city of Haifa, Beirut was nothing short of paradise.

Upon my return to Palestine, I immediately travelled to Jerusalem to organise an extension for my student visa. In the face of the ongoing Arab riots, Jerusalem had become somewhat unsafe. I looked European and spoke no Arabic, so naturally I grew concerned when darkness began to fall and I had not yet located the Polish Consulate. The narrow streets were almost deserted when I finally arrived at the building, which was located in the Arab sector of the city. I knocked on the solid gates. A small viewing window was opened and a dark set of eyes looked out at me. The gate was opened and to my surprise, an Arab gentleman in full robes stood before me.

'*Muumu*,' I addressed him cautiously, 'can I speak Polish? Do you understand Polish?'

'You can speak any language you wish,' he replied in perfect Polish, 'but I especially like to speak Polish.'

I was taken aback by the incongruity. This Arab man spoke Polish better than I did.

'The office is now closed,' he informed me, 'but if you want to stay, we can accommodate you. It is no good for you to be walking around now. Tomorrow morning, we will attend to your visa.'

I was hungry and tired, and I certainly did not fancy the idea of finding alternative accommodation at the late hour, but as always, I was guided by my pocket.

'How much?' I asked.

'You will have to ask the brothers about that,' he said as he led me inside. 'You are lucky; today we have chicken, and chicken soup.'

The brothers? I thought to myself.

As it turned out, the consulate was located within a monastery. My Arab escort ushered me into an office and introduced me to one of the monks.

'How much will it cost me to stay?' I asked him.

'Nothing at all,' he replied, also in flawless Polish, 'as long as you follow our prayers.'

It wasn't exactly the price of my soul, so I readily accepted.

It was the most comfortable accommodation I had experienced in Palestine. My quarters were neat, my bed linen clean and fresh, and the food outstanding. 'I could get used to being a monk,' I thought to myself as I drifted into a deep sleep. That option was quickly dispelled however, as I was awakened at six in the morning by the tolling of the bell calling all for prayers. I sat quietly, making sure that I appeared appropriately respectful, while the monks conducted the service.

The consulate office opened soon after, and my visa was extended. The monk with whom I had spoken the previous evening suggested that I stay for a few days. 'You look too skinny,' he said. 'You need to gain some weight.' I thanked him for his concern, but declined the offer. A monk's life was not for me.

En route back to Haifa, I decided to stop in Tel Aviv to visit my uncle, Shimon Lustig. Given my recent experiences in Drohobycz, and my realisation that returning to Poland was no longer a viable option, I felt that I needed to establish my relationship with my family in Palestine.

Shimon and his family had emigrated in 1936. In his haste, my father's brother and business partner had left considerable loose ends for my father to tie up. As I discovered on my return to Drohobycz, this was another reason for my mother to voice her disdain for Shimon. My father casually brushed this off, believing that it was a natural part of business and arguing that it was inevitable *some* amount of work would be left undone.

Shimon had always been sympathetic to Labour Zionism, and in Palestine, his involvement with *Mapai* had secured him a contract to represent *Tnuva*—the dairy producers' co-operative—in legal matters. It was a substantial account that formed the basis of his successful practice. Shimon was acutely aware of all that was politically expedient. In a gesture to further demonstrate his Zionist ideals, he changed his family name to Yaron, a derivative of *Rinah*, which in Hebrew means 'cheerful'—a direct translation of Lustig, which means the same in German.

I had had little contact with 'Shimon the Cheerful' during my first two years in Palestine. Anselm didn't like to discuss him. When Anselm lost his job, he travelled to Tel Aviv to see whether his uncle could help him find alternative employment. When my brother discovered that Shimon was clearly not interested in assisting him, he promptly severed his ties with that side of the family.

I stayed overnight with the Yaron family. Having left my parents behind in a Europe that seemed to be on the brink of disaster, I felt the need to speak with Shimon about the political situation there. But my uncle was unresponsive to my questions, choosing instead to lecture me on my father's personality traits.

'He may be a university professor,' he began, 'but he will never be a successful businessman.'

'Why is that, Uncle?'

'He has a decent understanding of theory and philosophy. In fact he is probably best suited to international matters, a post at The Hague perhaps. A good knowledge of *ethics*.'

There was a distinct tone of one-upmanship in my uncle's voice. And the ambiguity created by his emphasis on the word 'ethics' was not lost on me. He was suggesting that my father was too ethically minded to survive in the cutthroat world of business. His words struck me as all the more arrogant when I remembered my mother's complaints about Shimon taking advantage of my father in their shared practice. That these characteristics of my father suited my uncle's ambition was obviously not something Shimon was prepared to admit.

Shimon's assessment of Father upset me profoundly, but I suddenly realised that an age-old brotherhood rivalry existed between them. My father had taken responsibility for the family after the death of their father. He had paid for Shimon's university fees and had never refused him assistance. He had taken him in, into his own law firm, and had never requested anything in return. That was how I had always seen it. But now I looked upon my uncle as a child, driven by an intense desire to outdo his elder brother in any way he could. This competition may have even transcended the generations, which would explain his reaction, or lack of reaction, to Anselm's plight. Indeed, Anselm would have found more sympathy had he approached our aunt, Lonia.

I had always been fond of Lonia, a gentle and sentimental woman with a love of literature and poetry. Lonia was always very good with children. Back in Drohobycz, she would organise children's plays and poetry performances. Once a year she would stage a dramatic performance. As much as I hated them, she insisted that I be involved.

'Tedek,' she would say, 'your part this time will involve only two words, but you must pronounce them correctly and with feeling.'

Lonia was a natural entertainer with an outstanding reading voice. She had a remarkable ability to bring poems to life, and she was especially fond of reciting Mickiewicz, the great nineteenth-century Polish poet and leader of the Romantic movement. All the children liked these stories, especially those concerning the lives of the Polish nobles. One of our favourites was a comic poem that described life in the villages. A young student at the university comes home for summer vacation. An important guest from Warsaw is occupying the guest wing for the summer. The student is advised to speak and behave properly in the presence of this lady. She is older than he is, but she is very charming, and he finds her desirable. One day, they take a walk through the woods. She gets tired and has to sit down. Unfamiliar with the woods, she is unaware that the ground is crawling with living things. She suddenly jumps, feeling something creeping inside her panties. Of course the student then has to help her remove these creatures.

The woman in this poem was named 'Philomena'. Subsequent books were written about Philomena, creating a folklore around Miskiewicz's character, and every Polish boy was searching for a Philomena.

I was quite close to my Aunt Lonia and my three cousins. Alex was three years younger than me, Ludek six years younger, and Ilan nine years my junior. I saw a lot of them as I was growing up. We attended the same school and I enjoyed spending time at their house. Located on the outskirts of Drohobycz, it was a comfortable, lived-in, rustic home with huge gardens. Lonia loved animals and the family's unkempt dwelling resembled a freestyle menagerie.

It annoyed my mother how much I liked Lonia, whom she saw as a frivolous 'theatrical'. And my mother could not stand animals.

'But the whole house smells of dogs' urine,' she would say to me as I set off for the family zoo.

'I disagree.'

'You like dogs!' she would cry, hurling the statement at me as some kind of personally injurious accusation.

'Yes, I do,' I would answer sweetly, much to her horror.

Lonia's own family was Jewish, but almost totally assimilated. Her loyalty was to Poland, and Polish was the only language she spoke. It was only because of an unquestioning respect for her husband that she agreed to Shimon's plan to uproot the family and move to Palestine. We assumed that in time, Lonia would flee and return to her beloved Poland.

Instead, she undertook with remarkable dedication to learn Hebrew. In Tel Aviv, she met a poet named Czernykowski, a Russian Jew who would later become a well-known writer of Hebrew literature. Lonia studied with Czernykowski, who was of the opinion that listening and conversing while sitting in cafés was the best way to learn the language. She progressed rapidly and now, just two years after arriving in Palestine, she was almost fluent in Hebrew.

As we sat together in their apartment, Lonia seemed to detect my dismay at Shimon's words about my father, and she quickly changed the subject.

'You must stay overnight here, Tedek. We will have a special meal to celebrate your visit.'

'Thank you, Lonia. I will.'

'Now, tell me Tedek, how are Anselm and Lusia?'

I did not wish to divulge too much about my brother and his wife, and certainly not in front of my uncle. 'They are fine,' I replied.

'I believe that you have spent some time with Stephania?'

'Yes. It has been very pleasant.'

Stephania, Lonia's sister, was living in Haifa. She was a large woman, even larger than my large-busted aunt, and this was accentuated by the extremely tight clothing she was disposed to wearing. Stephania held a senior position at one of Haifa's banks, and as part of the job, she was assigned to take charge of a large bank-owned villa on *Har HaCarmel*. She had heard about Anselm's unemployment and was fond of Lusia, so she wanted to help them. She knew that they were going hungry, and invited them to dine at the villa. They ate a meal that only bankers could afford.

When I arrived in Palestine in 1936, she invited me to dinner. She seemed very happy to see me, and I was certainly happy to see the food she had prepared for me. After the meal, having noticed that I admired the table service, she presented it to me as a gift. I had a very nice table setting for one. Lusia saw it when I returned home. 'OK, you can give it to me. You don't need it,' she said, quickly claiming my prize.

Before arriving in Palestine, Stephania had held a similar position at a bank in Drohobycz. The bank was keen to have Dr Kaufman as a client, and Stephania was assigned the job of securing his business. There was just one complication: like so many women in Drohobycz, Stephania was intent on marrying the debonair Kaufman. When Kaufman told her that he needed money, she did everything she could, legal or otherwise, to get it for him. She then suggested that it might be more prudent for him to marry her than to be implicated in a case involving misappropriated funds. When Kaufman replied that he would rather go to jail than marry her, Stephania fled to Haifa, leaving the doctor to face the music. Kaufman was imprisoned, and Pani Dubiensky, the best chef in Drohobycz, took food to him daily.

I stayed overnight with my family in Tel Aviv, at Aunt Lonia's insistence, before returning to Haifa. I had visited in an attempt to establish a tie with my family here in Palestine. Now I understood that my relationship with my uncle would be uncomfortable, and visits sporadic at best. Perhaps I reminded him of his brother, for reasons known only to him; this did not elicit the best in his nature. Nevertheless, I was a little sad saying farewell, especially to Aunt Lonia. My aunt's rapid mastery of the Hebrew language had encouraged me, however, and I would make a concerted effort to follow in her footsteps. But other changes would have to be made—I had to move out of Anselm and Lusia's flat. I felt strongly that their refusal to integrate into Palestine, as well as my preoccupation with their personal problems, was retarding my own progress. It was time to move out on my own and live my own life.

The opportunity arose soon after I commenced my third year at the Technion, when I was invited to move in with Zinc and Grossman, two of my fellow civil engineering students. Zinc had suffered from polio as a child, and now his left arm was paralysed. While I thought that this would be a hindrance for an engineer who was required to draw plans, this proved not to be the case. Indeed, he had spent many years compensating for his handicap, and the right side of his body was now extremely strong. Grossman and Zinc lived with Zinc's family, in the small apartment above Mr Zinc's bakery. They welcomed me to their home. The three of us would be sharing the lounge room, which was converted into a bedroom at night.

I would live with the Zinc family for a number of months. Mr Zinc, the baker, spent much of his life downstairs working at the ovens. His specialty was *challah*, a sweet loaf eaten on the Sabbath. He baked it exclusively for his existing clients, and he was not interested in attracting new customers. Nobody was permitted in the bakery when he cooked his *challah*—the recipe was a jealously guarded secret.

In the heat of summer, when he wasn't occupied in the bakery, Mr Zinc spent his time walking around the house half-naked. He was barely five feet tall, and he reminded me of the stories of Italy's King Emmanuel II, who could not address a crowd without standing upon some article of furniture.

I never saw any evidence that Mr Zinc took a bath. Day in and day out, he wore the same pair of old slippers, adorned with the encrustations of his life's work. Some people wear their lives on their faces; Mr Zinc wore his life on his feet. Each Friday night, at the family's Sabbath meal, the stench of his feet slowly rose, as hot air does, to mingle with and gradually overwhelm the delicious odours emanating from the banquet of Jewish foods that had been set upon the table. While a little of the baker went into everything he cooked, a little of everything he cooked stayed with the baker.

13 A World at War

There was never a good war or a bad peace.
         BENJAMIN FRANKLIN

MY VISIT TO Drohobycz in 1938 had alerted me to the profound political changes that were taking place in Europe. The Nazi regime was gaining a foothold in the countries surrounding Germany, and anti-Semitic sentiment was gaining strength in Poland. I considered this to be a local crisis, however, and had no idea of the effects it could have on my own life in Palestine.

It soon became apparent that Britain was actually preparing for a war in Europe. The declaration of the MacDonald White Paper in May of 1939 effectively closed the possibility of any subsequent growth for the Jewish national homeland, a prospect first set out in the Balfour Declaration of 1917. The White Paper sealed off Palestine as a haven for all but an insignificant fraction of Jewish refugees at a time when European Jewry faced a mortal threat to its survival. Naturally, there was a reaction from Zionist circles, and violence from some factions of the movement. The Revisionist paramilitary organisation, the *Irgun Z'vai Le'umi*, bombed a number of government buildings in Jerusalem and Tel Aviv and sabotaged railway lines.

I failed to see what these attacks could possibly achieve. Over and above this, I actually interpreted the implementation of the British policy as a necessary and defensible act of self-interest. Facing the threat of war with Germany, there could be no question of allowing the Arabs to form an alliance with the Nazis, if only because a major part of the oil resources of the Commonwealth were in the Arab world. British interests had to be protected at a time when national survival was in the balance.

I largely ignored the Zionist rumblings and chose instead to concentrate on my studies. Even here, there were hints of the possibility of war. During my third year, in 1939, the Professor of Architecture announced a competition calling for the design of fortresses to be built along the mountains of Lebanon, a line of defence to prevent the enemy from advancing through to the oilfields of Iraq. While I did not realise it at the time, the project was addressing issues that would soon become all too real. Within two years, the Axis force would be engaged in a massive pincer movement, advancing towards Iraq by way of Turkey and North Africa. And by then, I would be working with the British on the construction of these very fortifications.

Students were not obliged to enter the competition, since a project of this size could have interfered too much with their curriculum work. I decided to enter, however, and soon became completely immersed in the project. Teams of three students were required. Grossman and Zinc joined forces with me, although their interest and efforts did not match my level of involvement. They were Israeli boys, not Europeans, and perhaps that is why they took less interest in the broader issues.

The competition involved far more in the way of engineering than architecture. I designed a series of towers of a certain height that provided an unobstructed view. All of this was to be built in the desert, which afforded me little in the way of useful geographical features. I calculated that if I built to a certain height, I could establish the necessary advantage in terms of reconnaissance. I made provision for the placement of the gunners and the armoury. Throughout the project, I imagined it as entirely factual. Therefore, apart from the construction of the towers themselves, I had to consider issues of accommodation, food preparation, supply lines, and sewerage. I studied all of this meticulously, asking myself the appropriate questions and assuming that I had little choice but to find the most suitable solutions.

Ten weeks later, the students of both courses—Architecture and Engineering—gathered in the auditorium for the announcement of the winner of the competition. Without any preamble, Professor Shapiro called out my name.

'The winner of the competition is Ted Lustig. Firstly, he has demonstrated outstanding architectural skill in locating the most suitable sites for the fortifications as well as the design of the defences themselves. More than this, however, he has expressed through his work an exceptional understanding of the logistical issues involved in this operation as well as an excellent grasp of the military scenario we presented.'

This was the first time in my life that I felt the satisfaction of expressing myself completely, and in the process I had identified those areas of my work that were of particular interest to me. In short, my strength was in assessing the bigger picture and organising the logistics accordingly.

Following the presentation, Professor Shapiro called me into his office. As I entered, he was sitting at his desk, dressed as usual in his tweed jacket and bright bow tie, a friendly smile on his face. Professor Shapiro was the archetypal architect. He was a most amiable fellow, a tall, broad Russian Jew who wore his long hair brushed back, creating a centre parting or *Wanzegasse*, which translates unflatteringly (and in this case irrelevantly) from German as 'a promenade for bugs'. He was an impressive teacher, a lively, animated lecturer with fierce dark eyes whose enthusiasm enhanced his ability to communicate a point. Apart from being Professor of Architecture at the Technion, he was also Associate Professor at the University of Moscow.

'Well done, Lustig,' he began. 'Very well done.'

'Thank you, Professor.'

'You have some talent in architecture, Lustig. I think that you should switch into the architecture course and get away from this absolutely shocking business of engineering.'

I knew that there was little chance of securing a job as an architect. And besides, there was nothing but stone in Palestine, no timber or other materials necessary to maximise the scope of the architect's craft as I saw it.

'I know that I will be looking for a job as soon as I finish the course,' I replied. 'Who needs architects when this country will be busy building roads and bridges?'

'Well, maybe you are right. I am an architect and naturally, I am biased. I would like to see everybody become good architects, but the decision is yours,' he said, with good-natured resignation.

I appreciated his sentiment, but continued with civil and structural engineering.

On 1 September 1939, at six in the morning, Germany invaded Poland. The newspapers and radio reports in Haifa over the previous few weeks had alluded to the possibility of this event, but at the time it was difficult to separate the propaganda from the truth. I was neither shocked nor shaken. To me, this was not an event of paramount concern. Uninterested in the debates that were raging among the political groups in Haifa, I did not really consider the implications. I was more concerned with my own immediate livelihood. There was only a whisper at that time that the implications were greater, and that the result would have a direct impact on Palestine.

I did not feel any great concern about Poland as such. Indeed, the Polish Jews who attended the Technion took the opportunity to express their anti-Polish sentiment. Many of their families had been forced to leave Poland as a result of harsh treatment dealt out by the successor-state government that was formed at the end of the First World War. A series of jokes began to circulate around the Technion, most of them alluding to the comic image of the Polish cavalry standing face to face with the German tanks and aeroplanes. 'Before I have even finished this sentence,' it was often mused, 'the Poles will be running for the hills.'

Perhaps there were a few who suspected that the Jews were in danger, but most people were not thinking in such specific detail. Besides, European boundaries were being crossed all the time. I didn't fear for my parents because I had confidence in my father. I had no inkling of what was to come; indeed, some weeks after the invasion, the Nazis withdrew from eastern Poland, leaving it under Russian occupation. It was only later events, under German occupation between 1941 and 1945, that proved how profoundly I was mistaken, not about my father, but about the extent of the threat posed to European Jewry.

A few weeks after the invasion I received a postcard from my father, instructing me not to write. In it, he explained that Drohobycz was under Russian occupation and consequently subjected to very strong communist control. He did not want to draw attention to himself as a Jew with the Russian administration, and receiving mail from Palestine could pose a threat. This was my last correspondence with my parents.

Actually, I considered the news of Russian occupation rather dour. I am ashamed to admit that, at the time, I would have preferred the Germans. Stalin's regime worried me more than Hitler's. There had been countless reports of disappearances of Jewish members of the intelligentsia in Stalinist Russia. Yet as far as I could tell, while the Jews in Nazi Germany were shockingly maltreated, they were not eliminated. Unfortunately, there were a number of Polish migrants in Palestine who believed that life in Russian-occupied Poland would be more rewarding than life in Palestine. Tragically, they returned to their homes in Poland.

I did not become fully aware of the atrocities inflicted upon the European Jews until much later, in 1944 when the term 'Holocaust' began to be used. When the news began to filter through, I was stationed in Damascus. I immediately returned to Haifa to see an uncle of mine, the husband of my mother's half-sister. Mr Grossman had recently managed to escape to Palestine after having spent most of the war in Poland. As far as he knew, my father had been shot while lying in a hospital bed. German troops had stormed the hospital and killed all the patients. Soon after, in the winter of 1943, my mother had been arrested and placed on a train for transport to one of the labour camps. He was unsure as to whether she had been shot while attempting to jump from the train, or simply died from the impact of the fall.

As my uncle spoke, I felt myself stiffen, my heart turning to ice. Now that my parents were gone, I missed them terribly. I realised how empty my life had been, devoid of the wisdom and guidance that my father had always been able to offer. As I was embarking on my own career, I felt alone and unsure, a ship without a rudder, left to the mercy of the tides.

Each morning, as I woke from vivid dreams of my mother and father, a harsh self-examination took place. Had I done all that I could to persuade my parents to leave Poland? I knew that in reality the blame lay elsewhere for the fate of my family, but the battle still raged within me. To temper my own guilt, I tried to imagine the life my parents would have led in Palestine, deprived of their creature comforts and sense of belonging. At least my mother had died in Drohobycz as a person with high social standing, with her dignity intact, and did not have to face the mundane realities of life as a refugee. Surely my mother could not have existed in this miserable world. Surely ...

In Palestine, the outbreak of war in 1939 had quickly dampened the disputes between the mainstream Zionist movement and the British over the White Paper. For the most part, Jewish efforts were geared towards British support. The Jewish Agency mobilised the community's resources for wartime agricultural and industrial purposes. Soil under tillage was expanded by 70 per cent, and within a year, 400 new factories were built, essentially related to British military needs.

The community's identification with Britain's cause assumed other forms. In the first month of the war, the *Va'ad Le'umi*—the executive body of the Jewish National Assembly—announced the registration of volunteers for national service. Within five days, 136,000 men and women enrolled. Their motivation was not simply a desire to fight the Nazis, but the expectation that an armed and active Jewish force would compel Britain to reconsider the Zionist case. The British, however, were averse to the idea of a Jewish legion, believing that it would provoke a renewed Arab uprising. The idea was shelved.

The Jews, however, found alternative ways of contributing to the military effort. At the onset of hostilities, General Sir Evelyn Barker, the British army commander in Palestine, suggested the formation of mixed Arab–Jewish companies of 'Pioneers'—actually truck drivers, storekeepers, and trench diggers—to be sent to the Western Front. It was understood that the number of Jews accepted was dependent upon an equivalent number of Arab recruits. The parity rule was soon eased, however, and the result was wholly Jewish brigades, with their own Jewish junior and non-commissioned officers. The first groups, each comprised of 500 Palestine Jews, arrived in France during the first months of 1940. They did repair and maintenance work. After the French surrender in June, most of them were returned to Palestine, where some worked as ground personnel for the RAF.

Through the efforts of Arieh Stern and Libertowsky, *Mapai* worked hard to recruit Technion students for the Pioneers, and their numbers were growing. Many of my fellow students joined the brigades, but once again most were attracted by the job prospects rather than ideology. A substantial number of British soldiers were arriving in Palestine from as far afield as Singapore and Malaysia. Australian, New Zealand and Canadian troops were also being mobilised. This all served to create new fields of employment: camps had to be constructed, sewers and roads built. Large numbers of those recruits who joined for idealistic reasons soon became disillusioned with their role in the war effort, and consequently, the Pioneers suffered a high rate of desertion. While these young Jews had imagined themselves as part of an active fighting force, they found themselves unarmed and responsible for mundane tasks such as building roads.

I took little interest in the idea of becoming a Pioneer, at least until I had completed my degree. My priority was to perform my best during my final year at the Technion. Besides, I would prove far more useful as a qualified engineer. As much as I would try to limit the impact of war on my studies, inevitably it still had an effect on my life in Palestine.

One of the more positive effects of the war was that it provided me with the opportunity to secure rent-free accommodation, at least for a while. With Jewish efforts turning to agriculture and industry, many commercial businesses ground to a halt. This left a number of large office blocks standing empty in downtown Haifa. One of my fellow students came up with the bright idea of squatting in one of these buildings in order to save ourselves the rent. I moved in, together with Lifshitz, Reichert, Abraham Meiri and two other students.

We had seven floors of office space at our disposal. Lifshitz, undoubtedly the dominant personality among us, demanded the top floor for himself. Nobody would have dared to challenge his claim; the rest of us found space wherever we could.

Another of the students, Schmulavich ('Shmulik'), an unremarkable boy, diminutive in stature and timid in temperament, looked upon Lifshitz as his hero, revering his projection of power and control. In time, Shmulik had adopted the role of messenger boy for our leader.

One day, Lifshitz was in his top-floor quarters entertaining three other students in a game of cards. I sat off to the side—while I was fond of playing bridge, I had never taken an interest in poker, and especially against Lifshitz who never lost.

Lifshitz turned to Shmulik.

'Fetch me a packet of cigarettes,' he barked.

Shmulik did not move. 'But we're on the seventh floor.'

Lifshitz persisted. 'I would like a cigarette. Go downstairs and buy some. Can't you see that I am busy here? Go! You have money.'

Shmulik held firm. 'What will you do if I don't?'

It was a suicidal response. We all knew that Lifshitz rarely hesitated before lashing out. Indeed, this was one of the keys to his strength. To our surprise, however, Lifshitz remained calm and gave his underling another chance to redeem himself.

'I am sending you downstairs to get me some cigarettes,' Lifshitz spelled out as if addressing a small child. 'If you do this and come back, that would be very nice. So stop arguing with me and just go. I can't concentrate on the game.' His tone was calmer, but far more menacing.

Shmulik's reply sent a wave of horror across the room. 'I'm not going.'

In a flash, before any of us had time to intervene, Lifshitz was standing at the open window. He had hold of Shmulik by the ankles, and was dangling him head first out the window.

'Are you going downstairs yourself or would you prefer me to show you the shortcut to the street?'

'I'm going, I'm going,' cried Shmulik.

Ephraim 'Fishel' Lifshitz was a hooligan; of that there is no doubt. But he was intelligent, and I respected him. 'It is common that for survival reasons we must appear to be a *kurve* [c - - t]. It is sometimes necessary in order to gain respect, as long as it just a camouflage,' he once told me in his wisdom.

Lifshitz had become a leader of the student movement, and he often addressed large gatherings. After hearing one of his speeches I realised that he was an eloquent and accomplished orator, and my sympathies grew. Later I came to realise that while he claimed to support the right-wing Revisionist movement, this was not actually the case. His ideology was eclectic. In reality, he had a cynical attitude toward life and politics, and was essentially a 'gun for hire'. 'Who is paying?' was the true, mercenary basis for his affiliations.

With his temperament, Lifshitz would make an excellent soldier. During the 1948 War of Independence, he would become officially recognised as a hero. In May of 1948, the Trans-Jordanian Arab Legion crossed the Jordan River, took control of the Judean Hills and laid siege to Jerusalem. For the 85,000 Jews in the Holy City, already weakened by an Arab stranglehold on their lifeline from the coast, the attack would prove disastrous. By 28 May, the Jewish quarter surrendered and the Old City fell. After weeks of fighting, and with the supply line from Tel Aviv cut, the defenders of the New City were exhausted. The water supply had been severed and the prospect of mass starvation was very real.

David Ben-Gurion, then Chairman of the Jewish Agency and a leading *Mapai* figure, insisted that full military priority be given to opening the Jerusalem highway. The Arab bastion controlling the road, Latrun, had to be assaulted. Repeated attacks were met by heavy artillery and mortar fire from the Arab Legion's Fourth Regiment, and Latrun very nearly became a graveyard of Jewish hopes for breaking the siege of Jerusalem. A single alternative remained for opening the Jewish supply line: a path south of Latrun could be widened to enable vehicles to pass through.

Engineers and hundreds of labourers were summoned from Tel Aviv and immediately put to work. Lifshitz had heard the radio announcements and was among the volunteers. The road to Jerusalem was completed within days. In order for this to be accomplished, several Arab defence points had to be overcome. Armed only with a revolver and facing Arab machine guns, Lifshitz led a group of 'volunteers' down the road and managed to secure a number of these positions. Ben-Gurion proclaimed these deeds as heroic. In fact, Lifshitz had forced these men into battle at gunpoint. 'Move, or I shoot you now, on the spot.'

During the months that we were able to live in the office building, before being discovered by the authorities and impolitely asked to vacate, I developed quite a close friendship with Lifshitz, as well as with Reichert, his right-hand man. Until then, I had remained friendless, preferring to look upon my colleagues as acquaintances, temporary and transient, people I would leave behind after completing my penance at the Technion, after leaving Palestine for greener pastures. Perhaps my growing realisation that I would not be returning to Europe had changed my attitude toward these people. I felt better for this—it had taken almost three years for me to feel that I had friends. The friendship I developed at this time with Abraham Meiri was particularly important.

Meiri soon became known to us all as 'Gandhi' for his uncanny resemblance to the great Indian liberator. He was an intelligent, well-mannered and trustworthy young man, one of the few people with whom I had an almost instant rapport. We would remain close friends long after our studies had finished. Indeed, he was my closest friend.

14 A 'WORKING-CLASS' MAN

We work to become, not to acquire.
ELBERT HUBBARD

I COULD NO longer rely on funds being sent by my father. By the end of the third year of my engineering course, war in Europe had broken out and communication had already been cut. Consequently, I would have to secure employment over the holidays.

Soon after the academic year ended, in September 1939, I approached Libertowsky about a job. Like Arieh Stern, Libertowsky had always thought of me as one of those 'bourgeois Poles'. So when I met him on the wharves that afternoon, he quickly dismissed my request.

'You're crazy,' he said, 'you already get money sent from home. Do you really expect to take a job from a student who really needs it?'

I was amazed that he had not realised the implications of the war. For somebody so involved with politics, this was incredible.

'There is a war on,' I explained. 'My father has had to cut contact with me. I need the job.'

He looked at me suspiciously. 'All right,' he said finally. 'I will get you a job. But you will pay me half your wage for the students' fund.'

I could not afford to be choosy, and besides, falling out with the leader of the student union body would surely see me among the very long-term unemployed.

'What are you trying to prove, Lustig?' he said petulantly as he herded me out of his office.

Surely I did not need to explain it again. 'I just want to prove that the bourgeois can work just as hard as these hooligans,' I answered, facetiously.

At six o'clock that evening I arrived on the wharves, ready for hard labour until six o'clock the next morning. Ephraim Lifshitz was in charge of the work crew. He stood me in front of a stack of boxes, each containing ninety kilograms of grapefruit, packed and ready for export.

'They have to be moved to the other end of the wharf,' he said.

The other students stood to the side, waiting to see how the new boy would cope. They must have been pleased because I could not budge a single box. Eventually, one of them approached me.

'Come on, you can have a trolley. We will stack three boxes onto it and you can wheel it down to the other end.'

Unfortunately for me, I had failed to notice that this area of the wharf was sloping slightly towards the water. As I edged the trolley forward, it gained momentum and was soon out of my control. I froze in horror as the three crates and the trolley plunged off the edge of the wharf and into the water.

One of the other boys let fly. 'You'll have to pay for that trolley, you idiot. And the boxes. You lost us three boxes.'

I apologised profusely, and in an effort to redeem myself, worked at a breakneck pace for the rest of the day.

When Libertowsky heard about the mishap, he turned to me with a victorious smile. 'You had better forget it. There are no jobs for you here. And you can forget about the pay.'

I was outraged. 'What do you mean? I was promised the money, and I was promised a job.'

He knew that I had performed admirably after my initial mishap, and decided not to argue with me. 'All right, I will pay you for the day and then I will organise something else for you.'

The following day I was sent to work for *Solel Boneh*, constructing a road in *Hadar HaCarmel*. This work was even more demanding than the job on the wharf. I was exposed to the sun from six in the morning until eight at night. There were no trees, no shade, just a relentless summer sun. By the end of the day, I was severely sunburnt.

Water was supplied, but it arrived in a 44-gallon drum, and was to be used for the construction as well. As the day wore on, the water became warmer, and was soon undrinkable.

On the third day of this job, I noticed that I was being watched closely by my foreman.

'Are you Lustig, the student?'

'Yes.'

'Come with me.'

He took me across to work with Stephen, a gorilla of a man from Salonika. He was brandishing a jackhammer. Our job was to take turns on the hammer and then fill a large basket with the broken rock. I couldn't even move the basket when it was empty, let alone when it was full of rock.

'Are you all right?' Stephen asked me.

I felt ashamed at my lack of physical prowess, and terrified that I may have been in his way.

'Look, just watch me,' he said patiently.

He broke the rocks with the jackhammer and pushed the rubble into the basket. Then he threw the basket onto the embankment. It had taken twenty seconds at most. Then he handed the hammer to me. Three minutes later, I had managed to shovel half of my pile of rubble into the basket.

The foreman returned, looked at the results of my efforts, and said to me, 'Maybe you shouldn't be doing this kind of job. I will get a hose and you can water in front of the steamroller.'

The steamroller, and its driver for that matter, were ancient and cranky. I would not have expected that I could go wrong with this simple and undemanding task, but the driver kept yelling: 'Lustig, Lustig. What's the matter with you? You are pissing too far in front.'

I lasted three weeks in this job. Libertowsky received his half of my wage and I received mine. I would have to find an alternative.

During my final year at the Technion, through 1940, I worked for the Palestinian police force. The war abroad had caused considerable local unrest, and the streets of Haifa were becoming unsettled. Many innocent people were subjected to harassment, even violence. My motives for joining the force were far from noble, however; I realised that this was the simplest way of securing six pounds per month, not to mention the added bonus of standard issue: boots, uniform, and a free meal during my shift. Furthermore, I was not required to 'stroll the beat'—my postings would be stationary positions.

It was only during my four weeks of basic training that I would be on foot patrol, and even then I was accompanied by two British constables. Despite my reasonable grasp of the English language, their cockney accents and guttural expressions left me dumbfounded. For the most part, I had absolutely no idea what they were saying. I learned later that these two policemen were actually convicts, sent to the 'colony' in response to severe overcrowding in the British prisons at home.

The two constables were made welcome by the local inhabitants, sometimes overly so. One night during my initiation, we stopped in front of a run-down old building, featureless except for a small, dimly lit doorway. With a glance across to his partner and a smirk, one of them instructed me to enter, to 'check it out'. Perhaps they had suspected that I was a little 'wet behind the ears', and my reaction to what I saw would surely have confirmed it. Before me stood a stage, and on it, a performer, completely naked. The appendage that hung low between his legs betrayed his gender. He was definitely a man, but the sight of his swollen breasts had me entirely confused. The constables must have noticed the wave of nausea that overcame me: they stood there laughing. It was my first exposure to the seedier side of life in Haifa.

I had always been well protected from the raw, harsh realities of life on the streets. My sheltered upbringing had ensured that I fraternised only with cultured, well-mannered, and educated people.

I was already sixteen when I was first confronted with 'life after dark' on the streets of Drohobycz. I had escorted Suza home one evening under the protection of my two students, the older boys who had managed to pass the school year under my tutelage. As we walked to her home, which was situated in one of the less affluent suburbs of the city, I saw people moving through the shadows, their swiftness and stealth suggesting that they wished not to be seen in these streets. On the way back, walking along the same street, I saw several women standing under one of the gas-fuelled street lamps. Suddenly, two of the women moved on to the sidewalk and stood in my path, blocking my way.

Of course I knew of the existence of prostitutes, but I had never encountered one before, and I did not know how to react. My mind raced—there were some rather rough-looking fellows around, and if I behaved like a prospective client, they might attack me for the money they would surely suspect me of having. Before I could formulate an appropriate response, one of the women opened her fur coat and flashed her naked body at me. The effect of the sudden confrontation, the darkness of night, and the eerie shadows of people moving around under the pale light of the gaslamps was to send me into a panic. I stood speechless for a few moments before bolting. I did not stop running until I had crossed the city and arrived safely at home.

My only other experience of note came two years later, while visiting my mother's step-brother in L'vov. He was the son of Kuhrmärker who was, for a very short time, Grandmother Elbaum's second husband. A dapper blonde gentleman with a charming personality, young Kuhrmärker was quite the ladies' man. This dedicated and experienced socialiser decided to take me to a nightclub to celebrate my completion of school and introduce me to 'the scene'.

We entered the darkened room, where I saw a dozen women sitting at the bar.

'You see those ladies?' he asked.

'Yes.'

'Invite any one of them to dance and then take her back where you picked her up. This is all you need to know. And don't be so tense. Relax! Go with the flow.'

As I danced with one of the young women, she started to talk to me. I felt embarrassed—Kuhrmärker's instructions had made no reference to a conversation! When the tango ended and the foxtrot began, the beat was much too fast for my awkward feet. The foxtrot was certainly not part of my training for the debutantes' ball.

'You can enjoy the dancing,' she remarked, 'it won't cost you much more.'

I started to wonder about this. What is this costing me in the first place? Is Kuhrmärker paying? As it turned out, he hoped that I would not find out about the payment because it was a gift from him. Nor did he want me to know that he had arranged for this woman to invite me back to her home.

'Nothing will be said,' he told me when I approached him about her offer. 'No problem at all. A very fine woman.'

Thoughts did cross my mind as to what was expected of me, but this exercise would prove a complete waste of time. I did not feel any attraction towards her, and besides, I was already in love with Suza. I spent the night on a sofa in my dancing partner's freezing apartment, and could hardly wait to make my getaway in the morning. She gave me a dry piece of bread for breakfast, and I left.

This, then, had been the extent of my experience of life on the streets, and it certainly did not include that which stood before me now—a person who was half woman, half man. In this respect the constables were correct: I wasn't just wet behind the ears, I was saturated!

It did not take long in the force for me to realise that certain assignments, or postings, were more 'comfortable' than others. One night, I was assigned the job of standing guard at the Haifa hospital.

Two Arab prisoners were receiving treatment and were placed in adjacent beds in an otherwise empty ward. My job was to guard them, from ten o'clock at night until six in the morning. I was seated outside in a position where I could watch them through the glass door.

The nursing duties in the Catholic hospital were performed by an order of nuns, who went well out of their way to make sure that I was comfortable and, to my surprise, provided me with a very satisfying meal. I had spent a long day at the Technion and faced the prospect of another the following day, and after a few hours on the job, I felt myself drifting into sleep.

It occurred to me that a job like this—one that would provide me with dinner, and then allow me to sleep through the night—would complement my daytime life at the Technion perfectly. But a strict rule of the force stipulated that anyone caught sleeping while on duty was docked half of the month's pay. The possibility of getting caught was substantial, given that a team of inspectors did the rounds each night. So I had to find a way of eluding the inspectors.

The inspectors had developed a keen strategic advantage. They wore rubber soles, enabling them to move in on their prey undetected. In order to seize the advantage for myself, I struck an alliance with the nuns. They agreed to lock the main door to the ward, thus depriving the inspector of an opportunity to catch me literally off guard.

A week elapsed. I heard that my sergeant suspected that I was sleeping, and he swore to the English constables that he would catch me out and 'fix me up'. After about a month, the sergeant instructed me that I was to report to Inspector Nicholl. I thought my time was up. 'He knows,' I thought to myself.

The sergeant escorted me to the inspector's office and issued his final instructions: 'Stand straight and speak properly when you are in the presence of the Inspector.'

Nervously I entered the room, where before me sat Inspector Nicholl. Even seated, I could tell he was a tall man, six foot two perhaps, very skinny, very straight—but with a vacant look in his eye, a glazed expression that must have taken years of alcohol abuse to cultivate.

'Why is it, Lustig, that you apply every day for night duty, and always in that hospital? We are aware that you have warm accommodation, good food, and that you are locked in by the nuns. What is behind all of this?'

'I am in my last year of university,' I replied with an honesty born of fear. 'I am going to be sitting some very difficult exams. It is crucial that I attend the lectures, and they are all conducted during the day. That is why I am applying for night duty.'

It occurred to me that he was more suspicious of my request for night duty than of my requests for the hospital posting. After all, nobody else in the force *wanted* to do night duty; they only took an occasional night shift because the roster demanded it. The inspector mumbled something, and I jumped to attention. He scribbled his address on a piece of paper and handed it to me.

'I am living in the German colony of Haifa. I want to meet with you at my house.'

Early that evening, after finishing at the Technion, I went to his home. I was met at the door by an extremely attractive young German girl. She showed me inside to the lounge room, where the inspector was reclining on a leather sofa. We all sat down to a pot of tea.

'I liked what you were telling me, Lustig,' the inspector said. 'I wanted you to meet my girlfriend.'

I felt important.

'I am impressed by your honesty and your work ethic. I think that if you chose to stay in the police force under my supervision, I would put you through the police exams, and in six months you would become a sergeant.'

I was stunned. 'Thank you, Inspector.'

I thought it unwise to tell him that he must be 'off his bloody rocker'. I was going to be an engineer. Who would want to be a policeman? But I appreciated his compliment. I was kept on the force until the end of my engineering exams, September of 1940, when I passed my diploma and resigned from the force.

I had seen little of my brother since moving out of his apartment. I continued to keep an eye out for possible jobs for him, but was unsuccessful in my efforts to interest potential employers or contacts.

I finally found a job for Anselm through my maths tutor, and the opportunity arose as a direct consequence of the war. At the outset of hostilities in Europe, the oil refineries in Haifa Bay were ordered to triple their production of petroleum. This would require extra manpower.

My maths tutor was a young man who had recently completed his engineering degree at the Technion. After graduating he worked with the refineries developing a signalisation process, the success of which had propelled him to a senior position. Somewhat dissatisfied with engineering as a full-time profession, he turned his attention to other pursuits, including teaching. He had remained on the Board of the refineries, however, and a professorship at the Technion was in his sights. An extremely handsome and immaculately presented man, he had climbed to the top of the social tree in Haifa. He lived on *Har HaCarmel* and owned a very impressive automobile.

He was helping me to prepare for my final exams in mathematics when I broached the subject of my brother. He had taken me under his wing, offering me advice on all of my subjects, not just mathematics. I felt that I could confide in him.

'There is something weighing heavily on my mind,' I began, 'so much so that I am finding it difficult to concentrate on my work.'

'What is the problem, Tedek?'

'I have a brother. And he hasn't been working for the last four years. I am terribly concerned about him.'

'Why is that?'

'I could explain why, but it is a long story and you may not believe it. Suffice to say, he couldn't get along with his foremen. He went from one job to another.'

'That is a concern.'

'I know. But I can assure you, he's a very nice guy. And honest. Would you be prepared to meet him at least?'

'Of course, Tedek.'

The following day he met me at Anselm's flat. After a short discussion with Anselm, he decided that he would give my brother a chance. This gave Anselm a new lease on life. The following day, he began to take Hebrew classes, and within a week, my brother was working at the refinery. He was started in a position that paid him five pounds more than anyone else in his intake and he was the happiest man in the world, thrilled at the opportunity to finally take care of himself and his wife. Anselm would keep that job for the next thirty years.

15 Engineering a New Fate

Miracles sometimes occur, but one has to work terribly hard for them.
CHAIM WEIZMANN

BY SEPTEMBER 1940, I had completed my degree, and the small piece of paper I held proudly in my hand on graduation day proclaimed me a qualified civil engineer. I could not get a job, however. I had borrowed a typewriter from the Technion—a museum piece that had been used to demonstrate the mechanics within. I was typing at least ten applications per day, for jobs that were advertised on the notice-board at the Technion.

With my ear to the ground, I caught wind of the fact that *Solel Boneh*, the country's largest construction firm, was undertaking an enormous amount of work. It was mostly projects that arose out of the need to accommodate the many battalions of soldiers who were moving into Palestine as the battles in Europe and North Africa raged. There were jobs for carpenters, bricklayers, electricians—countless opportunities for all manner of tradesmen. But for the fresh new engineer there was *babkes* (nothing) and it was back to the old drawing board.

Soon after Italy's entry into the war, 1400 Jews were permitted to join the 'Pioneers' as members of the Royal Air Force ground crew. The vast majority of Pioneers were being used as labourers in camp, road and sewer construction, and these positions with the air force were considered the best jobs available. As an engineer, a job with the RAF would be a fine education for me, and so I decided to apply.

The prerequisite for a job with the RAF was the ability to pass a test on the electrical workings of an automobile, of which I knew nothing. I joined forces with two of my friends from the Technion who were also preparing for the examination. We borrowed a number of books on the subject from the Technion library and studied them in detail. We bombarded each other with questions to test our knowledge. A fortnight later, I took a bus to Sarafant, fifty kilometres east of Tel Aviv and the largest and most important British military camp in Palestine.

The bus driver called out, 'Anyone for Sarafant?'

I raised my hand.

'Joining the forces?' he asked.

'Yes.'

'Bravo,' he said good-naturedly. 'Another idiot.'

In an attempt to increase my chances for selection, I had dressed in what I considered to be a British uniform. Khaki shorts and shirt were actually the Palestinian fashion, but I had added a few British touches—long sleeves and long socks.

On arrival at the camp, I found myself standing in a queue ahead of an acquaintance from the Technion. Mazer stood about five foot six inches, and was well known for his neurotic temperament and his lack of nerve. I had little to do with him at school since we studied different subjects. He had qualified as a mechanical/electrical engineer. I wondered why he was in this queue—after all, he had already passed the examination.

'How was the exam?' I asked. 'Did you answer all the questions?'

'Yes,' he replied, 'but why are you standing in the food queue?'

I did not wish to alert him to my blunder. I thought fast. 'I am hungry. I haven't eaten a thing all day.'

We sat together and ate. The food was excellent, by local standards at least. I was starving anyway and perhaps that is why it tasted so good. I turned to him and continued our discussion.

'So, what is it like here?'

'Look,' he replied, 'we are all stupid. This camp is bullshit. You sign, you are in, no questions. But you're not in the RAF. You end up doing whatever they want. Toilet cleaning, anything.'

This was not good news. I realised that I had to get out of there. Fast.

'Can I just walk out of here?' I enquired.

'I don't know. You look like you already belong here wearing all that khaki.'

Two large Senegalese soldiers stood guard at the gate. As I approached, they crossed their rifles, barring my exit. Instinctively,

I adopted the best English accent I could muster and screamed, 'Attention!' They jumped with a start, and I saluted them as I passed through the gates. I returned to Haifa, grateful that I had not been charged as a deserter and ready to continue my search for a job once again.

By this time, my rent-free existence as a squatter in an office block had come to an end. Now four of us were living in a single room in a three-bedroom flat, paying extravagant rent. One and a quarter pounds per month, each.

Our landlady was a dumpling of a woman who was as wide as she was tall. Her loud, obtrusive manner was that of a 'fishwife', and indeed, her piscine odour further justified the label. She rarely afforded herself the cost of a shower, if at all. Her husband, an employee of the Palestine Electricity Commission, always looked weary and withdrawn, like a man who had endured decades of browbeating.

One afternoon, as the four of us sat out on the balcony of the apartment, I noticed an extremely attractive young woman sunbathing on her terrace in the building across the road. As I watched her, I caught her eye, and she returned a smile. Curious, I asked our landlady about this woman. I was informed that her husband was an important man who supplied labour to the British forces.

At that moment, I decided to take an enormous risk. I was determined to meet this man, and I would do so through making contact with his wife. If I succeeded, I would have a job; if not, I could always hurl myself head first off their third-floor balcony. I was truly 'playing the rock', as in Monaco, where the casino stood conveniently next to a cliff. Winners could rejoice; losers might as well jump.

I told our landlady that I needed to take a shower.

'You will pay?'

'I will be no longer than five minutes.'

'Five minutes! Do you realise how long a time that is?'

'Okay. I will take only three minutes.' It was an investment, after all.

I still had my light grey suit from Poland. I had to look my best. This was important when dealing with a woman. My room-mates were laughing at me. They thought I was crazy.

I climbed to the third floor and knocked on the door. It was chained, and it opened slightly.

'What do you want?'

From her Hebrew I could tell that she was Polish.

'I have finished my studies, I have a diploma. I have no money. I cannot find a job. I am hungry.'

I had found that this always made an impression, the hunger part. She asked me in.

'You are Polish?' she asked.

'Yes. And you?'

'My husband and I are from Cracow.'

'I believe your husband may be able to help me with a job.'

'This is true. He is supplying labour to the British and is very well paid for it. I can tell him about you, but he is a jealous type and we cannot make any mistakes.'

I noticed her use of the word 'we'.

'Why don't you tell him that we are old friends from Cracow,' I suggested.

'Okay,' she continued, 'but be careful, he is very suspicious. You must exercise control, and for heaven's sake, don't compliment me.'

'Don't worry, I wouldn't dare,' I replied, realising my chances of employment lay in maintaining an active neutrality towards her obvious charms.

'You stay out on your balcony. He comes home at about seven. He is always tired. You may be able to talk to him, but sometimes it is very difficult. Watch my balcony. I will give you a signal. If you see a falling piece of paper, you know it is all right to come.'

Hardly a foolproof plan, I thought to myself. What happens if there is a gust of wind?

'Just be ready,' she urged.

'I am ready right now,' I announced. And I was.

The other guys sat out on the balcony with me waiting to see what would happen. They joked among themselves that this gorilla would throw me out of his window. I watched and waited, training my eyes on the terrace doors.

Finally the paper fell, and I made my way nervously up to their apartment. It was a brief session.

The young lady invited me in with a string of fake greetings that implied we were long-lost friends. What a surprise to discover that I lived across the street! She introduced me to her husband.

The boys had been joking about a gorilla, but it was no joke. Before me sat an ape-like hulk of a man, short but built like a tank. His

Neanderthal face supported a heavy brow and he was covered with hair, from head to toe. He was wearing nothing but a towel around his waist. His perspiration seemed to have a life of its own, feeding upon itself as rivulets moved like dam-busters, searching for a home in any crevice they could find, or simply streaming to the ground.

'Who are you?' he demanded. 'What is your name?'

'Lustig.'

'What do you want?'

'I thought that you might be able to help me with a job.'

'What are you qualified to do?'

'I am an engineer.'

'Do you know how to work with instruments?'

'I have just completed four years of study,' I replied.

'Do you know anything about naphtha?'

'It is a refined crude oil product that is used for residential heating.'

He considered my answer. The interview was over.

'Okay. I may be able to help you. A lorry will be here at six tomorrow morning. You be here. And when I say six, that means that I want you here at five to six. Do you understand? We have to be on site by seven.'

'I will be here at five to six.'

'And don't wear that suit. Dress like me.'

Dress like him? He was wearing a towel with a hole in it. I guessed that he was referring to khaki work clothes.

'Thank you very much,' I gushed as I backed out under his wife's supervision.

'Don't thank me,' he grunted, 'and you don't need to thank my wife.'

That was it. I returned to my flat, and reported the result to my room-mates. They could not believe it.

'Ted. You are hallucinating. You must be ill.'

Perhaps I was. Spending the money I had yet to earn, I took them all out to dinner that evening to celebrate. We ate like human beings, almost.

The next morning I was on that lorry, heading north. We arrived at an isolated camp. The area was completely unsettled. Open space for as far as the eye could see, except for a small hut which served as an office. My new employer instructed me to wait outside while he spoke with the British air force officer inside.

Half an hour later he emerged with the news that I would be starting work the following day.

'Really?' I exclaimed.

He looked at me with disdain. 'Don't ask me, just listen. You told me that you were familiar with engineering instruments. You will be required to set out an airstrip. Be here at eight tomorrow morning.'

'Okay.'

'It's a six-month job. If you get through this one, you will be on your way. And they will pay you eighteen pounds. Take it or leave it.'

'Eighteen pounds a year?' I asked, wondering why this figure was a little low.

'A month,' he snapped disdainfully, as if he were addressing a simpleton.

Eighteen pounds a month! I had never dreamt of earning that much money.

'What do I pay you?' I enquired, sensing a catch.

'Nothing,' he replied, 'you are a friend of mine.' After a short pause, he continued in a more serious tone. 'Just don't mess with my wife.'

The following morning I reported to the officer in charge.

'What's your name?' he asked.

'Lustig.'

'We are here because we need to build an airstrip,' he continued. 'They must have told you what we want to do.'

'Where does it start?' I enquired.

'Over there. There is a marker somewhere. I have been here the whole night and I have not slept. I am going now. I have had enough. Get everything done.'

He then stepped into his jeep and drove away. I was left alone. I was hopelessly out of my depth and did not have the foggiest idea of what to do. While I was aimlessly studying the maps, I heard a car pull up. A young man stepped out and walked towards me. From a distance, he looked tall and straight, his head held high: a posture that bespoke a position of importance. Strangely, as he came closer, his image did not seem to be getting larger and when he stood beside me, I realised that he was very short indeed, even shorter than I. The tone of authority with which he spoke was betrayed by the unnaturally high pitch of his voice. It was quite absurd.

'*Shalom*,' he squeaked. 'I want to speak to the officer in charge.'

'He will be coming later,' I replied, not wanting to alert this man to the fact that my superior had gone for a nap.

'What are you doing here? You speak Hebrew.'

'I am an engineer.'

'What are you doing?'

'Setting out an airstrip.'

'You know how to do this?'

'Yeah.'

'You know, my name is Diskin. You know who I am.'

Indeed I did. His family owned one of the largest construction firms in Palestine.

'Yes, the builders in Jerusalem.'

'Oh, you know of us then? Do you know land surveying?'

'Yes. I have been doing it for four years.'

'I have a proposition for you. We have got a big job in Beirut coming up. What do you say?'

I remembered my stop in Beirut on the way back from Drohobycz. It had appealed to me greatly.

'It sounds very interesting.'

'There is one problem. Do you have your own surveying instruments?'

'Yes,' I lied.

'Are you sure? You know that we can't buy these instruments.'

'Yes, I'm sure.'

'Are these instruments here yours?'

'No. They belong to the military.'

'So you will borrow them, or steal them perhaps?'

'No. I don't do that kind of thing. So what about Beirut?' I asked, trying to turn the subject from larceny to opportunity.

'No problem, if you have the instruments—here is my address in Kingsway, downtown Haifa. Come to my office at six tomorrow evening. Wait for me if I am not there.'

'How much do I get?'

'If you have the bloody instruments, you will be looked after. If you are talking bullshit, don't bother to come.'

I had several hours left that day. I simply waited for the lorry to pick me up. I did nothing on that airstrip. On the way back to Haifa I thought about my employer, the gorilla. He is going to kill me. I thought. He will crush me like a peanut in his bear-like hands.

But more importantly, where the hell was I going to get hold of the instruments?

It suddenly dawned on me. The Technion.

During wartime, the number of students would be down, so there must be a surplus of instruments. They had about fifteen or twenty sets there, and maybe they could make some money by leasing a set out to me. It was a good idea. It was the only idea. It was already six in the evening. The Technion would be closed. I took the bus to *Bat-Galim* (daughter of the waves), to the home of my Professor of Geodesy and Surveying.

I knew Professor Steinberg quite well. In fact, I also knew that he was interested in me as a husband for one of his daughters. What would I tell him? It was a unique opportunity for one of his students. I had to impress this upon him. He would *have* to help.

His house was built from rocks, and it was the only house in the area. He lived there with his wife and two daughters. The elder daughter opened the door. Boy, was she ugly! What could the Professor have been thinking?

'I would like to see the Professor please.'

'What is your name? What is it about?'

'It is a very important matter and I would rather speak with him personally.'

'Does he know you?'

'He taught me surveying for four years. If he does not know me by now he needs medical attention.'

She showed me in and directed me to the Professor's study.

Professor Steinberg was an English Jew, having been raised in the east end of London. He was a tall man who smoked a pipe and had developed the characteristic smoker's twitch in his nose. His mannerisms had been cultivated to give the effect of British aristocracy, and he seemed to belong in the House of Lords. No one would have dared remind him that his family had originated somewhere in Eastern Europe.

'Lustig, what a surprise! What can I do for you?'

I told him my story.

'When do you need an answer?' he asked.

'Tomorrow. I have to be in Diskin's office at 6 p.m. with an answer.'

'I will see you tomorrow morning at eleven at the Technion. I will speak to Krupnik.'

The following morning, Professor Steinberg saw me in his office.

'I spoke to Krupnik,' he said. 'I think that you may have a chance, subject to conditions. I recommended to Krupnik that he lend you the instruments because your job depended on it. He wants to see you.'

Krupnik, the Head of Administration at the Technion, was a Polish Jew with heavy eyebrows and short-cropped black hair. His piercing dark eyes were always watching, whether he was talking or listening. I liked him, and his attentiveness was a rare trait among the people I had met in Palestine.

'Where is the job, Lustig?' he asked.

'Beirut,' I replied.

He was very impressed.

'Really? That *is* good. OK, you can have the instruments, but you have to pay. It will cost one pound per year.'

Later that day, I met Diskin in downtown Haifa. I told him that I had the instruments, and he told me that I had a job.

'Thirty pounds per month,' he informed me, 'plus twenty pounds per month for the instruments.'

Twenty pounds per month for the instruments! And I was paying a pound per year for them. The mathematics were tremendously appealing. My room-mates were still sitting around in that apartment, out of work, and I was heading for Beirut on fifty pounds a month. My mind was in a spin. Everything was happening so quickly around me; I was being thrown from one place to another. But I had found the surveying instruments.

Before I left, I knew that I had to approach my neighbour, the gorilla, and present him with a gift. I had left his job after just one day, and I felt the need to convey my appreciation for what he had done and perhaps stave off my own demise. I bought him a beautiful light green vase with a copper collar and respectfully presented it to him. He accepted it with grace. In that moment, I established a different level of relationship with him. I had achieved more than he could offer me, and at some time in the future, I would be his client rather than his employee. I would be creating the jobs and utilising his labour force.

Two days later I was in Beirut. It was early 1941. The job was based in Baalbeck, the ancient Roman city located north-east of Beirut, between the mountains and the sea. The job involved the construction of a British airstrip. With France out of the war and Syria in Vichy hands, the British now had to devise methods for blocking possible avenues of German invasion into the Middle East. German Stukas had already begun flying over Lebanon, and the British airbases had to be protected. This meant huge excavations to accommodate the planes with suitable protective cover: effectively bunkers for planes, with sloping entrances and exits.

My stay in Baalbeck would be short-lived, however, and this time my fate was determined by the weather. Three of Diskin's employees were working on this project—a project manager, a finance manager, and myself (the surveyor). We were staying together in a hotel near the site of the proposed airstrip. After two days, work was halted because of the rain. The ground had become too soft and unworkable. The deluge persisted for the next three weeks, during which I spent more time playing cards in the hotel room than anything else. The job was becoming more complicated and expensive, and eventually Diskin arrived and reassigned the other two men.

Diskin was prepared to redeploy me elsewhere too, but I had heard about *Solel Boneh* constructing an enormous convalescent camp in Tyre. British soldiers were withdrawing from areas of South-East Asia, returning to Europe through the Middle East. Large numbers of them were suffering from a variety of tropical ailments, as well as battle fatigue, and the facility at Tyre would provide them with treatment and respite.

Ever since I was a young boy, I had been aware of the benefits of keeping my ears to the ground—quite literally. The cowboy movies had taught me that. I had always been fascinated by the idea of listening for the vibrations of approaching horses, and I often experimented in the fields that lay beyond the outskirts of Drohobycz. I imagined that I was under the threat of an Indian attack and wanted to see if I had enough time to prepare my ambush.

Now my preparations had paid off. *Solel Boneh* was offering even higher pay than I was receiving from Diskin, as well as a guarantee of two years' employment. Sixty pounds per month. I sent out my résumé and to my amazement I was called for an interview in Beirut. I was accepted and sent immediately to the camp at Tyre, a fishing village south of Beirut, approximately halfway to the Palestinian border. The small town was almost deserted as a result of the war, and I was housed, together with a number of workmates, in an Arab dwelling. The highlight of this posting was definitely the food. In stark contrast to Palestine, it was in plentiful supply. More importantly, for the first time since leaving Poland, I was served my traditional breakfast each day—two soft-boiled eggs. And when I had eaten them, there were two more if I so desired. I stayed in this job for the next three months, happily well fed and comfortably well paid.

Very little could have motivated me to leave this job, but sure enough, three months later, one such opportunity arose—an opportunity to work directly for the British armed forces, and not as a labourer with the Pioneers, but as a civilian engineer. As a long-time admirer of the British, dating back to the days of my spirited debates with Father, I could not and would not let this opportunity pass.

16 For King and Country

It's them that take advantage that get advantage i' this world.
GEORGE ELIOT, *ADAM BEDE*

He that leaveth nothing to Chance will do few things ill, but he will do very few things.
GEORGE LORD HALIFAX

AT THE ONSET of the Second World War, the British had reason to be confident of triumph in the Middle East. The French were solidly based in North Africa and the Levant, and the British themselves were in firm control of Egypt, Palestine, Transjordan and Iraq. Their assurance was shaken, however, by the Nazi *blitzkrieg* of Europe, the collapse of France, and the subsequent entry of Italy into the war. Almost overnight, a thousand miles of North African coast, the entire Syrian littoral, and the French Mediterranean fleet fell into an uncertain Vichy neutrality. When Hitler despatched General Rommel to Tripolitania in March 1941, and his armoured divisions crossed the Cyrenaican border later that month, Britain was put on the defensive and ultimately placed in jeopardy at the very nexus of its Mediterranean-Suez lifeline. Were Alexandria to fall, the Suez canal would be unable to be defended. So too would Palestine and Syria.

Throughout the ordeal, which would continue until mid 1942, Britain derived little encouragement from its Arab treaty partners. The Egyptian government refused at the outset to declare war on Italy, even when Italian bombs were falling on Alexandria. In Iraq, a virulently anti-British government was installed under the premiership of Rashid Ali. A series of expensive military expeditions—in May 1941 to overthrow the Rashid government, and the large-scale invasion of Vichy Syria the following month—were required to halt a growing Nazi presence in the Levant.

Following the occupation of Damascus, and with the Axis forces still advancing through Europe, the Mediterranean, and North Africa, British attention turned to the construction of fortifications through Lebanon and Syria, designed to prevent the Germans from reaching the precious oilfields of Iraq and Iran. The theoretical subject matter of my third-year engineering competition was now becoming a reality.

By July of 1941, the British were calling for civilian staff to work on these projects. I had recently organised a job for my friend 'Gandhi' (Abraham Meiri) through my first employer, 'King Kong', the labour supplier. He had been sent to work for the British at the oil refineries in Kirkuk, northern Iraq, but was unable to cope with the severe desert climate, and soon returned to Lebanon. Now the British wanted to recruit their own staff. Gandhi was working in Beirut when he noticed such an advertisement in the daily newspaper. He immediately sent a copy to me in Tyre.

I discussed the opportunity with a fellow engineer at *Solel Boneh*. He was from Cracow and had completed an architecture degree in Bergamo, northern Italy. He had taken a liking to me after hearing about my adventures with Diskin. He was considerably older than I, and highly intelligent. I had found a friend in him, and a confidant. We often spoke about worldly matters, concerns I had harboured privately in the absence of an understanding and wise companion. I appreciated his counsel. He advised me to avoid questions about the future.

'To reach distinction,' he said, 'you do not delude yourself with dreams and imagination. Take care of the present and the future will look after itself.'

He wished me well in my attempts to find work with the British army.

I responded to the advertisement and within two days I received a telegram specifying the date of my appointment in Beirut. I arrived at a ramshackle old building with small windows: a commandeered warehouse.

A sergeant led me through to the rear of the building. He opened a heavy door that led to a small, dingy room with iron bars over a small window, a kerosene lamp, a table and a chair. He handed me a folder, on which was written 'Codename Stonehenge'. Inside were plans for a construction using precast concrete.

The sergeant spoke quickly and was obviously not a student of the art of oratory. His instruction was minimal and to the point, but he swallowed most of his words, making it difficult for me to understand what he was saying.

'This is a test of specification, bill of quantity, and construction,' he began. 'Instructions. I am locking you in here. If you want to get out, you knock on the door. If you want to go to the toilet, you knock on the door. If you want to go to lunch, you knock on the door. The examination concludes at four o'clock. Do you understand?'

I understood.

'Good. You are being watched.'

He closed the heavy door and left me in the silence and gloom of my cell-like cubicle.

I looked down at the plans in front of me and realised that I had no idea where to begin. I was completely out of my depth. I thought about knocking on the door immediately, putting an end to the charade, and returning to my job at *Solel Boneh*. But, I reasoned, I had come all this way and concluded that I ought to stay until lunchtime at least.

I wondered about the 'classified' material that lay in front of me on the table. My mind wandered. It wandered everywhere but where it should have focused itself.

My main concern was how to occupy myself for the next four hours. I stood up from the desk and walked around the room. I began to browse through a small pile of folders that sat on the primitive shelving against one of the walls of the room. Many of the folders were sealed, and marked 'classified'. To my amazement, one of them was also marked with the name 'Stonehenge'. When I opened it, I found a set of plans identical to those on which I was being tested. The only difference was that these plans were accompanied by typed specifications and the bill of quantities: a complete set of answers.

My head was in a spin. Surely the British army could not err to this degree. I could have been an Axis spy for all they knew, and yet here I was privy to their secrets. No, it had to be a trap. He had told me that I was being watched, and this must have been part of the test.

I had little choice, however. Without the aid of the answers, I would never have been able to pass the test. If I was caught, I could always argue that I was simply showing tremendous initiative. They could throw me out; but really, what else did I have to lose? I decided to proceed.

I sat down and spread the pages of the 'borrowed' file across the table in such a way that I could cover them up quickly if the sergeant returned to the room. I began to copy the answers exactly. Then it struck me that a perfectly worded answer would appear too anomalous with my somewhat imperfect aptitude for the English language, so I began to insert a few small errors—not in the numbers, but rather in the technical terms and grammatical expression.

Shortly after midday, the sergeant returned to check on my progress. He leaned over my shoulder and examined my work.

'You're doing all right. Do you want to go to lunch now, or would you prefer to keep working?'

'Forget lunch,' I replied, to impress him with my apparent diligence. 'I just want to get this done.'

I continued copying out my answers until just before four o'clock, when I gathered up the template, returned it to its file and replaced it on the shelf. I had been writing vigorously all day and my arm was severely cramped. My supervisor returned once more. I was nervous and afraid. Now I would discover if I had been caught in their trap.

'How far did you get?' he asked me.

I pointed towards my work.

'That's enough,' he said in a pleasant voice. 'You have done an excellent job. It seems that we are lucky here. We will send you a telegram for another appointment.'

I returned to Tyre that evening, thinking about Professor Yedlinsky leaning over and whispering the answer to me during my matriculation exam. Had he not done so, I might still be in Poland, and I certainly would not be a qualified engineer in Palestine. My guardian angel had a name and a face that day. I could not help wondering who my guardian angel had been today, and where he was leading me this time.

The following day, the army telegram arrived, requesting my presence at a further meeting two days later. I afforded myself the luxury of a taxi ride to my second appointment, and this time I was greeted by a major, not a sergeant. I was progressing through the ranks.

'Mr Lustig, good to see you.'

The major's office was a small room, but it boasted two normal-sized windows. Comparing it with the black hole I had worked in a few days earlier, I saw this as a luxury, a privilege of rank. He introduced himself as the officer in charge of civilian staff.

'Your performance on the test turned out to be very satisfactory.

On this basis, Mr Lustig, we have three locations where your services would be needed. Aleppo, on the boundary of Turkey and Syria; Shtora, a small town on the border of Lebanon and Syria; and Damascus.'

'Have you been in Damascus before, Mr Lustig?'

'No, I haven't had the opportunity.'

'Well, it is a very nice place.'

With my typical *chutzpah* I replied, 'If you wouldn't mind, I would rather stay in Beirut. It is also a rather nice spot.'

'I understand, but please, we have no choice. I recommend Damascus because you will enjoy the nightlife. I have no doubt.'

'Damascus it is then, sir.'

'By the way, you will have a car and a driver. Be ready to leave the day after tomorrow.'

'How long will it take?'

'Six hours, perhaps eight, depending on how many times you have to stop. On your arrival in Damascus, you will meet the colonel responsible for the area.'

Two days and a formidable road journey later, I was deposited in Syria. The colonel was in his mid forties, a huge man, tall and broad with a commanding presence. He greeted me with a smile.

'Ah, Mr Lustig, I saw the results of your test. Congratulations. I received them yesterday by wire. I have been anxiously awaiting your arrival.'

'Thank you, Colonel.'

'Have you been to Damascus before?'

'No.'

'It is a very nice spot. But since you don't know the place, I will make some arrangements to have you shown around. Corporal Nikorian is the clerk, Mr Lustig, and he will organise your accommodation and anything else you request. If you need anything, please telephone.'

I assured him I would do so.

'You will be paid sixty pounds per month and you will be provided with a driver. You now have fourteen days free to become acquainted with Damascus.'

Nikorian took me to the French Quarter of the city where, like all the British in Damascus, I would be residing. The apartment was situated in a very attractive French-style block, and boasted three-metre ceilings. Nikorian introduced me to an elderly Armenian lady and her daughter, with whom I would be living, and whose job it was to cook, clean, and serve me. I was shown to my room—the master suite—a large chamber with a glazed door and heavy plush drapes, and a very comfortable king-size bed. Cushions, rugs, ottomans and chairs decorated the parlour. As the miserable living conditions and continual hunger I had endured for the past four years flashed through my mind, I could not help but smile at this opulence. So this was where my guardian angel had sent me.

My only concern at that moment was how I was going to occupy myself for the next two weeks. I stole a glance at the young Armenian woman beside me, and sensed that I would not be suffering from boredom. She was truly beautiful, a dark, exotic-looking girl with sparkling black eyes. She was wearing a pale blue slip dress that clung tightly to her curves, and around her neck she wore a fine double cross, signifying her Armenian Orthodox faith. Neither she nor her mother spoke English—only Armenian and French—so our communication was limited, but sure enough, after a few days, I came home late one night to find her in my bed awaiting my return, whereupon she claimed me as her own.

After being served a very healthy breakfast on my first morning in Damascus, I decided to take a walk to get acquainted with my new home. Initially, I moved only within the safety of the French Quarter, which boasted beautiful parklands and wide, tree-lined avenues in the European style. Trams shuttled up and down these streets and the sidewalks were lined with stylish boutiques set beneath blocks of apartments. The entire area was spotlessly clean.

When my young Armenian house-mate invited me for dinner to see Damascus at night, we ate at the Orient Palace, the most modern hotel in the city. While our conversation was restricted by the language difficulties, we managed to communicate through signals and mime. For most of the next two weeks, she would act as my guide throughout the delights of the city.

The Arab sectors of the city were considerably older than the French Quarter. The streets were narrow and cobbled, designed to accommodate the four-legged varieties of transport—donkeys, mules, even camels. We visited the Arab market, *Souk HaMedeir*. It was my first experience of such a trading floor (I had not visited the *souks* in Jerusalem) and I would later recognise this as a forerunner to the modern shopping centre—with all the stalls set around an open area, and no partitions, as opposed to a strip of shops.

I was taken aback by the beauty of Damascus, an oasis city with seven rivers running through it. The desert was only about 60 kilometres away, but Syria's capital was lush and green.

The cost of living was incredibly cheap, and given my wage, I was privileged, able to live like a king. The food was outstanding, and for the first time in years, I was able to eat extremely well. I dined in the restaurants at the Orient Palace and at the Omayar hotel. But my regular haunt became the Oasis restaurant in the French Quarter. Jacques, the *maître d'*, was indeed a professional, but what truly converted me to the Oasis was my first experience of chateaubriand. I tipped Jacques well, and from that day on we looked after each other. He would make sure that I had extra side dishes with my meal, and I would continue to show my gratitude when it came to paying the bill. Eventually he would serve me the side dishes even when I was not eating a main meal. Over the next four years, I would become a regular customer at the restaurant. I would eat there almost daily.

A week after arriving in Damascus, while eating lunch at the Oasis, I noticed a group of men sitting at a nearby table conversing in Hebrew. They were all considerably older than I. Their conversation seemed to be dominated by one character in particular. He instantly reminded me of Weidenfeld in that he never seemed to let anyone else have the last word. His manner was aggressive and arrogant, and it was obvious that he believed himself to be superior to his colleagues in every way. I took an instant dislike to him.

Jacques must have guessed that I was Jewish because without any prompting, he ushered me over to the table for an introduction. As it turned out, these four men were civilian engineers and architects, and they would be working for me.

Bruchner, an architect from Vienna, was in his mid thirties. A promising career had been interrupted by war, and it was clear that Bruchner did not want to be here—he wanted to be in Austria, back on the road to success. Bodor was Hungarian, a bald, uncomfortable-looking man in his mid forties, who represented a group of builders in Haifa and Tel Aviv. He spoke English but with a pronounced Hungarian accent. Marcel Kuhn was also Hungarian, but had been raised and educated in Vienna. He was younger than Bodor, somewhere in his thirties. His claim to fame was an alleged affair with a well-known actress in Vienna.

At the head of the table sat Maslovaty, a large and boisterous fellow of Jewish Lithuanian extraction, with a lisp and a redoubtable belief that he was truly an outstanding wit. I would never be able to confirm this, since more often than not he would ruin the punchline of his story with an outburst of laughter that sent chewed food flying across the table. Maslovaty looked about 45, but I would learn later that he was only 30. He was born in Petah Tiqvah in Palestine, and his manner suggested to me that he was a Sabra. His arrogance had at least part of its source in the fact that he had travelled to Italy to complete his degree in architecture and engineering.

Despite my being considerably younger, I would take charge of these men for the next three years. We would meet again the following week after I reported for duty, and we would remain a close-knit group during our stay in Damascus. When we weren't working, we would eat together, and we would regularly enjoy a game of bridge at Maslovaty's apartment.

After my two-week acclimatisation period, I reported to my superior, Captain Paynter, to begin work. The captain was in his forties, an immaculately groomed man who smoked constantly. Even when his pipe was unlit or empty, it protruded regally from the corner of his mouth, a permanent feature set beneath his trimmed English moustache.

He looked me up and down before returning to the report on his table. He seemed mystified by my appearance.

'How old are you, Mr Lustig?' he asked at last.

'Twenty-four,' I stammered, attempting to rise to the occasion.

'I am sorry,' he continued, 'but we cannot put you in the position of garrison engineer. In order to occupy that position, you have to have a minimum of fifteen years of practical experience.'

'I see,' I replied, trying to hide my disappointment.

'So, we will appoint you acting garrison engineer, but generally you will assume the duties of the garrison engineer. Welcome aboard, Mr Lustig,' he declared, pumping my hand vigorously.

I was placed in charge of constructing defense structures and hospitals, and in selecting positions most suitable for aggressive attacks and defences. My fellow civilian engineers were not overly happy about the fact that a 24-year-old had been appointed as their superior. It was not simply a question of age, but of experience and understanding, of being able to negotiate exchanges to procure materials that were difficult to acquire. With no experience, and based solely on my phony test results, I was now managing engineers who were twice my age. Fate had dealt me an interesting hand.

'How on earth did you get this position?' protested Maslovaty.

'I don't know,' I replied. 'I passed a test. Did *you* pass a test?' Turning the tables on this bullish man seemed the best course of defence.

'What test?' he demanded suspiciously.

'A test of quantity surveying.'

I had been studying at the Technion for four years and nobody had learned quantity surveying. It was a purely British system. You had to know what went into a project, and how much it cost—labour and materials. Estimation, procurement. I didn't know anything at all about it, and only Bodor suspected this.

'How *did* you pass the test?' he asked me quietly one day.

'I don't know. It just happened.' And this was largely the truth.

Ladislav Bodor was the one who came to my rescue. He had been working with British Royal Engineers—the sappers—in Palestine, primarily in the Tel Aviv and Gaza regions. He knew the British system and was able to tell me exactly what they wanted. So it was easy for him to direct me, and by doing so, to win my support. Kuhn would also prove an ally, working with Bodor in teaching me the trade and assisting me in keeping my ignorance well hidden.

Years later, as a property developer in Tel Aviv, I would repay their loyalty. They would work with me on a number of building projects and by that time, we were all well versed in the practicalities of quantity surveying. Experience *is* the best teacher.

17 SARAH

They gave each other a smile with a future in it.
RING LARDNER

A FEW WEEKS after beginning work as 'acting garrison engineer' for the British forces, I managed to secure a five-day pass to return to Palestine. On hearing this news, Maslovaty requested that I deliver a gift to his wife in Haifa. With his usual gruff manner, he handed me a very ugly pair of shoes that were workman-like and extremely unfeminine. He extracted a photograph of his wife from his wallet and showed it to me, just in case I was to hand this priceless gift to the wrong woman. She looked rather plain, a brunette with dark eyes. Her name was Sarah.

The journey from Damascus took a little more than three hours by jeep. I arrived on late Saturday afternoon and went directly to my old apartment, where I had shared the single room with my three room-mates. They were all still unemployed and their lives had remained rather grim. The highlight of their week came each Saturday, when they took to their bedbugs with lit matches, a rather practical form of recreation.

A few months earlier I had been sharing this same experience with them each week. Now I was living like royalty in Damascus, and my stories now provided them with a vicarious thrill otherwise absent from their world. I am sure that they believed only half of my tales, but their eagerness for excitement made this irrelevant.

'Why on earth are you back in Haifa?' one of them asked me.

'I wanted to play bridge with my friends,' I replied good-humouredly.

I had also come back to see my friend Gandhi, who had returned from his jobs in Iraq and Beirut. I used the trip to arrange for him to join me in Damascus.

On Sunday morning, I walked to *Hadar HaCarmel* to deliver Mrs Maslovaty's hideous shoes. Bent over and trying to catch my breath after a trek through the midmorning heat, I was caught off guard when she answered the door. Before I could compose myself, the door was open and I was staring at a pair of feet. I suppose it was not all that inappropriate given that I was there to deliver a pair of shoes for those feet. I looked up slowly, and to my surprise I saw an extremely attractive woman in front of me. I quickly realised that the photograph I had seen had not done her justice at all. Absent from that image was the smile with which she greeted me now, her perfect white teeth and full red lips complemented by an almost heavenly sparkle in her eyes.

When I introduced myself and explained the reason for my visit, she invited me inside for a drink. She offered me a 'jarrah', a fine clay porous water container with a longish neck, and when I had finished I asked for another. It was not that the first had failed to satisfy my thirst; rather, I wanted to watch her walking around. Her graceful movement was something else lacking in the photograph I had seen, and it mesmerised me. Her hair fell sensuously around her slim shoulders, revealing a narrow, elegant neck. She sensed me watching her, and she enjoyed it. Sarah was quite beautiful, and a coquette.

We sat down to talk.

'How do you like the shoes?' I began, my tongue planted firmly in my cheek.

'Please don't say anything, but I don't think that I will wear them. But,' she sighed, 'when my husband comes back, I am sure he will expect me to.'

We spoke for about ten minutes. Sarah said little, perhaps because she was somewhat shy, but more likely because I did most of the talking. Before leaving, I tentatively suggested that we meet that evening to go to the air-conditioned cinema, where we could find respite from the oppressive heat. She agreed, and I arranged to collect her at 6.30. I left, feeling a very pleasant sense of anticipation and not at all troubled that I had just asked Maslovaty's wife on a date.

After spending the early afternoon with Gandhi, I returned to the apartment to shower and change. My room-mates had prepared some food and were sitting down to a game of bridge. They asked me to join them. So absorbing was my passion for the game that I completely forgot about Sarah. It was already nine o'clock when I realised what I had done. The three boys around the table laughed uncontrollably—

I had given up a night of romance for a silly game of cards. I was appalled by my own lack of manners, despite the fact that European sensibilities were not common in Haifa at the time.

The following morning I bought a large bouquet of flowers—the largest I could carry—and proceeded to deliver them to Sarah. As she answered the door, I hid my embarrassed face behind the massive profusion of petals. When I peeked through them, I could see her smiling.

'This time,' she announced, 'you will take me out for dinner *and* the movies.'

Over the course of the next few days, I spent a considerable amount of time with Sarah, during which she told me about her life, her family, and how she came to be with Maslovaty. She seemed determined that I understand exactly how she came to be in her present situation.

Sarah's father, Joseph Lipshit, had emigrated from Russia to Palestine in 1905. It was during the Russo-Japanese War, and inexperienced young men were being used as cannon fodder for Japanese attacks. Many young Jews were moving south to Turkey, and some even further: to Palestine, which was at that time under Ottoman control.

Mr Lipshit soon built a very lucrative business supplying water to Jewish and Arab settlements, and he married the daughter of the Jewish community representative in Jaffa. Water in Palestine was a valuable and scarce commodity, and supplying it for agricultural purposes was a highly profitable business. An energetic and dedicated worker, Mr Lipshit was able to compete successfully with Jewish organisations already in the business. He was even more successful than *Mekorot*, the Zionist-operated water planning authority.

Sarah's father developed a liking for films and each Saturday night he would take the family (his wife, two sons and four daughters) to the cinema. During the week, he would often travel to Jaffa in the evenings to find a different sort of satisfaction in the arms of a bellydancer.

Mr Lipshit was working on a new well when tragedy struck. The family was alarmed when his horse returned one evening without its rider. One of the family's Arab employees, Abukhnin, rode out to find him and returned with tears in his eyes. There had been a collapse in the course of digging the well, and Mr Lipshit had been buried beneath the rubble. It took more than a week to recover his body.

Sarah's mother decided to take control of the business, much to the chagrin of her two sons, who had been working with their father for some time. When the brothers hired lawyers to challenge their mother, the family was torn apart. The daughters stood by their mother against their own brothers, and eventually the brothers turned their hostilities on each other.

The matter was decided in court and Sarah's mother won the lion's share of her late husband's inheritance. The two sons left the business and each of the daughters was granted one thousand Palestinian pounds.

While he was alive, Sarah's father had forbidden her to associate with Maslovaty, whose family was very poor. But as is so often the case, her father's warnings served only to drive her toward him, and they were married within nine months of Mr Lipshit's death. No sooner had the marriage licence been signed than Sarah, trusting her husband with all financial matters, lost control of her considerable inheritance.

Maslovaty decided to take Sarah to Turin, Italy, where he would study engineering for three years. His degree had led him to Damascus, and now Sarah was back in Palestine without a penny to her name. She was sewing dresses for acquaintances in order to carve out a meagre living.

Maslovaty had told Sarah that wives and family were not permitted to visit the men in Damascus. I knew that he had good reason for this deceit. He was living with a Christian Arab family. When he had arrived, the husband was unemployed, but Maslovaty found him a job so that there would be no one at home during the day except for the wife.

I knew straightaway that I wanted to save Sarah from her brute of a husband, and I also sensed that she wanted to be saved. Perhaps I was already in love with this woman, for my following actions would undoubtedly sabotage their marriage.

'That's not true, Sarah,' I explained, 'and I will tell you what. Not only will I organise a permit for you, but I will also arrange for you to come and see him.' What was good for Maslovaty would be even better for me.

On my return to Damascus, I called on Maslovaty. He was in an affable mood and appeared to be grateful that I had run his errand for him, until I confronted him with a question that changed his expression.

'Why is it that you have never brought your wife to Damascus?'

A shadow crossed his face and his brow furrowed into a menacing scowl. 'What is it to you, Lustig?'

'I would like to know why you told her it is not permitted.'

'It's not safe for her to come. She would have to travel by bus, with Arabs.' His answers were prickly and prepared.

'That's no excuse, Maslovaty.'

'This is war, Lustig. She's better off in Haifa.'

'Do you think so? She's better off starving in Haifa while you are living it up in Damascus?' My antagonism knew no bounds.

'Yes,' he declared triumphantly, completely unaware of where our exchange was heading. I had of course, saved the best barb for last.

'Well, I don't agree. And what is more, I have made arrangements for her to visit.'

'WHAT?' Maslovaty turned purple with fury.

'It's already done, Maslovaty. Now, don't argue with your superior.' With that, I turned on my heel and left.

The evening Sarah arrived, she joined us for dinner at the Oasis. Maslovaty looked suitably disconcerted. Jacques, the *maître d'*, waited for an appropriate moment and whispered to me, 'What is this beautiful woman doing married to that pig? What an odd couple!'

Later that evening, after dinner, my Armenian girlfriend questioned me about my noticeable lack of interest in her charms since my return from Haifa.

'I'm just very tired,' I explained. 'I have a lot on my mind with work.'

Within two days of arriving in Damascus, Sarah discovered that her husband had been unfaithful to her. Oblivious to her new-found knowledge, Maslovaty expected his conjugal rights, but they were no longer forthcoming. His frustration soon gave way to threats of violence, and Sarah sent one of the servants to my apartment with the message that I had to get her out of there. It was impossible to have her to stay with me—after all, my suspicious Armenian girlfriend seemed ready to kill me already. Instead, I booked a room for Sarah at the Orient Palace.

Maslovaty seemed to care little about Sarah's departure or about my involvement in it. By this time, he had become suspicious that my attention to matters concerning his wife was a little out of the ordinary, that my interventions suggested more than a platonic interest. His only concern was Sarah's continued presence in Damascus, and he demanded that I find him a job in Palestine to get him away from his wife. Their marriage was over.

Within two days, I had arranged for a transfer for Maslovaty, but as it turned out, Sarah would return to Haifa to stay with my brother Anselm while her lawyer began divorce proceedings.

Kuhn volunteered to drive us to Beirut overnight. From there, we would make our way back to Haifa. Maslovaty sat beside him in the front while Sarah and I shared the back seat. Like a couple of naughty schoolchildren, we explored each other under the heavy fur cover that protected us from the cold of the desert night. Our touching turned to silent lovemaking, and were it not for the utter disdain with which Maslovaty had recently behaved towards his wife, I may have felt a pang of guilt about this flagrant indiscretion. As it was, he showed no interest in what may or may not have been taking place, literally behind his back.

As I sat self-satisfied and sated in the back seat, reflecting on the surreal scenario, I was reminded of a short story I had once read, a comic tale written by Minhousen in the seventeenth century. An elderly and somewhat absent-minded professor returns home after a long day of lectures and decides to go straight to bed. His considerably younger wife is already asleep and he is not inclined to wake her. He approaches the bed, looking at her with loving eyes, when he notices two pairs of legs protruding from the sheets. 'Am I drunk?' he asks himself. 'I haven't had alcohol for a week.' He climbs into bed, and now counts three pairs of legs. 'This can't be right.' The professor stands up and walks to the foot of the bed, taking yet another look. 'Oh, everything is in order now, two pairs of legs—hers and mine'. We see only what we wish to see and Maslovaty, like the professor, had selective myopia.

On our arrival in Beirut, Sarah and I checked into a hotel and Maslovaty went his own way. It was the last I ever saw of him. When Sarah was finally granted her divorce in February of 1942, she returned to Damascus and we moved into an apartment together. When I proposed marriage, however, she seemed somewhat reluctant. While she insisted that she loved me, she was afraid that marriage might place me in an inconvenient position.

'We are of such different backgrounds,' she said hesitantly. 'I will have to start learning how to behave, how to communicate with others. I am sure that I will cause more problems than satisfaction.'

I insisted that these were minor obstacles, and that my love for her was strong enough to overcome them.

A number of my friends in Damascus tended to agree with Sarah—after all, I would be the only one there with a wife by his side. Boris Kaminsky and Abdul Hajar were partners in a construction business that was carrying out work for the British forces. Both of their names in their respective languages translated as 'stone'. Kaminsky, a large Russian Jew, an extrovert whose round face always wore a jovial expression, had no hesitation in voicing his opinion on the matter.

'You're crazy, Lustig.'

'It's a matter of honour,' I replied.

'If I started talking about duty and honour, the officers would send me for a medical. Nobody does this kind of thing during war.'

'I'm not nobody,' I insisted.

'Take a look at me, Lustig. Do you know where my wife is?'

'No.'

'Well, neither do I. I last saw her two years ago. In Tel Aviv, I think.'

Over the next few weeks, Sarah's reluctance receded, and a decision was finally reached one Saturday morning when she sat me down and told me that she thought she was pregnant. I was absolutely delighted. For me, this was just one more reason to get married. I kissed her gently on the forehead and reiterated my desire for matrimony.

'Tomorrow, we will go into Abli Ou [the Jewish sector of Damascus],' I began. 'We will find a rabbi there. Let's not make a big deal of this; let's just do it.'

At ten o'clock the following morning, having requisitioned a jeep and a driver, Sarah and I travelled to the Jewish quarter to marry. I was to meet with a construction crew in the afternoon, so there was no time to waste and we did not plan to stand on ceremony. I wore my usual garb: my khakis and an officer's stick. Sarah wore a plain summer dress but looked beautiful as always.

The street at the heart of Abli Ou was extremely narrow, closed in on both sides with high walls. We were heading towards a miniature square, where I noticed three men scurrying around, frantically closing the heavy timber shutters over the windows. Obviously, news of a military jeep having entered the main gates travelled faster than the jeep itself, and these men were 'battening down the hatches'.

Afraid that they might disappear before I could explain the

situation, I instructed the corporal to speed up. Noticing the jeep accelerate, the three men turned to run, but before they could, we had already stopped outside their premises—a barber shop.

'*Anna ibn Yahud* [I am a Jew],' I shouted.

By the terrified looks on their faces, I assumed that they hadn't believed me.

'*Anna behuve madam* [I love the woman],' I continued, pointing towards Sarah.

Still they did not understand. '*Imshi yallah* [start moving],' I implored, beating the side of the jeep with my stick, but this served only to frighten them more. They stood silent and stock-still.

Finally, I showed them the gold ring I had bought for Sarah. When Sarah finally turned to them and said 'wedding' in Arabic, they understood. They smiled with a mixture of relief and sentiment.

'We will find the rabbi and come back,' they said.

Concerned that they would be too frightened to return, I instructed the corporal to go with them. A few minutes later they returned, practically carrying a withered old man. 'This is the rabbi of our community,' they explained, indicating the wizened, trembling form.

The holy man was shaking like a leaf, obviously terrified of being dragged before a man in military uniform. At first he could not utter a word. '*Anna ibn Yahud*,' I repeated, pointing to the ring and the woman with whom I wished to be joined in marriage. We entered the barber shop, where he placed a parchment document on the table and sat down. He began to ask a series of questions in Arabic. I answered in broken Arabic and Hebrew.

'Name?'
'Theodore Henrik Lustig.'
'Born?'
'Vienna.'
'Married?'
'No.'
He turned to Sarah,
'Name?'
'Sarah, daughter of Joseph.'
'Born?'
'Petah Tiqva.'
'Married?'

'Divorced.'

The rabbi stopped. He did not understand.

'No,' Sarah quickly corrected herself.

The rabbi seemed agitated. He needed to know more information. I hit the table with my stick. He proceeded with the ceremony, intermittently mumbling, 'Bar Minan, Bar Minan.' I did not know what this meant, but judging by the expression on his face, he was asking God's forgiveness for performing a marriage without first ascertaining all the necessary facts. He finally signed the document that made us married in the eyes of the Orthodox synagogue. It was written in Arabic and dated 15 May 1942. On the back of the parchment, a clause stated something along the lines that in the case of separation, my wife was entitled to two donkeys and a camel.

Sarah and I would remain happily married for the next forty years, though in many ways, our first three years, in Damascus, were the happiest and most uncomplicated of all. We lived in luxury, with four servants to cater to all our needs, and our apartment soon became the most popular meeting place for the British officers. We held a dinner each Friday night, before settling down to a serious game of bridge, and Sarah took delight in her role as Damascus' most perfect hostess.

It turned out that Sarah was not pregnant when we married, but by November 1944, we had a daughter, Iris. However, she very nearly did not have a father.

Sarah was nearly a week overdue, and unfortunately, I had to be out on site for an urgent job. When she called me with news of her labour, I implored her to hold on for half an hour, by which time I would have returned. I immediately grabbed a motorcycle and began to make my way back to Damascus. The road to Damascus was congested with convoys of trucks and in an attempt to hasten my journey, I decided to get off the road and take a short cut through the open fields. The sun was setting and in the fading light, I failed to notice an open anti-tank ditch. My only thought as both motorcycle and rider flew through the air was that I had to land well away from the bike, and luckily I did. I picked myself up and brushed myself off, not stopping to check whether I had sustained any broken bones, and raced over to the road to flag down a passing convoy. Despite my civilian status, my lack of rank, I barked out orders like a man possessed.

'Attention!'

A truck stopped and I was approached by a corporal.

'Sir.'

'Fix my motorcycle.'

'The convoy, sir.'

'Don't worry about the convoy. I need that motorcycle, now!'

He lifted the bike out of the ditch and made sure it was in working order, whereupon I continued on my way.

I was late for the birth. By the time I arrived, Sarah was resting and our daughter was lying in a cot by the side of her bed. I looked into the cot.

'Lift her up, Tedek. She is your daughter.'

I was afraid to touch her. I looked at her tiny fingers and her microscopic fingernails. She was too perfect, everything was so correct. Deep within me, I felt a need being fulfilled, a desire to be part of a family—no longer alone. I was a father. I thought of my own father, and as I held my daughter for the first time, I began to cry.

18 The Tender Age

Egypt: Where the Israelites would still be if Moses had been a bureaucrat.
LAURENCE J. PETER

The illegal we do immediately. The unconstitutional takes a little longer.
HENRY KISSINGER

THE FIRST MONTHS after my marriage coincided with the most dangerous period of World War II. By the summer of 1942, Rommel's forces in North Africa had reached the gates of Alexandria and the Germans were approaching the Caucasus on the Russian front. It was feared that the Axis' European forces would violate Turkish neutrality and advance in their usual blitzkrieg manner to the sources of oil in Iran and Iraq. They would be supported in a huge pincer movement by Rommel who was threatening to move through Egypt, Palestine and Jordan.

The fortifications designed to repel this movement were to be constructed along a line which ran from the port of Beirut through the mountains of Lebanon to Palmyra in Northern Syria. It was a huge operation that stretched across hundreds of kilometres. Access roads, trenches, pill-boxes, bunkers and hospital facilities were required all the way along the line.

Captain Paynter was in charge of construction. I was on supervision to ensure that contract conditions were imposed and preserved. It was my job to assess and control the quantities of materials used in the constructions. All the plans were prepared in Cairo by British engineers who would visit periodically for inspections. Building contracts were awarded on the basis of tenders. There were about a dozen construction firms on the War Department list, and these were the only firms permitted to tender. There were a number of local firms, as well as Jewish-run businesses. Some, like Kaminsky, had established partnerships in Damascus specifically for the purpose. Others, like Diskin, were Palestine-based, but were large enough to compete for the work. *Solel Boneh*, an obvious candidate, already knew me from Tyre and pleaded with me for work.

'Any work at all,' said their representative.

'By bidding on anything that comes along,' I explained, 'you are only going to damage your name. You had better think about what you want to do, and what you are able to do.'

I had just two meetings with their representative before they decided instead to deal with the British forces directly through Kaminsky's firm.

Competition for tenders was fierce and Kaminsky had always been keen to have me on his side. He was a shady character who had fled Palestine after being declared bankrupt, and on more than one occasion, he had brazenly offered me *bakshish* in exchange for certain information. I was loyal to the British, and the idea of taking this kind of money appalled me. Furthermore, I was smart enough to know that had I done so, I would then have been at Kaminsky's mercy. He would have had something over me, and I could never allow that to happen. Besides, I never really had the constitution of a thief. My father was a man of the law and a man of honour. His words had always rung true to me.

'Why don't you approve of a capable thief?' I once asked him.

'If you want to do something illegal, go ahead,' he replied, 'but before you do, remember to assume that you will be caught and convicted twenty-five years hence. That is the statute of limitations, and it is an awfully long time to watch your back. Even longer if they discover new evidence, in which case the statute no longer applies.'

'I see,' I said, romantic visions of myself as the gentleman thief swiftly dashed against the rock-solid logic of my lawyer father.

'You needn't worry yourself about these things, Tedek. I am sure that you are too clever to get yourself involved in some idiotic scheme.'

I did nothing to help *Solel Boneh*, primarily because of this basic concern. I was too young and had far too much at stake to become involved in this kind of wheeling and dealing.

What I did learn from my meetings with the representative from *Solel Boneh* was that shortly after my departure from Tyre, the firm began to encourage many of its employees to join the Jewish war effort.

By the middle of 1942, the ranks of the 'Palestine Buffs'—the 'official' Jewish participants in the British Army—had swelled to almost 18,000, and nearly a third of them had been given front-line combat positions. In addition, a second, parallel Jewish military role had developed. When the war erupted, the Jewish military underground—*Haganah*—command decided to cooperate with the war effort, but at the same time it maintained its clandestine training activities. As a result, forty-three of the *Haganah*'s best officers were arrested, among them Moshe Dayan and Moshe Carmel. As the military situation turned against Britain in 1941, the government eased its policy towards the *Haganah*. With France out of the war and Syria in Vichy hands, the *Haganah* were invited to cooperate with the British in preparing lists of bridges and tunnels that were vulnerable to sabotage in Lebanon, Syria, Turkey, and Iran. Other joint efforts followed. It soon became apparent that there was a need for a permanently mobilised Jewish task force. Such a unit was established by the *Haganah* in May 1941, and classified as the *Palmach*.

With this increased Jewish involvement, *Solel Boneh* took the opportunity to supply fighting men from its ranks, and by doing so, was able to claim substantial financial compensation for its own loss. Had I walked out of my specifications test in Beirut as I had planned, and returned to Tyre, I too may have been with the Buffs, fighting on the front line. Perhaps the lesson of fate is not so much where it has led you, but what it has saved you from.

The British operation in Syria and Lebanon was proceeding with a fair degree of efficiency, despite the enormous quantity of alcohol that was being consumed. It was extremely rare that a construction was unacceptable, of poor quality, or in the wrong location.

There was only one occasion on which a successful tenderer was found to be deficient and had to be struck from the War Department list. A road was to be built at Qatana, forty miles east of Damascus, and the job was awarded to an Arab construction firm. A few weeks later, one of the company principals, an Arab dressed in a European suit, came to my office to collect a progressive payment. His firm had already received £6000, and I was instructed to travel to the site and inspect their progress before authorising the next payment. It was October and the road had to be completed before the winter set in. It was a matter of some urgency.

I expected to see heavy machinery, steamrollers, and teams of Arab labourers hard at work. When we arrived, there was not a single Arab worker in sight. Instead I saw teams of shirtless workers wearing diggers' hats. They were Australian soldiers. I approached the officer in charge. The contractor lingered in the distance.

'This man is asking for more money,' I explained, indicating the rogue who was looking at me.

'Money!' bellowed the officer. 'We requested that this job be completed three months ago and nothing has been done. We are in a dangerous situation—if it starts raining tomorrow, we're in real trouble. Heavy machinery will be lost. It's obvious now that we have to do the bloody job ourselves!'

As I tried to calm the officer, the Arab contractor slunk back to his car and drove away, leaving me with thirty irate Australians. After some investigation, I came to realise that the tenderers were in fact a company of butchers and had no experience in road construction or any other construction. They had been more than happy to accept the weekly payments for as long as they could maintain the charade.

Captain Jackson, a tall, slim Londoner whose lack of muscular definition belied his military stature, was our resident expert in camouflage techniques. Indeed, he was hardly a soldier; his successful civilian career in theatrical set design had qualified him for the job, and he had been granted the rank of captain shortly prior to his arrival in Damascus. His job in Syria and Lebanon was to develop and implement a method for concealing the line of defence that was about to be built. His task assumed even greater importance after Italian planes began to fly over the requisitioned land, dropping leaflets with the message, 'Give up! We know where you are.'

After a six-month bout of intense drinking and deep contemplation, Captain Jackson formulated his plan. The areas surrounding the land in question were being farmed by the local Arab population, who cultivated healthy orchards and grew grains and vegetables. In order to conceal the planned fortifications, the captain realised that this land also had to be farmed. In this way, it would blend seamlessly into the surrounding areas.

A tender was issued for the management of this project. The military staff did not understand the tender at all. It was a very expensive tender and there were a lot of considerations. I received a pile of papers setting out the conditions and the method of payment. Somebody had to negotiate with the appropriate Arab *Muktars* to take control of the land, and then ensure that the land was being farmed properly. Not a single firm on the War Department list submitted a tender. They were all construction firms and did not have the slightest idea of what this tender was about. The only application I received for this job came from Palestine, from a strange little Jewish man by the name of Efron.

Efron and his family lived in Metullah, in the most northerly Jewish settlement in Palestine. The area, situated in the Golan Heights on the border between Palestine and Syria, was something of a no man's land. Nobody from either side—Jewish or Arab—took much interest in this region since the land was largely untillable, and the precise location of the border was not an important issue at the time.

A number of Jewish families had established a *moshav* in this area, a cooperative, after fleeing the Russian pogroms during the early 1880s. Here they had lived a poor and very primitive existence, and even now they had no electricity or running water. The community was largely illiterate, and given the poor quality of the land, their source of sustenance had always been a mystery. Yiddish was their primary language, but most also spoke fluent Arabic. Progressively, the community had lost contact with the main Jewish centres and settlements. Safad and Tiberia, the northern-most townships, had offered some protection against Arab attacks. But attacks were very rare on this settlement, if they occurred at all. The reason for this was that this isolated community was on friendly terms with the neighbouring Arabs, and now this would prove to be of enormous benefit to both Efron and the British forces.

Efron had first come into contact with the British forces a year earlier, as Australian troops were moving north into Syria and Lebanon. The roads leading through this territory were unmade, and while the transport of heavy vehicles caused few problems in the dry season, the rainfall rendered many of these passes unusable. The Australian troops encountered these problems as they progressed through Metullah towards Syria. To their amazement, they came across an ancient machine standing idle by the side of the road. It was a stone-crushing machine, a remnant of Napoleon's visit to Acre in northern Palestine, and acquired by Efron's grandfather.

Efron had used the machine to clear the fields around Metullah, but now the Australian officer in charge recognised its value in repairing the flooded roads. He enquired as to whom it belonged, and Efron stepped forward. He spoke in Yiddish.

'It's mine,' he said proudly.

Efron's eldest son, Zvi, spoke basic English and managed to translate for his father.

'We need to requisition this machine,' explained the officer. 'We have to clear the roads in order to pass through.'

Efron subsequently had the tool of his livelihood taken away from him, but in time he would receive ample compensation.

He arrived at my office with his son. I had heard about his archaic stone-crusher, and when I saw the man, I could not help but wonder if he too was a relic from a distant past. He wore traditional Arab clothing and despite his long and unkempt beard, I could see that his skin was leathery, permanently parched by the long years of hard toil in harsh conditions. He addressed me in Yiddish.

'*Iss int a yid* [Are you Jewish]?'

I nodded.

'*Vus machtse? Here, mit de goyim* [What's going on? Here, with the gentiles]?'

'Yes,' I replied, the extent of my Yiddish comprehension already exhausted by the first question.

Zvi broke in, speaking English, and we conducted the negotiations. He bid a certain price per *dunam* for the job, and wanted the government to pay. He then guaranteed that the entire area would be taken care of on the basis of a ten-year lease. Naturally they won the tender—they were the only ones who applied. The British paid them handsomely for their services.

Efron spoke fluent Arabic, and he was already on friendly terms with many of the Arab *Muktars*. All he had to do was ride his horse from one town to another and organise the Arabs to work on the land. Efron was a smart negotiator, and he knew the Arabs well enough to know that they would be thrilled to obtain permission to farm the extra acreage, prohibited until now. Consequently, he assumed the guise of a benefactor, bearing news that he could obtain permits for them—for a price. The *Muktars* were to pay him a certain amount of money per *dunam*. In this way, Efron managed to secure payments from both parties, and in the course of the next two years, he amassed a huge fortune.

Efron was not the only one who managed to cash in on the spoils of war. For Jewish builders, the war was a bonanza. An honest bonanza. For each construction, I had a set of plans, and the builder had a set of plans, and I would always wonder why they were not identical. It took me some time to understand what was going on. The British system of construction meant pricing in order to get the tender. Builders were able to price low because of the British system of quantity surveying. When pricing for a door, for example, builders would not quote on the finished product, only the door itself. The door frame, the handle, the lock, and any decorative adornments were separate items, treated as add-on value. The door may have been quoted at one hundred dollars, but by the time the extras were added, it may have cost up to five hundred dollars. When quoting, these extra costs did not have to be included in the summary—they were considered later by the quantity surveyor, Captain Paynter, who then decided whether they were to be added or not.

The builders learned this very quickly. Consequently, variations were always present. Not improvements, but *variations*. And everybody benefited, except for the British army coffers.

Another area of exploitation involved water tank construction. The tank was constructed and would be approved, provided that it had no leakage. If there was leakage, the builder would work hard to stop the leak. However, to refill this tank after repairs, and to keep it full, twenty or thirty camels were needed to cart the water. The builders soon realised that repairing the leak was costing them money, and they demanded remuneration for the costs of the camels (with a little profit built in). The British knew that they were occupying a difficult country and went out of their way to keep peace with the locals. They agreed to the demands. By paying the costs of the camels, however, they ensured even greater profits for the builders, and eventually, the smart ones began constructing tanks that had latent leaks. Then they would seal the tank and build in another leak. This became known as the 'leak business', and it was a very profitable enterprise.

By the end of 1942, a rumour began to circulate that some of the officers and the builders were rorting the system. One day, after returning from one of the building sites, Bodor burst into my office.

'Did you hear what happened?' he asked breathlessly.

'No.'

'Captain Paynter has been arrested and they are waiting for three judges from the Justice Department to arrive for the court martial.'

I was flabbergasted. 'You're kidding?'

'No. They are sending another captain from Cairo to take Paynter's place. And I hear that he is not exactly a gentleman.'

When I thought about it, I realised that it would have been quite simple for Paynter to have abused the system. He was a very capable man, and he was in complete control of the supply of materials and the management of the construction firms. And there was variation in everything—plans, materials, time. He was far too smart to put himself at risk by accepting bribes, but he could certainly hide his profits in the variations.

Captain Paynter was the only officer who resided outside the barracks. He shared a flat, and a bed, with a local Arab woman. When the police searched the premises, they discovered a box under the bed containing jewellery, a small amount of cash, and the stub or receipt part of a ten-pound banknote. They realised that if they found the other half of that note, they would find the booty. They went from bank to bank in Beirut, Damascus, Tel Aviv, and Bersheva. Eventually they found it in a small bank in Tel Aviv. The captain was found guilty and sentenced to the front in the most dangerous hot spot, Italy.

In 1945, as I was strolling down Allenby Street in Tel Aviv, somebody called out to me.

'Lustig!' I turned to see the disgraced captain, alive and well.

'I cannot believe it. Captain Paynter. I am glad to see you alive.' We exchanged pleasantries for a while, when suddenly his tone became low and confidential.

'You know, Lustig, I made over thirty thousand pounds from all of that business in Damascus.'

'But you were caught,' I reminded him. He was not the 'capable thief' of my vernacular.

'So I was, Lustig, but I didn't rob anybody. It was all just part of the building process. They had to let me keep the money.'

I'd never heard that the British army maintained such a *laissez-faire* approach to their military criminals, but still I wasn't quite sure whether to dismiss his claim.

Captain Beverley was the man who arrived to replace Paynter. His reputation preceded him—the word was that he was a bastard of the highest order, a man who made life difficult at every turn and who was capable of causing problems even when he slept. He was reported to have said that the civilian staff in the Royal Engineers Corps were a bunch of thieves and must be discharged at once.

Two days after his arrival, he summoned me to his office. He got straight to the point with his businesslike manner.

'What about these structures in Qatana, Lustig? What is the status?'

'They are under construction now, Captain Beverley.'

'Tomorrow morning, o-eight-hundred. We are going out there to take a look.'

'All right, Captain.'

The following morning, his driver took us to the site of the undergound hospital. The British had calculated that Qatana could be the point through which the Germans were likely to break, and had begun preparing for the contingency. We began our inspection of the work site.

'What's that pipe, Lustig?' Beverley demanded.

'That's to drain the blood away from the operating theatre, Captain.'

'It looks very long.'

'If I remember correctly, sir, the plans called for one hundred metres.'

'I want to see the plans.'

A builder handed him the plans. Then he instructed the builders to measure the pipeline. It was 110 metres long.

'Check it again,' barked the Captain. 'How much did you pay, Lustig?'

'We paid for one hundred metres.'

His tone suddenly softened, and a smile crossed his face. 'Mr Lustig, I would like to have a word with you, privately.'

He took me aside.

'It is most uncommon that a civilian employee in the army would try to do something extra for the army, free of payment. Actually, this is the very first time I have come across it.' When he continued, he raised his voice to ensure everyone's undivided attention. 'Mr Lustig, on behalf of the British taxpayers, thank you very much for putting yourself to the trouble of saving us some money. Very good.'

On the way to the work site, Captain Beverley had not uttered a word to me. On our way back to the barracks, he was all smiles and joviality.

'I am very pleased, Lustig. I see now that what I have heard about you is correct. I think that we can work together and save ourselves a lot of money. You know what I am talking about, don't you.'

Clearly, Captain Beverley had been sent to Damascus as a 'fix-it' man.

'Yes,' I replied.

'Where are you living here in Damascus?'

I told him about Sarah and our apartment.

'How do you spend the evenings, Lustig?'

'Generally at night, I play bridge.'

'Oh, really? I have not played for years. Would you allow me to join in?'

'Of course. Tonight, eight o'clock.'

'It seems to be very close by, your apartment.'

'Yes. In the French Quarter. Shall I arrange for some food or drink?'

'Well, I wouldn't mind a drink, Lustig, but don't go to any trouble.'

'No problem, Captain.'

We became friends, and the dreaded Captain was nowhere near as fearsome as we had thought. Indeed, that night at my apartment, I put him in his place. Since he brought the number of players to five, I sat out of the game. He didn't seem to be doing well, until I isolated the problem.

'Captain Beverley, some advice: if you concentrate on the cards instead of on my wife, you may actually win a hand or two.'

19 The Tide Turns

When you're on top of the world you should remember it turns over every twenty-four hours.
Tamie Fraser

He that resolves to dealing with none but honest men, must leave off dealing.
Thomas Fuller

By the spring of 1943, the Germans had been defeated at Stalingrad and El Alamein. The tide was turning to the Allies' advantage, but the German force remained formidable and we were not yet sure that the war was won. Just as the Germans were on the receiving end of sustained strategic bombing of their synthetic oil plants, the Allies had to maintain a constant flow of oil to serve their growing war effort. Not surprisingly, the Germans were aiming for the massive oilfields at Kirkuk and Mosul in northern Iraq.

After the suppression of the Iraqi fascist government in 1942, and the retreat of the Germans from Egypt and the Caucasus, the only interference with the 600-kilometre pipeline that ran from the Kurdish oilfields to the Mediterranean refineries at Tripoli and Haifa came from Bedouin tribes moving freely between Syria and Transjordan.

A number of the Bedouin tribes were led by the renowned Emir Fauer el Fauer. He was not an especially important emir, nor were his tribes numerous, but his repeated sabotage missions, which often involved destroying sections of pipeline with explosives, were causing considerable concern. It was unclear as to whether this activity was born of genuine anti-British sentiment, or was simply a diversion for the Bedouins from the boredom of the Syrian steppe. Indeed, it appeared to be treated by them as some kind of sport. On the other hand, Damascus, like Casablanca and Lisbon, was crawling with Axis agents, and it was suspected that the Emir was hiring out his services.

A new face began appearing regularly at military headquarters. While he wore a pilot's uniform, it soon became clear that he was not merely an air force officer; he was a member of MI6, British military intelligence. He had been brought in to solve the problem caused by the Emir. Clearly it was impossible to place guards all the way along the 600-kilometre pipeline, and so a plan was formulated to strike a deal with the Bedouin leader.

A rumour began to spread among our ranks that a large convalescent camp and hospital were about to be commissioned. This struck me as rather odd—after all, construction had slowed with the recent Allied victories, and I had seen no plans from Cairo for such a project.

I was summoned to see Lieutenant-Colonel Williams, commanding officer of the Royal Engineers. His instructions were brief and to the point.

'Mr Lustig, there is going to be a new tender,' he began. 'You will be placed in charge of this tender. You will be told who is going to win the tender. Do you understand? This is a political contract. You need not know any more about this. You will be advised.'

'Yes, sir.'

'The winning tenderer will want to go through the usual procedure, the requisite pomp and ceremony. You will escort him to the site, introduce him to the site operation, and explain the basic conditions of the contract. Then you will return to base.'

The tender was sizeable: two hundred and fifty thousand pounds. I wondered whether this had anything to do with the mystery camp and hospital. When I was informed that the Emir was to be announced as the winning tenderer, I realised that this was the payoff for his cooperation. The *bakshish*. Of course, the difficulty had been in establishing how much the Emir would be paid and, more importantly, how the payment could be disguised so as to avoid any questions from Headquarters in London.

On the given day, I received a call and made my way down to military headquarters. At about 11 a.m., the spectacle began. A cavalcade made its way down the street and stopped in front of the office. Six Arab guards on horses led the parade. They were dressed in full regalia: immaculate white ceremonial robes and red *kaffiahs*. There followed more horses, then camels, and then the cars—eight brand new shiny white American Buicks. The last car was equipped with two flags, one the Emir's and the other British. At the rear of the cavalcade, there were half a dozen mules with riders. And on both sides of the street rode two columns of fierce Arab fighters on horses, brandishing rifles, bandoliers strung across their chests. There must have been two hundred Arabs in this parade.

The rear door of the flagged car opened and a tall European gentleman stepped out. He entered the office and spoke in an official tone.

'Who is Mr Lustig?'

I stepped forward. The Armenian man introduced himself as Fabrionian, the Emir's engineer. He reminded me of a character from a Peter Lorre film, and not an attractive one.

'Mr Lustig,' he oozed, 'I understand that you will be handing the site over to us. Please come with me.' I duly followed in his repugnant wake.

As we approached the car, I could not help but wonder why I had been chosen for this specific task. It was unusual, especially considering the eminence of the Emir. My instincts told me that something was not right. I was suspicious.

Fabrionian opened the car door and there sat Emir Fauer himself.

'Please sit down,' said Fabrionian. 'The Emir does not speak English. If he wants to say something, I will translate.'

'*Shukran*,' I said. 'Thank you.' The Emir smiled.

We sat down, and with a wave of the Armenian's hand, the door was closed and the entire procession began moving, leaving Damascus for the site.

A few moments later, the Emir leaned across to Fabrionian and muttered something in Arabic.

'The Emir would like to know how it is that you are not British and that you are not dressed in a military uniform.'

'I am a civilian engineer. I have the title of Acting Garrison Engineer, and I am the one who knows the details of the contract.'

'That is all right,' replied the Armenian. 'The Emir is interested because you spoke in Arabic. How long have you been working with the British?'

'Three years.'

'Where do you come from?'

'I was born in Vienna.'

'Is this a town or a country?'

'Vienna, Austria.'

'And where did you study?'

I knew that the answer to this question could have landed me in serious trouble, so, discretion being the better part of cowardice, I decided to avoid the issue.

'Oh, around here,' I vaguely offered, gesturing towards the land beyond the vehicle.

It was then that I discovered that the Emir not only understood every word that I had uttered in English, but that his own English was perfectly appropriate for a polite conversation. I hoped that ours would remain so.

'And what is the name of your university?' the Emir asked.

'The Institute of Technology.'

'Where?' he insisted.

I hesitated for a moment. The options and the possible outcomes began to flood my mind. Then I recalled how well honesty had always served me in the past.

'Haifa,' I said reluctantly.

The Emir was quiet. Then he gruffly said something in Arabic to the Armenian, who turned with instructions to the driver. The car came to a sudden stop before the driver performed a rather hurried U-turn.

The Emir did not look at me at all.

'What is going on?' I asked Fabrionian.

'I am sorry, Mr Lustig, but the Emir is offended and we are returning to your office. The Emir understands that you are a Palestinian Jew, and he refuses to deal with you. He will deliver you back to your superiors at the Royal Engineers.' So much for honesty.

We spent the return journey in silence. The Emir stared angrily out the window. I wondered what humiliation would befall me upon my return. I could have lied, but then it would have been worse had the Emir discovered my identity. I was angry with the Lieutenant Colonel for not having briefed me.

My exit from the car was as perfunctory as it could possibly be, short of being physically hurled into the street while still in motion. No ceremony. No pleasantries. No farewells, fond or otherwise.

I leapt up the stairs to the commander's office, humiliated and ready for a confrontation. After all, my honour was at stake.

The Lieutenant-Colonel was waiting for me, beaming from ear to ear as if he had anticipated my return. The MI6 'pilot' stood by his side, also looking suspiciously smug.

'Mr Lustig,' the commander exclaimed, grasping my hand. 'Jolly well done. Thank you.'

He made a great show of looking at his watch. 'And your reappearance is right on time, just as we calculated.'

'What is this all about, sir?' I demanded, my wounded pride surpassing all protocols.

'You, Mr Lustig, have just saved the British government an enormous amount of money. I would suspect that the Emir is very offended that we granted our Jewish employee the privilege of handing over the site of a camp that we didn't need to build in the first place.'

'I should have been told!' I protested.

'I couldn't tell you. But don't worry, you did a wonderful job. Now we begin stage two of our negotiations with this fellow.'

Two weeks later, I was informed that the 'pilot' had concluded an alternative deal with the miffed Emir. He had settled for £25,000 up front, saving the British a cool two hundred and twenty-five thousand.

It was the last I heard of Emir Fauer el Fauer until the Israeli War of Independence in 1948. He led the Bedouin attacks on the Jewish settlements in the Galil before being soundly defeated.

By early 1944, the threat of German invasion had almost completely subsided, and our work on the construction of fortifications had slowed considerably. It did not stop completely, however, and the work that ensued was rather a waste of British money. For within two years, tenders were issued for the demolition of these very structures.

Besides continuing with the construction of fortifications through 1944 and 1945, albeit on a limited scale, the British continued to tender for the construction of roads and bridges, primarily between Damascus and Baghdad.

By mid 1944, I had been approached by a local construction firm to join them as a partner. With a number of the civilian staff leaving the employ of the British army, I decided to take up their offer. The two partners, Bettingani and Quweitar, approached me because of my intimate knowledge of the British system and the personnel in control of awarding the tenders. They came to my home and offered me £100,000 plus a twenty-five per cent share of the profits. It was an opportunity too good to pass up, though at the time, I did not know that I would see little of the promised lump sum, and none of the profits.

Bettingani and Quweitar were both Syrian, though Bettingani was a Christian and Quweitar a Muslim. It was an uncommon partnership. As a Jew, I thought that the three of us would create a quaint little trio, a model of cooperation for the peoples of the Middle East. Bettingani had studied engineering for four years at the American University in Beirut, and while he was clearly more sophisticated than his partner, neither of them was fluent in English. I agreed to join them, but added a number of conditions of my own. One of these was the employment of my friend 'Gandhi'. When he arrived and informed me that Fishel Lifshitz was in trouble with the police in Palestine and needed a speedy escape route, I insisted that Lifshitz join us too. I placed Gandhi in charge of finances and administration, while Lifshitz took control of construction.

The nine-month experiment with Bettingani and Quweitar bore little fruit, for a number of reasons. While we were successful in winning a number of tenders, many of the projects were cancelled because of the British army's diminishing interest in the area.

One tender that proceeded involved the supply of pure river sand for a number of experiments with precast concrete. This project would fall through for different reasons. It was fraught with problems. When we applied for the job, Quweitar had assured me that he knew where to find this sand. But he had not taken delivery of the sand into account, and I did not find out until after the tender had been won. The job came out of Beirut, and I had to travel there with Quweitar to see the Major-General in charge of the Royal Engineers.

'How can I help you, Mr Lustig?'

'I need trucks.'

'How many?'

Quweitar looked at me excitedly. He took this to mean that we could have as many vehicles as we needed free of charge, but I understood that the chief was thinking only about availability, and would only consider an offer against payment.

'I need twenty-five three-ton trucks.'

'This is unusual, Mr Lustig. I am prepared to lend you twenty-two of our new trucks. But you will have to pay for the Lebanese drivers.'

'Thank you, sir.'

This was indeed a coup. The other construction firms had to rent trucks, but somehow we had managed to secure these trucks free of charge. On the way back to Damascus, I told Quweitar to take me to the site where he intended to procure the washed sand. When we arrived, I realised to my horror that we had nowhere near enough to satisfy the terms of the contract.

'Where is the sand, for Pete's sake?'

'Here,' exclaimed Quweitar gesturing at an outlandishly small deposit.

'You're kidding me. We don't have a tenth of the amount we need.'

We managed the first delivery, for which we earned good money, but soon our pure sand was beginning to run out, and there was no more to be found. Given that we were paying nothing for the use of the trucks, we could probably have afforded to wash the impure sand for delivery, but things were becoming too complicated now. I decided to return to Beirut with Quweitar. He was embarrassed that he could not deliver, and I was trying to figure out what I could say to the chief that would make sense to explain on what basis we quoted, and how it happened that suddenly we didn't have the goods. Once again, as had been the case with the Emir, I felt that honesty, with myself and others, was the best policy. If I could find a good, convincing lie, that was all right; but otherwise, I would be straight. At least the truth was always internally consistent.

We arrived in Beirut in the evening and stayed overnight. We were supposed to meet the chief at ten in the morning. At breakfast, Quweitar was very anxious and I suggested that he stay there drinking coffee while I saw the chief myself. He remained silent. Finally, at ten minutes to ten, he agreed to stay, but only on the condition that I call him with the news straightaway.

'I am sorry,' I told the Major-General, 'I have a local partner, and he told me the location of the sand. I had calculated that if I had a certain depth of sand over that area, we would have enough. On that basis I quoted. When I saw the location I realised that there was not sufficient volume, but the administration had moved very quickly, and here I am. I have the job but I don't have the sand.'

'What about the trucks? You have twenty-two new trucks.'

Here I saw my opportunity to turn a negative into a positive.

'When I was given these trucks, I assumed that after supplying the wet sand, the trucks would be ruined, and of no value, so at least you get your trucks back in one piece.'

The chief smiled.

'Look. I don't want to appear like a pupil at school in front of the headmaster. The facts are clear. If I don't supply the sand, I won't damage the trucks.'

'No problem, Mr Lustig.'

At that moment, in the eyes of Quweitar and Bettingani, I became a hero.

While the British jobs were gradually grinding to a halt, we were able to find work on road construction through the Syrian Board of Works. Bettingani concentrated his efforts in this area, and was successful in winning a number of tenders. Lifshitz claimed to be an expert on road construction, and so he took charge of the work. Then he suddenly disappeared from the face of the earth—with two truckloads of steel.

I was alerted to the fact by two military policemen from the British army who came into my office asking after Lifshitz and the missing trucks. I had helped Lifshitz out of a crisis in Palestine by employing him in Syria, and now he was repaying me by robbing me of a fortune. Besides the fact that the steel itself was worth more than gold, he had made off with the trucks as well.

After Lifshitz's disappearance, I sensed that my two Arab partners felt they had made a mistake in asking me to join them. And perhaps I had made a mistake too. The business had grown, and we were all making a considerable amount of money, but the arrangement was hardly equitable. Each week, they would come into the office and withdraw funds. I soon realised that they perceived our operation as a means of earning spending money rather than building a business. It would soon be time to leave.

That time arrived as I sat in the Oasis and began to overhear sophisticated, Westernised Arabs making derogatory remarks about Jews. They were isolated incidents at first, but soon became regular occurrences.

The war was nearly at an end and I now had an infant daughter. My future became crystal clear to me. I would return to Palestine and begin a career as a builder and developer, employing the skills I had gained in the military.

One chapter of my life was drawing to a close and I had to think about the next. I calculated that I needed £3000 to start anew in Palestine. I did not have this kind of money and I knew that I would receive little joy from Bettingani and Quweitar. I was not broke, but I would need to double my money quickly if I was to realise my newly formulated plan. Consequently, I accepted an offer made to me by Boris Kaminsky.

At one of Kaminsky's famous parties, he had begun to tell me about 'his way' of making fast money. I had my reservations about his theories, but I had nothing to lose by listening. In reality, his theories were nothing more than ideas about speculative trading: finding the appropriate goods and selling them to the appropriate people.

'Ted—you don't mind if I call you Ted?'

'Go ahead,' I answered, wary, but my curiosity piqued.

'I know where I can get my hands on some *fantastic* silk stockings from Turkey. You know how difficult they are to come by, Ted. Invest together with me and we will make a killing.'

There was something charming about this big Russian, something irresistible. And I was not able to resist. I invested £400 in his scheme. It was a considerable proportion of my savings.

Two days later I was told that my money was gone.

'I'm really sorry, Ted. I had no idea that the goods were faulty. Goddamn it! One stocking in lieu of two, and when there were two, they were different sizes! Ted, I am as disappointed as you are. I lost money too, you know. Look, Ted, we can make up for the loss. Both of us. I have been offered a shipment of playing cards. Ted, you can't get them anywhere. It's a surefire gain. Let's do it!'

'Once bitten …' they say. If only. I fell for the same trick twice, handing him another £200 of my hard-earned savings.

Sarah had warned me against it. She understood that I was trying to invest. While she was rarely inclined to interfere in these matters, she quietly suggested that it might be a better idea to invest in land in Palestine. Not land that needed tending, like orchards, but a piece of land that could just sit there and accumulate in value. This she had learned from her father. In my arrogance, and my urgent need for a quick return, I spurned her idea. Indeed, at the time I thought that her ideas were a bit simple—to have solid, good, high-quality cash and then dig a hole in the land somewhere and throw your money into it! Of course it did not occur to me that this was exactly what I was doing, only I would have nothing to show for it. I was taking very good cash and burying it deep in Kaminsky's pocket.

Naturally, I was let down once again. Either Kaminsky was the world's most stupid speculator, or I was. I suspected the latter.

'Goddamn it, Ted. How was I to know that the decks were faulty? Fifty-one cards in one deck, two jacks of clubs in another. We haven't had much luck, have we, Ted? I'm *really* sorry.'

It did not take me long to realise that I had now been given a personal demonstration of Kaminsky's method of making quick money. I had never seen the goods—for all I knew, there were never any goods. There was simply a con man, cashing in on the naïvety of his fellow man. I felt ashamed that my appetite for easy money had landed me in this situation. After four years earning good pay and living the high life in Damascus, I would be forced to return to Palestine, family in tow, without a job and with hardly a nickel to my name, my savings irretrievably lost on odd stockings and decks of cards rife with jokers. I'd been dealt a most vexing hand, and the stakes were way over my head.

20 War of Independence

... Take my mother-in-law. Please.
HENNY YOUNGMAN

'ARE YOU SURE he's a Jew?' Sarah's mother asked her sarcastically, peering at me from across the small dining room in her Tel Aviv flat. With her characteristic lack of grace, and her compulsive propensity to kick a man while he was down, she was now referring to my lack of funds and my present inability to find work.

In Damascus I had become friendly with Janowsky, a Jewish architect and engineer from Haifa. He had informed me of a tender for the construction of a block of apartments in Haifa. I submitted a bid, but it was deemed too high and I didn't get the job. In the meantime, however, I organised for Janowsky to have my name registered on the list of official tenderers in Haifa. I was bidding on a number of jobs by the time we returned to Tel Aviv, but this was not good enough for my mother-in-law.

Sarah did not dignify her mother's question with a response—she knew all too well how embarrassed I was to be relying on the charity of her family. Indeed, Sarah was herself reluctant to have us move into her mother's apartment, even temporarily. She knew her mother better than I, and I always detected a slight embarrassment when she spoke of her.

I had not met my mother-in-law prior to our return to Tel Aviv. Sarah and I had met in Haifa and had married quickly in Damascus. There hadn't been an opportunity to meet her family, and I don't think that Sarah was sorry for that.

I *had* met Sarah's sister, Hassia, however. Soon after our decision to leave Damascus for Palestine, and curious about my standing with Sarah's family, we made a reconnaissance trip to her sister's home in

Petah Tiqvah, outside Tel Aviv. Hassia had married into a well-known, wealthy Haifa family, certainly one that would have been considered local 'establishment'. The patriarch, Hassia's father-in-law, was Commissioner of the Palestine Railways.

We arrived for lunch at the designated hour—around 1.30 p.m.— to find the apartment empty, except for a housemaid who knelt on all fours cleaning the floor, and a young girl who we presumed to be Hassia's daughter. Atop the table sat a huge, uncovered bowl of potato salad. While I was somewhat shocked by the absence of our hosts, Sarah's unperturbed response that we should simply sit down and wait for their arrival suggested that this was not an uncommon occurrence in her family. Within fifteen minutes, Sarah's brother-in-law arrived home. He was a big man, polite but slow and leaden. Hassia's family did not mind this; they considered Hassia lucky to have married into his family's money. When Hassia finally arrived home almost an hour later, her child was crying, her salad was spoilt, and her husband was furious. But his mood left little impression on her, and even less effort was made to disguise the obvious problems that clearly already existed in their union.

Indeed, Hassia's marriage would not last long. She soon fell in love with Ziggy Schwartz, a strapping man from Podolskiy in Poland, who stood six foot four and boasted movie star looks. They met on a beach in Netanya, north of Tel Aviv, and while Ziggy could have had his choice of any woman on the beach, he was taken by Hassia's exotic Eurasian appearance, her athletic but feminine figure, and most of all, by her ability to match him stroke for stroke over a five-kilometre swim.

Within weeks, Hassia had filed for divorce from her husband. It was an unpleasant episode in which Hassia had to claim impotence on the part of her husband. As soon as the divorce came through, and after a campaign by the first husband, featuring threats of suicide and further threats aimed at Ziggy, Hassia and Ziggy were married. Shortly after, and with relations between the Jews and Arabs straining in the uncertainty of the pending British withdrawal from Palestine, Ziggy began work for a *Haganah* munitions factory. While he was testing a new hand grenade, it accidentally exploded, leaving his hand and face permanently disfigured. This affected Ziggy profoundly—until this time, he had been somewhat of an Adonis, and his captivating looks had not merely fed his vanity, but had kept him alive. Through the

Second World War, he had walked from Russia to Budapest, staying alive and fed by 'servicing' local women along the way. And upon his arrival in Palestine, he had settled on Netanya beach and eked out a living in the same way—Ziggy's gigolo service.

The lunch at Petah Tiqvah with Hassia and her first husband was an uncomfortable introduction to the Lipshit family, and at the time it strengthened Sarah's and my own conviction to avoid relying on them for anything at all. It was all the more depressing since I had lost my hard-earned money to Kaminsky and was forced to seek the help of my mother-in-law upon our return to Tel Aviv.

My small family was obliged to occupy the dining area of my mother-in-law's third-floor apartment in King Street, in downtown Tel Aviv. Our only possessions were a cot and pram for Iris and three Persian rugs that we had brought from Damascus.

Sarah's mother had recently remarried. Her second husband was a happy-go-lucky fellow from Warsaw who had everybody believing that he was a professional house painter. Indeed, the small blotches of paint that decorated most of his clothing suggested that this was in fact the case, but after marrying my mother-in-law, he settled into a life of leisure, spending his days cycling around the city and whistling incessantly. It was essentially a marriage of convenience—on more than one occasion, he took me aside to complain about his new wife, particularly her less-than-ordinary looks and her 'foul odour'.

Sarah and I were clearly an intrusion upon my mother-in-law's new-found domestic bliss, and she was never reticent about telling me that she wanted us out of her house as soon as possible. With this ulterior motive, in a rare display of charity she decided to help me find work. She went to see an acquaintance—the chief of the British police force in Tel Aviv. An hour later she returned, looking most satisfied with herself. Addressing Sarah, she said, 'He has to see the chief tomorrow morning.'

The police chief introduced me to Fogel, a thickset Russian Jew who worked as the inspector of design and construction with the Tel Aviv Town Planning Authority. He was an accomplished structural engineer and an excellent mathematician who specialised in the economics of structural design and construction. The interview was brief.

'You studied where, Mr Lustig?' he asked me.

'Haifa Technion.'

'And you completed your degree?'

'Yes'.

'Okay. You can start tomorrow morning.'

That night, Sarah and I celebrated at a restaurant. It was our first meal out since our return to Tel Aviv. We savoured every morsel.

The following day, I fronted at my new employment. Fogel asked me some basic questions.

'What system do you use when you have forces that exceed … ?'

Once again, I was faced with the familiar situation in which honesty would reveal my ignorance, and once again I simply hoped for the best.

'I really don't remember.'

'Okay, I'll ask you another question.'

'You are wasting your time, Mr Fogel. I simply don't remember.'

'Excellent,' he said. 'I do not have to *un*teach you, which means that you will be more capable of learning something from me. I am very thankful to our chief.'

After six weeks with Fogel, I was sent to work with Vandrov, the engineer responsible for overseeing construction in the North Tel Aviv area—the *Myhandes* of the North Tel Aviv Council. He was responsible for issuing all the requisite permits, and I was sent to work with him as a building inspector. There was a high degree of town planning involved. It was more than simply structural integrity; the building also had to improve the streetscape.

Landing this new job would prove to be a landmark for me—the first big 'break' in my own professional advancement. Vandrov was a renowned bureaucrat—a pedantic and extraordinarily stubborn man who would not approve plans for a project until he knew everything about every single detail involved. Consequently, developers often had to wait inordinately long periods of time before being granted the most routine of building approvals. Before long, I realised that this could be of great benefit to me. Word spread quickly that a new building inspector had started at the council, and that this young man was capable of supplying permits in half the time it took to obtain one from Vandrov.

Developers began to seek me out, if for no other reason than to avoid Vandrov. Within months, many of these developers had begun requesting my own design and drafting services, fully aware that my familiarity with council requirements would further accelerate the process of obtaining permits. Since my working hours at the council were 7.30 a.m. to 3 p.m., I had ample time to complete these private jobs. Drawing up plans for these clients was not an entirely 'kosher' activity on my part given the potential conflicts of interest, but Vandrov diligently watched over my shoulder to ensure that no unsound plans passed through the office, and that *bakshish* did not figure in the equation.

A more immediate benefit of the council job came in the form of accommodation for my family. Sarah's mother had grown increasingly impatient for our departure and had even threatened to call the police and evict us. It was an ugly situation, but unavoidable since the city was suffering from a housing density problem and obtaining an apartment in Tel Aviv required a substantial sum to be paid as 'key money'. I did not have that kind of cash.

Shortly after I had commenced work for the council, the city's architects, engineers and building inspectors went out on strike for more than six weeks. During this time away from my desk, I decided to examine the entire North Tel Aviv area, to become acquainted with all the projects that were under way. I soon noticed that many developers were taking advantage of the absence of inspectors, moving quickly to add new and unapproved areas to their buildings. Notices had been placed in the newspapers informing developers that any unauthorised construction would have to be demolished at the developer's cost, but many of them took the chance that once the buildings were completed, the law would not be enforced. As I strolled down Motzkin Street, a small cul-de-sac, I noticed that an extra apartment was being constructed on the roof of one of the existing buildings. From my knowledge of engineering, I knew at once that such an addition could not possibly have been authorised. The concrete slab that had been poured as the roof of that building would not have been engineered to bear any load, let alone the weight of an entire apartment.

I found the name of the builder and owner. A Mr Fink leased the lower floors and was now developing the roof. I went to see him on the job, and told him that I was from the council.

'You understand, Mr Fink, that you now face the cost of demolishing this construction. If you leave it, the council will demolish it themselves but you will have a black mark against your name.'

'I will get the permit …'

'No, Mr Fink, if you apply now, after you have started, I can assure you that it will take another twenty-five years to get a permit.'

I watched his face. Here was the opening and I took my chance.

'On the other hand, you can complete the job and earn some small rent from this apartment. I expect to be able to move in within two weeks.'

We came to an agreement. I had secured a small apartment for my family. One room, plus a bathroom and small kitchen. No key money, and *very* flexible rent conditions. My only concern was that someone would find out and denounce me to the council. My fears intensified when Finkel, the *Myhandes* (engineer) for the entire Tel Aviv area—and Vandrov's boss—embarked on a campaign to check all permits at the conclusion of the strike. But as the developers had anticipated, once the buildings were standing, it was almost impossible for the council to enforce their demolition. Sarah, Iris and I lived in that apartment for many years.

Here I would build a new future, starting with nothing but a job and three Persian rugs. In time I would work for myself as a developer. But for now I was simply an employee of the council, with a small design and drafting business on the side, and soon even that work would begin to dry up. The period of uncertainty prior to the British departure from Palestine saw building slow dramatically. As a building inspector, I had little work to do, and late in 1947 there was a three-month period where no one at the council was paid a salary or any fees.

War was on its way. Ill feeling towards the British began to escalate after the end of the Second World War. After having made a significant contribution to the Allied war effort, the Jewish community of Palestine felt betrayed by British legislation to restrict Jewish immigration into Palestine, especially at a time when hundreds of thousands of Jews were suffering as post-Nazi refugees in Europe.

While I was sympathetic to the cause of the European victims, I cannot say the same for my feelings towards the extreme Zionist underground groups which embarked on a vigorous campaign against British installations and the British themselves. I was staunchly anti-nationalist. I had been raised in Europe—a region where such patriotism resulted in hatred and bloodshed—and I could foresee the dangers of Jewish nationalism. I could envisage no positive outcome resulting from this extreme anti-British tide, and in fact this proved to be the case. Reactions from both sides intensified. The bombing of ten of the eleven bridges connecting Palestine with surrounding nations in May of 1946 led to the 'Black Sabbath'—the most far-reaching cordon and search operation in modern Palestine's history. The Black Sabbath resulted in the bombing of government offices that were located in the King David Hotel in Jerusalem, prompting the British to enforce curfews in Tel Aviv and Jerusalem. These actions only served to prevent us all from getting on with our lives.

Through 1946 and 1947, as it became clear that the British would withdraw from Palestine, leaving the Jews and Arabs to their own devices, I began to plan for my family's emigration. Sarah had long expressed a desire to leave Palestine, and since our years in Syria, had had her heart set on moving to Australia. I knew little about this far-off land, but my wife had been charmed by the Australian troops who were stationed in Damascus during the war. They were a friendly bunch and Sarah was left with the lasting image of them playing with the local children in the streets. They were easygoing, free-spirited, and non-partisan, and Sarah was intrigued by the sort of country that could produce such specimens.

For my part, I knew that there were other destinations, possibly more accessible than Australia. I had discovered evidence of this soon after arriving in Tel Aviv, while strolling down Allenby Street.

'Well, well. Here comes our millionaire. Hey, Tedek! I'm talking to you!' A familiar bellow stopped me in my tracks.

It was Weidenfeld, my old acquaintance from the Technion, the Polish snob whose sport was bullying his friend Brauder. I was never particularly fond of him and seeing him did not evoke any great pleasure.

'Weidenfeld,' I replied, 'what do you want?'

'I need some money. I'm going away.' Tactful as always, Weidenfeld had not changed one iota.

'Where are you going?' I enquired, hoping the journey would be long, distant, and commence immediately.

'Venezuela. Listen, I can tell you how to get there. But I need some money.'

I knew that a visa to Venezuela was worth a man's weight in gold, and despite my own financial straits I agreed to give him fifty pounds, a considerable amount of money.

'First of all,' he began, 'you have to have a skill or occupation.'

'That's not a problem.' I began to feel the first stirrings of excitement.

'Secondly, you have to be a Catholic.'

'And herein lies the difficulty.'

'Not really. It is simply a matter of spending six months at *Stella Maris*, the Catholic monastery on *Har HaCarmel* in Haifa. You just convert. But the monks cannot guarantee passage to Venezuela after six months. It is still a risk.'

We travelled to Haifa and Weidenfeld took me up to the monastery, where he recommended me for a visa. In return, I handed him fifty pounds, with the parting remark, 'The only chance I have of seeing this money again is if you make it to bishop.' Naturally, I never saw Weidenfeld, or my money, again. To my knowledge, Weidenfeld never distinguished himself at the Holy See.

I abandoned the idea of converting to Catholicism. Marvell's trope about a man's dedication to his 'coy mistress' is an apt one: 'I will love you until the conversion of the Jews'. Even the lure of a visa was not enough. Apart from the fact that it offered no guarantees, I was reminded of my stay at the Polish consulate in Jerusalem. The food was good but the hours were terribly uncivilised.

Twenty years later, while visiting Brazil with my family, it came to my attention that the then Archbishop of São Paulo was none other than the rabbi's grandson, the young boy at the Technion who had been victim to Weidenfeld's taunts so many years before. Although never a convert himself, Weidenfeld proved a more effective tool than the Spanish Inquisition when it came to others in his circle.

Sarah had an aunt and uncle who had left Palestine during the 1920s and now lived in Perth, Western Australia. Sarah contacted them, and her uncle went to the trouble of obtaining entry visas for us. By May of 1948, I had arranged for my family's passage to Australia, via Rome. All that remained was for a family to take occupancy of our apartment (for key money, of course), and I was also awaiting payment for a recently completed design job. There were a few remaining commissions that I hoped to complete in order to maximise the funds available to re-establish ourselves abroad. Then I would have to arrange for the money to be sent to New York. These plans were interrupted on 14 May, however, when Ben-Gurion read the independence proclamation to announce the birth of the State of Israel.

Sarah burst into tears when she heard the announcement. They were not tears of joy, but tears of frustration. She was fully aware that this development would hamper our attempts to leave the country. That day we strolled through Tel Aviv, mingling with the crowd who sang and danced in the streets. But we did not dance, nor did we sing.

The pressure Sarah placed upon me to organise our departure intensified and I knew that I had to act quickly, before the inevitable repercussions of Ben-Gurion's announcement—war—began. I felt somewhat ashamed, and frightened, about standing in the queue outside the American Consulate in Arlozoroff Street. The Jews finally had their own country, and it struck me that the idea of leaving at this stage amounted to an act of treason. But I had not really wanted to stay there, and I remained true to myself, despite feeling that such personal integrity was not necessarily a smart idea. Sarah, a *Sabra* herself, had no such reservations at all—she was desperate to leave.

Within eight weeks, the arrangements had been finalised. I resigned from the council job, and handed my unfinished personal projects over to Ladislav Bodor, who would complete the works and forward my share of the payments to me.

Within hours of the Declaration of Independence, Arab forces broke forth from all sides—Syria and Lebanon to the North, Iraq and Transjordan to the East, and Egypt to the South—standing as one against the new Zionist state. The Jewish forces held firm and a truce was negotiated on 11 July. Two days earlier, Moshe Dayan's mechanised infantry had broken through and secured Lydda with its international airport, situated ten miles south-east of Tel Aviv, and within Arab territory. Lydda airport was to be our point of departure.

We joined a group that hired an armoured truck to take us to the airport. It would be a dangerous trip through Arab-occupied territory, and as soon as we were outside the area of *Haganah* protection, we were attacked. The driver immediately turned the vehicle around and returned to Tel Aviv. Our attempt to leave was unsuccessful.

Arriving back at our starting point, I immediately returned to our old apartment in Motzkin Street and within three hours, I had negotiated with the couple who had occupied it and secured their promise to depart. I returned their key money, along with a handsome profit, and suggested a building where they might find alternative accommodation. I called Bodor and told him that there had been a change in plans. I was not leaving, and I would take back the projects I had left with him.

The following night, at around 1 a.m., as I sat working on the drawing board in the tiny hallway of our apartment, there was a knock on the door. I answered it to find myself face to face with a young man in military uniform, brandishing a submachine gun.

'Are you Lustig?' he asked curtly, pointing the gun in the direction of Sarah and Iris in the living room.

'Yes,' I replied without hesitation.

'Come with me.'

'Tedek! Tedek!' Sarah cried out as I was escorted down the stairs.

The young soldier was *Haganah* and I was taken immediately to a military training camp. I had been recruited by force, and I knew that my only recourse was to make contact with my cousin Alex Yaron.

Alex had returned to Palestine from London about a year earlier. After having shot down an Italian fighter plane while serving in the British forces in Palestine during the Second World War, Alex had been sent to London to attend officers' training school. After completion of his course, he attended a ball where he met and fell in love with an attractive and wealthy young woman, and the couple were married soon after. Upon his return to Tel Aviv, I invited them to lunch in our apartment. I helped them to find an apartment to buy in *Shikun Ha-Kzinim* (settlement of officers), the old German area of the city where, as a major in the British Army, he was granted a price privilege.

Alex was now an influential member of the *Haganah*, and fortuitously for me (though I did not know this at the time), he was currently in charge of recruitment to this and a number of other training camps.

'I demand the right to make a phone call,' I protested to the *Haganah* officer.

'You have no such right.'

'I demand to speak with Alex Yaron.'

The sound of this name stopped the officer dead in his tracks.

'What has he got to do with *you*?' he sneered.

'We are family,' I answered simply.

Finally, I had Alex on the other end of the phone.

'Alex, I am in trouble. I am in this training camp, and Sarah has no money and no food.'

'Where is the camp?' my cousin asked.

I conferred with the officer and passed the information on to Alex.

'Okay, Ted. I will send a man right away with instructions for your immediate release.'

'Thank you, Alex. And by the way, how is your wife?'

'Don't worry about the small talk now, Ted. I have thousands of people to supervise here.'

'Very good, Bombardier.' I almost saluted as he rang off.

When I arrived home later that day, Sarah was the second happiest person in the world.

Every able body was recruited into the war effort, and while I managed to avoid being conscripted into the fledgling army, I was employed as a civilian camouflage expert, based on the knowledge I had acquired in Syria during the Second World War. I attended a seven-day course in the science of concealment run by two German Jews.

For the next few months, I served in the camouflage detail. Only once did I come close to losing my life. I was sent by truck to a location off the main road between Tel Aviv and Jerusalem. We came to an embankment on one side of this wide road, where we met a regiment of around forty men, all over fifty years of age, and all armed with ancient rifles of what looked to be Napoleonic vintage. They were holding a position some fifteen metres above the road, and an Arab regiment was positioned on the other side of the road, about thirty metres away. They were close enough to see each other, even without field glasses. Like the British and French before the battle of Agincourt in Shakespeare's *Henry V*, 'each … sees the other's umber'd face'.

My job was to assess camouflage requirements before returning to Tel Aviv to procure materials: nets, dummy anti-aircraft guns, a dummy tank. Weapons and ammunition were not easy to come by for the Israeli forces at this time and place, given limited funds and availability. The commanding officers believed the camouflage ruse to be the best alternative in the circumstances. I knew that dummy guns could not be relied upon for long, but I had been informed that nobody actually expected the Arab regiment to advance.

As dusk set in, we moved the camouflage equipment in under the cover of night. The Arabs were to assume that this mobilisation was real, as were the fortifications and munitions that they would face come daybreak. With the job done, and with no orders for me to remain, I returned to Tel Aviv. The following morning at seven o'clock, the Arab forces did attack, and all forty Jewish soldiers were killed. The Arabs had been ordered to move, and they would have attacked whether the munitions were real or not. Their guns were genuine; ours were fake. Had I stayed overnight, I too would have perished.

With the signing of the armistice agreement in early 1949, I was transferred from the camouflage unit to a civilian engineers detail, situated in the underground offices of *Shikunim Al Ideh*, a large building concern that had lain idle since the start of the war. I sat for some days in these offices, this bomb shelter, watching engineers and architects drinking coffee and playing cards while the drawing boards sat unused. Before long I began to implore my colleagues to start thinking about the future. With the armistice holding, the arrival of large numbers of immigrants was imminent, and they had to be housed. Within two days, I had secured three orders for the design of residential apartment blocks. Resurrected again, like the land around me, my career was up and running once more.

21 A Grand Design

The reality of the building does not consist in the roof and walls, but in the space within to be lived in.
LAO-TZU

IRIS WAS ALWAYS a headstrong, somewhat defiant child. By the age of three or four, she already had, down to a fine art, many and varied ways to send her poor mother into a frenzy. Like many children, Iris learned that a particular high-pitched scream could overpower Sarah's will and often result in the indefinite postponement of something Iris did not want to do. Sarah was a good woman but had little confidence in her abilities as a mother, and had absolutely no idea of how to deal with her daughter's histrionics. Sarah was at her wit's end, to the extent that she sought the help of a counselor. Her regular consultations helped to ease the strain on her mental health, but it placed a considerable strain on our finances. It was a very difficult time for us.

Much of the time I was at work and Sarah was left to her own devices. When I was at home, I managed to enforce some discipline but I was only slightly more adept at handling the situation. For a short period, I managed to control Iris with the use of reverse psychology—'No, you are *not* allowed to go to bed'—but she soon became wise to the ploy. On one occasion, Iris was dressed up to attend a friend's birthday party and was sitting up on the table so that Sarah could put on her shoes. Not only did the child refuse to allow her mother to finish dressing her, but she resisted my attempts to get her to finish her meal.

'Open your mouth and swallow,' I demanded, 'your mother wants to finish dressing you.'

I forced a spoonful of food into her mouth, whereupon she froze, stubbornly resisting the natural urge to chew or swallow. Then she took a handful of the food from her plate and smeared it onto her pristine dress. Sarah was reduced to tears.

My temper rising, I then did something I would remember and regret for the rest of my life. With an open hand, I slapped her on the cheek. We both stared at each other in shock. She swallowed her food. With this, I had established a terribly unhealthy method of discipline. Iris began pushing me to the limit each and every time I instructed her to do something: for some reason, she had to see how far she could go before her father raised his hand.

Apart from her troublesome temperament, there were times when Iris's health caused us tremendous concern. During 1949, when Iris was five years old, she travelled with her mother to Chicago, to visit Sarah's elder brother. During their stay, Iris fell ill with a fever of 42 degrees, and for some days, the doctors felt that she might die. Eventually, they resorted to laying her outside in the snow to bring her temperature down. I was on the telephone with Sarah throughout this procedure and I could hear my small daughter screaming in the background. It was heartbreaking and I was helpless to relieve her pain or her fear.

We had actually planned that I would join them in Chicago after some weeks. As it turned out, Sarah's brother was not particularly welcoming; he believed Sarah and Iris were there because they wanted money from him. Two weeks after their arrival I received a letter from Sarah, the ink-stained pages smudged with tears. In a bizarre and unjustified leap of logic that betrayed my wife's deep-seated insecurities, she asked me whether I was actually going to join them as planned, or whether I had another woman in Israel and was taking the opportunity to abandon her while she was in Chicago with her brother. He thought that was my plan, and that he would have to take care of them.

I answered Sarah's letter, including a brief note to her brother that was intended to disabuse him of his misconceptions—and that was, I admit, not overly polite. By the end of 1949, my wife and daughter had returned to Tel Aviv. We were together again, and Sarah was deeply and profoundly relieved.

As 1949 drifted into 1950, our plans to emigrate to Australia began to fade, and while Sarah felt somewhat heartbroken that this goal had not been realised, life was beginning to improve. For one thing, I was beginning to build a reasonably successful business for myself. The influx of immigrants and the consequent need for new housing resulted in a rapid growth of the building industry. My knowledge of town planning laws and requirements enabled me to secure permits quickly, and the contacts I had gained through my work with the council provided plenty of projects. Before long, I was inundated with work, and was employing two draughtsmen to assist me.

In my fourth year at the Haifa Technion, I had successfully completed a thesis that involved designing a five-kilometre bridge connecting Lydda to Beer-Yaakov in central Palestine. As was the case when I had won the competition in my third year, I tended to perceive civil engineering as merely one part of total town planning. My own interest lay in the bigger picture: how a township could best be designed to make an area not just habitable but livable.

While completing my thesis, it had dawned on me that town planning and design in Palestine involved a very particular social coexistence: integrating the culture of the incoming Europeans with that of the *Sabras*. I doubted that this would be easy, or maybe even possible.

Designing residential properties in Tel Aviv presented me with a unique set of challenges, not the least of which resulted from the fact that Israel was devoid of almost all conventional building materials. Timber and steel had to be imported at extraordinary expense, leaving concrete as the only viable building medium. The climate, too, imposed significant limitations and presented problems. Measures would have to be introduced to prevent the apartments from becoming hot-boxes, requiring the careful analysis of airflows in order to maximise the sea breeze that provided the city with its only relief for a few hours of each day. Another consideration was the best method for the storage of water at reasonable temperatures. And since the harsh climate forced inhabitants to live much of their domestic lives on the balconies, privacy became a critical factor.

Several other unique elements distinguished my designs from others that were being built at the time. With a European clientele in mind, I drew heavily on my knowledge of living conditions in Poland. For example, rather than having open access to each individual apartment, a security entrance was provided in the block. Furthermore, in anticipation of the increased importance of the motor car, I sacrificed the ground floor of many blocks for under-cover parking. Over a period of two years, I refined a formula for my apartment blocks, one that could be simply adapted to each specific block of land, thus further reducing the time it took to draft the plans and secure council approval.

I have always believed that clients will pay a little more in order to ensure a quality product. I hasten to add that there have been many occasions on which I have questioned the wisdom of this approach. While two buildings can look very similar from the outside, they may differ greatly in their quality, with this difference imperceptible to the untrained eye. I have often had to compete with those who are all too willing to compromise, and who may gain an edge simply because of their lower price.

I tended to be very critical of myself, and was always disappointed with the results of my labour. This perfectionism was undoubtedly inherited from my father. As I was finding my feet in Tel Aviv and formulating the ideas that I would carry through my career, I often felt that I was stabbing away haphazardly in the dark, with no professional guidance. In the absence of a mentor with whom to discuss my views, I missed my father all the more.

Towards the end of 1951, the opportunity presented itself for me to take a significant career step—from being a designer to becoming a developer. And, as had been the case with so many opportunities, it came about through sheer luck: simply being in the right place at the right time!

The place was the Café Tifferet, which stood at the intersection of *Shderot Keren Kayemet* and *Rehov Allenby* in downtown Tel Aviv. Tifferet and its competitor across the intersection, Café Attara, formed a *gelder*, a type of real estate stock exchange, where builders and developers sat in an acrid smoke-filled environment, drinking Turkish coffee and exchanging sensitive information—sometimes genuine, mostly gossip. This was where the deals were done. Everything was whispered across the tables in a shroud of secrecy, as if the information imported would ultimately affect the balance of world power.

There was no institution of real estate agents at that time; liaison between vendors and developers, developers and buyers, was a free-for-all dominated by *shmuklers*—a group of wheelers and dealers. *Shmuklers* had to find the available land, and then find the buyers, without informing the buyer as to the identity of the vendor lest the middleman be cut out of the deal. Sometimes two *shmuklers* were granted permission to act as agents for the same piece of land, resulting in a fierce competition between them. Theirs was a delicate operation in a cutthroat business.

Information about available land never really came my way. I was neither a buyer nor a developer. I was merely scavenging for design work. In doing so, I utilised all avenues. Some of my designs were commissioned by developers who had the land for use and wanted to start building. At other times, I was commissioned by the *shmuklers*—on behalf of the owners—to prepare plans that would 'dress' a piece of land for sale. More often than not, I would be required to overdress the land—include more apartments than was feasible. The sketches would then form the basis of how much a developer would pay for the land. It was a dubious business all round, and the lessons I would learn from these smart operators in Tel Aviv would prepare me for anything.

On one particular occasion, as I was 'networking' over coffee at the Tifferet, a fellow came in shouting my name: 'Lustig!' A burst of adrenalin surged through my veins. I was actually being sought out rather than seeking. It was a major turning point, but had to be handled correctly. I turned to my companion with as casual an air as I could muster.

'Did he say "Lustig"?'

'I think so,' came the reply.

'Lustig? Lustig?' came the cry once again across the room.

I rose slowly and approached the man.

'Are you Lustig?' he asked me in a conspiratorial whisper that seemed in absurd contrast to his previous tone.

'I am Lustig,' I replied with what I hoped was a similar gravity.

'Go outside,' he continued. 'Walk a little way up Allenby Street. I will find you.'

I followed his instructions and waited in a small lane—a *Simta*—behind the café.

After a few minutes the elderly man approached me. We spoke in a mixture of Hebrew and Yiddish.

'I don't think that we will be heard. I have a piece of land …'

He suddenly cut short his speech and eyed me suspiciously.

'Are you really Lustig?'

'Of course I am. Here is my identity card if you want to take a look.'

He examined the document with a cursory air.

'All right. I believe you.'

He continued.

'My name is Boborovich, and I have a piece of land that nobody knows about.'

'Where on earth did you get a name like Boborovich?' I asked him casually, attempting to conceal my excitement. I had never seen him before in my life, had never heard of him. He was an absolute nobody, yet he knew my name.

'You are lucky. You have the name of "Lustig". I am Boborovich, and nobody gives a damn about Boborovich.'

It suddenly dawned on me that this man thought I was the *other* Lustig—a highly sought-after Tel Aviv land developer of some renown. But I was not going to let this opportunity pass; instead, I would behave with a nonchalance that would leave no doubt whatsoever that I was indeed a successful developer. I was, when all was said and done, Lustig. And I was involved in building.

'You shouldn't say that, Mr Boborovich. After all, *I* give a damn. I am interested in whether you have something worthwhile, or whether this is just another of the many bullshit stories that are flying around this town. Now, where is the land?'

'*Shderot Keren Kayemet*,' he replied.

A *shderot* was rather like an avenue, wider than a normal street and lined with trees, although the trees of Tel Aviv were not entirely healthy. Nevertheless, it was considered to be a good location.

We walked approximately half a mile to the block of land. On it stood a ramshackle old house, suitable only for demolition, and even then, heavy machinery would hardly be required for the job. As a result of poorly designed land subdivision, the block had three street frontages. The avenue was the main elevation, but it also fronted onto two other narrower streets. It was most unusual and my interest was piqued.

Boborovich stood beside me, trembling with obvious emotion.

'Have you ever seen such a piece of land before?' he asked, looking past me towards his odd tract of soil as if it were a beautiful woman of bountiful assets.

'Frankly, no,' I replied, 'and as a matter of fact it looks to be difficult because each of these three streets would demand setting the building back, which leaves very little room for development.'

Obviously, he had not considered the constraints of town planning, because when I told him this, his feverish excitement turned to a deep concern. His brow furrowed as he silently faced the realities of his attachment. The object of his affection was not such a prize.

Eventually, he spoke.

'What do you think?'

'Well, Mr Boborovich, I am certainly not prepared to discuss design or price until I have got some basic information from the council.'

It was midday, and I knew that if I hurried, I could reach the council in time to make contact with the right person. But herein lay another major concern. By virtue of their necessary exposure to property deals, each and every city engineer in North Tel Aviv was also a *shmukler*, selling sensitive information about available blocks of land. It was a risk I had to take.

I knew the council engineer very well since I had worked under his authority as building inspector three years earlier. My concerns were raised when he remarked, 'This is a very interesting piece of land. Really, I never paid much attention to the fact that such a nice block was ripe for development. Are you handling the affair?'

'Yes, I am.'

'I would like to see a sketch.'

I stalled. 'I will bring one in for you.' Blustering now, I tried to distract his attentions.

'What I am most concerned about, however,' I continued, 'is the requirement for setting the building back from the street frontages.'

'You only need to set back from the *Shderot*, Mr Lustig. The other two streets are not a problem.'

I discovered that the land actually belonged to *Keren Kayemet*—the Zionist Foundation Fund—but was sold on an extendable lease. And ninety-nine years of that lease remained. Effectively, the leaseholder had control over the land for as long as he wished. I began to get excited. For the first time, I realised I was now confronted with the very situation I had been dreaming of for years. All that remained was to meet, through Boborovich, the leaseholder himself.

The *shmukler* and I sipped our coffees at Tifferet, and for the first time, I was paying. There was no shilly-shallying or mistaking the intent of the meeting.

'I would like you to pay me, Mr Lustig, and then I will introduce you to this *Yiddel*. You will then tell him, and me, what you want to pay for the land. Meet me at the house at six this evening.'

Naturally, I did not have any money to pay for the land. But it was quite common for developers to work with the landowners in an agreed arrangement—for example, with payment to the owner coming in the form of a number of apartments in the development *after* the building is completed. I hoped and prayed that I might be able to make such an arrangement.

Before entering the house, Boborovich turned to me and asked about his payment. He hoped that there would be a £500 windfall in it for him. 'I will speak with you separately on the matter,' he concluded, reacting to my lack of response.

'Mr Liberman,' began Boborovich, 'this is Herr Lustig. I bring you the developer.' I was presented to him with something akin to the fanfare of a screen idol.

Liberman, the leaseholder and a retired tailor, was a frail man in his mid seventies. His hair was thinning and his sight and hearing were beginning to fail him.

'Oh, it is an honour, Herr Dr Lustig,' he croaked.

'The honour is mine, Mr Liberman,' responded the 'real' Lustig, suddenly in possession of my speech and demeanour.

Dispensing with the formalities, I immediately directed the conversation to matters of business.

'What is the asking price, Mr Liberman?'

He replied slowly. 'Herr Lustig. I have a daughter and a son. They are each looking to get married. I want them to get married. I want to be around to see my *Einikle* (grandchildren). But neither of them can marry because they have nowhere to live.'

Boborovich interjected.

'I will explain this to Mr Lustig. He needs a two-bedroom flat on the middle floor for his daughter, another on the top floor for his son, and a one-bedroom on the ground floor for himself.'

'Mr Lustig, do you think you will have the room to accommodate us?' asked the old man.

'Of course,' I replied in my most businesslike manner, trying to contain my urge to leap out of my skin with happiness. 'As long as there is no more, then that's it.'

Two days later, Boborovich and I met with Liberman and his lawyer to finalise the deal. The lawyer opened proceedings.

'Gentlemen, this is not such a simple matter. Mr Liberman needs to have some assurances that the whole thing can and will be built.'

'What are you talking about?' I asked incredulously, hoping that he was not referring to some enormous cash payment. I had already prepared a series of sketches and referred to them as if they were already a *fait accompli*. Boborovich then came to my defence, perhaps frightened too at the prospect of this deal disintegrating before our eyes.

'Mr Liberman, you know I would not bring a nobody here. Lustig is a big firm. The best buildings in Tel Aviv. I am right, you know.' He turned to me. 'Am I not, Lustig?'

'Of course,' I said.

The lawyer continued. 'What arrangements are going to be made for Mr Liberman to move out so that the house can be demolished?'

I had not anticipated such a request, and my ability to improvise at that moment took even me by surprise.

'I am in close contact with the municipality of Tel Aviv,' I began, 'and I expect that I will get permission for Mr Liberman to occupy one of the old houses on the beach which is currently occupied by a group of squatters.'

In fact, the house I spoke of was one of a number of condemned houses along the beach strip. Fortunately, it did not take much to convince the city engineer to bury the plans for its demolition. I then approached the squatters who occupied the house and told them that they could remain in their squats if they provided the old man with a room and looked after him. If not, I warned them, they would be out. Liberman stayed there for the next nine months while I completed the development.

With the deal signed, Boborovich approached me about his payment.

'I am sorry,' I told him. 'I have no money. But when I sell all these apartments, you will be paid.'

'I cannot wait,' he demanded. 'You have the best piece of land here. You have plenty of jobs and plenty of money. Everybody tells me that.'

And so, inevitably, the charade was precipitously close to a revelation.

Clearly, he still believed that he was dealing with the other Mr Lustig—the 'Big Lustig'. I thought about this. How would the 'Big Lustig' react to such a situation? With the arrogance that came with being big.

'Look, Boborovich. Understand this. I will not be paying you a cent until I have sold at least three of the apartments.'

Boborovich backed down.

He eventually got his money, and I sold all of the apartments for an average price of £5000, providing me with a considerable profit. When the building was completed, Liberman and his children were so happy that they held a party in my honour. It was a proud moment for me.

Importantly, with this project under my belt, I was admitted to the close-knit circle of Tel Aviv developers. Under the guise of the 'Big Lustig', the small Lustig had bluffed his way onto the scene, then made his mark. Good things come in small packages.

22 ALL FOR ONE? ONE FOR ALL.

All I know is that I am not a Marxist ...
KARL MARX

MY FIRST BUILDING development did not proceed without its share of problems, and my career in property development was almost cut short before it had begun. A crisis in the Israeli economy had led to legislative changes that all but crippled the private developer.

In the early years of statehood, Israel's economic infrastructure was woefully underdeveloped. With its enemies still under arms, the Arab market, which had represented 15 per cent of Palestine's exports, was closed. Haifa's oil refineries lay idle. The Dead Sea potash works was damaged by war. The needs of the all-important army and the growing local market deprived the country of sources of export. The victory in the War of Independence saw donations from the diaspora ease. There were difficulties in luring foreign investment—and high taxes dulled incentive for increased productivity.

A balance of payments crisis occurred in 1949. The threat of inflation became unmanageable and in 1950, the then Prime Minister, Ben-Gurion, introduced rigorous austerity measures: rationing, and cost and wage controls. These deflationary measures enabled Israel to function on a minimum, but a large supply of unspent, progressively cheaper money began to find its outlet in the black market. In 1951, there were protests and shop closures. There were prolonged work stoppages in factories for lack of raw materials and electricity. Black market prices almost completely dominated the economy.

In desperation, in February 1952, the government inaugurated a 'New Economic Policy'. Inflationary credit expansion would end. The currency was selectively devalued. Immigration was slowed.

Israel was exerting more governmental or quasi-governmental

influence on the national economy than any other nation in the world, apart from the communist countries. As early as 1954, the *Histadrut* was the nation's single largest industrial employer. There was virtually no economic or social activity in which the labour federation was not represented.

Histadrut's sheer size and its complex interlocking of functions allowed it to operate virtually as an economy within an economy. For the first ten years of statehood, the federation controlled the labour exchanges. The left-wing *Mapai* leadership in government and the *Histadrut* were comrades in arms, and together they regarded the enactment of social welfare and labour legislation as one of the nation's priorities. A labour exchange law required employers to hire workers through official labour exchanges. *Solel Boneh*, the *Histadrut*'s construction arm, achieved a near monopoly of public works contracts, and controlled so large a supply of building materials that it became a huge trust, able to freeze out the private builders and developers.

While I was in the midst of my first property development, the supply of building materials dried up. The only way to obtain the necessary goods was through agents of *Solel Boneh*, and at black market prices. Furthermore, the Builders Labour Union raised wages by approximately 25 per cent. Ultimately, I had to call a meeting of prospective buyers and raise the sale price of the finished apartments in order to complete the project. I was fortunate enough to sell them at the higher price and make my profit. But I would have to think very carefully before embarking on another project.

Each Friday night, Sarah would cook dinner and we would entertain guests at our apartment. Generally our visitors were unmarried men, colleagues of mine, who would enjoy a good home-cooked meal before settling into a game of bridge. On one occasion, my good friend Bodor, who was married with three children, decided to join us. He was now working with *Tahal*, a partially government-owned company charged with the task of designing the country's water supply systems. *Tahal* worked in tandem with *Mekorot*, the country's Water Authority, which carried out the construction. That evening he questioned me on the subject of my future career in property development. His own projections were unambiguous.

'Ted, the situation is lousy. Untenable. Now is not the time for residential developments, for taking risks. Have you thought about joining *Tahal*?'

Proud of my recent achievements and fond of financial independence, I felt somewhat offended by my friend's suggestion that I take a step backwards to become a 'nobody' within a large organisation. His suggestion was actually a compliment, however. *Tahal* had performed poorly in terms of its financial controls, and Bodor felt that my skills might be of use to the organisation.

'Just promise me that you will talk to the chief engineer tomorrow,' he asked in the face of my objections.

Sarah had listened intently to Bodor's words and after our guests departed, she pleaded with me to take his advice.

The following day, true to my word, I entered the *Tahal* offices and announced that I was there to see Mr Balaban, the Chief Engineer. I was escorted down a narrow hallway and led into a dark room. One small window produced a narrow shaft of light, illuminating a small desk. For a moment I thought I was back in Beirut at British headquarters, so much was this room like the small cell in which I had completed my entry exam. The stocky man sitting at the desk continued to write a series of notes and did not raise his head even on reflex as I entered. I stood waiting for a response. When the instruction 'sit down' arrived, it was delivered with such gusto that it nearly blew me into the chair.

Finally, Balaban looked up from his work and appraised me. He had been born and educated in Germany and was revered as a man with a superb knowledge of ideas in civil engineering.

'Tell me about yourself,' he said.

'Which period?' I asked.

'The clever period, one of those periods you are satisfied with.'

I told him about my experience with the British army in Damascus, embellishing it to a certain degree, especially in details about my work on water supply and pumping systems.

'Do you speak any English?'

'Of course. After spending more than four years with the British army working in technical fields, I must remember something.'

After testing me on a number of technical terms, he seemed satisfied.

'Can you start tomorrow morning?'

'Yes. What are my conditions?' I asked.

'It is not my business to know conditions. My business is to know whether to keep you or throw you out of here. With regard to your wages—if that's what you mean—you will have to speak to Lowenthal. He is in charge of quantity surveying. Do you know what quantity surveying is?'

'Of course I do.'

'Good,' he said brusquely, indicating that our discourse was at an end. 'I will advise Lowenthal, and you will see him.'

The expertise in quantity surveying and the tendering process that I had gained in Damascus ultimately saw me employed as a financial controller at *Tahal*. I was hired on a full-time basis, but being reluctant to abandon my design practice completely, I requested that I be permitted to carry on a certain amount of personal business outside of the company. *Tahal* took the unprecedented step of approving my request. As building restrictions were gradually lifted over the next two years, as conditions for private enterprise began to improve, my own design firm continued to grow.

I had about forty men working under me at *Tahal*, predominantly engineers and technicians. Very few had any financial background or business sense. And all were European immigrants.

There was a clear separation between the European—*Ashkenasi*—Jews and those of Middle Eastern background, the *Sephardim*. Even the *Sabras*, those born in Palestine, were treated with a level of disdain by the highly educated Europeans. It was almost an unspoken law that an Ashkenasi Jew be given preference over a Sephardic Jew in employment. It was a situation I found to be absurd, and much against the trend of the day, I found myself employing quite a number of Sephardim at *Tahal*. What impressed me most about them, particularly the ill-treated Iraqi Jews, was their grasp of financial issues, which offset any lack of technical skills. It was almost a streetwise intelligence, an unteachable talent that was generally lacking in the European engineers.

The work being undertaken by *Tahal* and *Mekorot* at this time was of an enormous scale. From the earliest days of Jewish settlement in Palestine, no one had doubted that irrigation was the indispensable key to economic survival and growth. Rain fell only in the winter, and largely in the northern part of the country. The Jewish Agency had been studying the possibilities of irrigation throughout the period of the British mandate. Under its auspices, Dr Walter Lowdermilk, a distinguished American soil conservationist, prepared a report that laid the basis for all subsequent water planning in Israel. In it, he asserted that the harnessed flow of the Jordan River, combined with the exploitation of ground water, would enable Israel to support a population of up to five million people. Later, American engineers James Hayes and John Cotton would endorse and refine the blueprint, which would be adopted by *Mekorot*. Its priorities included the intensive utilisation of ground water; reclamation of flood overflow and sewage; tapping the Yarkon and Kishon Rivers; and finally, the mighty Jordan Valley Project itself.

The first stage of this enormous undertaking involved the drainage of the Lake Chula swamplands and the construction of a canal to channel the waters south to the Sea of Galilee. It was fraught with danger since the work sites were initially situated in the demilitarised zone between Syria and Israel. It was brought to fruition in 1953 after the Israelis devised a complex means of completing the project without using Arab land.

My own work was primarily on the second stage of the project, which involved the establishment of sewage purification plants, the Yarkon-Negev and Kishon Valley projects, as well as the construction of a number of underground hydro-electric and oil-driven power stations. The Yarkon was a small stream that wound its way around Tel Aviv. With underground dams, pumping stations and pipes, one hundred million litres of the Yarkon's flow were rechannelled southwards to the Negev desert. The Kishon Valley project, in turn, used catch-basins and pipes to trap the rivulets and streams of the Galilee Hills and direct them to the Valley of Jezreel.

The concrete pipes that transported the water were more than three metres in diameter, and the factory that manufactured them was mobile—it moved along the pipeline as it produced the pipes. The technology was imported, and had been recently used in Morocco. The construction had to take into account the enormous temperature changes in the desert, and had to be fitted with manholes for easy access. It was in this setting that I learned so much about precast concrete—knowledge that would provide me with an advantage as a property developer so many years later.

By 1955, after two years with *Tahal*, I was considered a bit of an expert in all aspects of structural design, including budgets and costing. And *Tahal*'s financial performance had improved dramatically in that time. Small wonder then that I was quite confident of my prospects when rumours began to spread that the company board was about to be overhauled, and my name was being touted as a possible candidate. It was the career break I had been hoping for.

Tuvia, a Czech engineer, was company chairman at the time; the three-man board also including Balaban and a *kibbutznik* named Weiner. According to the rumours, Weiner was to be replaced. While I did not want to get my hopes up too much, I found it impossible to ignore the fact that my colleagues were hailing me as a 'shoo-in.'

A few days later, I received a telephone call from Tuvia, who requested my company for lunch. We sat in a dark corner of the small restaurant while he spoke of the company's situation and praised my work.

'I hear rumours, Tuvia, about a new arrangement of the board.'

'Oh, yes, I am glad that you mentioned it.'

He paused for a moment before continuing.

'I know of the rumour too. But you know how it is with rumours. They are always ... misleading.'

My heart sank. 'Misleading?' I probed.

'Yes. Misleading. That's right. I like you, Lustig. That is why I am giving you this straight. You are not going to be appointed to the board.'

'Tuvia, are you serious?'

'I am serious, Lustig. But you could not possibly be serious about advancing to the board.'

'Why not?'

'Don't be ridiculous, Lustig. It's obvious. You are not a member of *Mapai*.'

'But Tuvia, surely you have some say in this?'

'Don't worry, Lustig. Your current position is not in jeopardy. Everybody knows that you are a good man. Just don't expect to be elected to the board.'

At that moment I realised with frightening clarity that my future in Israel was over. All those years, through my time at the Technion, during the Second World War, through the Declaration of the State of Israel and the War of Independence, I had never fully appreciated the true power of political affiliation. In choosing my work above patriotism, I had compromised my future. Like my own father, who was more concerned with the pursuit of knowledge than the pursuit of social contacts, I now found my personal ambitions dashed.

At that moment, regardless of how and where, I decided to leave Israel once and for all.

Part III

Australia

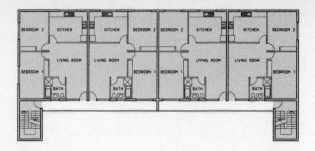

LEVEL 1 PLAN

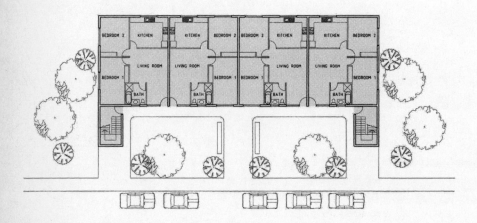

GROUND LEVEL PLAN

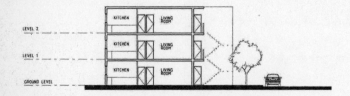

SECTION

A generic residential flats design from around 1956

Ted Lustig's innovations in apartment block design in the 1960s were a break away from traditional generic postwar apartment developments (see above). His apartments were characterised by openness and flow in the main living areas and increased amenities for the residents. The external design allowed for the inclusion of undercover parking, a landscaped forecourt and an intercom for public access. Internal design features included open-plan kitchen, living and dining rooms, natural cross-ventilation, views, ensuites and separate toilets, and discrete entrances from the main living areas.

(See, for example, pp. 227-8, 231-4, 235-8)

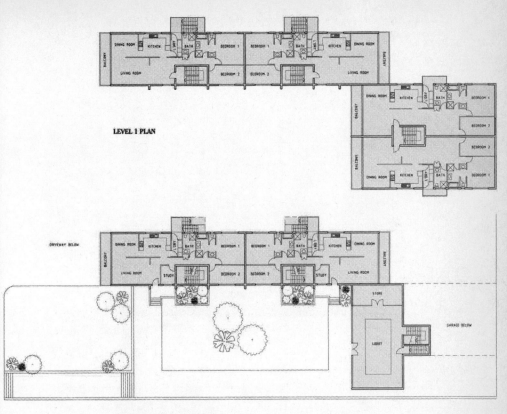
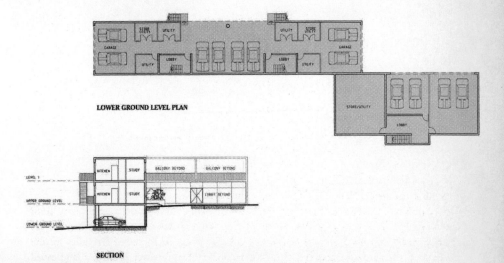

Design of one of Ted Lustig's high-quality apartments

23 Alone in the Most Isolated City in the World

'You feel free in Australia'. And so you do. There is a great relief in the atmosphere, a relief from tension, from pressure. An absence of control or will or form. The sky is open above you, and the air is open around you. Not the old closing-in of Europe.
D. H. LAWRENCE

IT WAS HARDLY possible to emigrate from Israel without feeling some degree of guilt. In many respects, the Jewish homeland was even more patriotic, more nationalistic than the 'old world' Poland I had left behind twenty years earlier. Despite my distaste for Israel's extreme nationalism and my lack of interest in her all-pervasive politics, I felt some remorse about leaving. To abandon her was considered traitorous. Nevertheless, it was precisely my lack of interest in political involvement that had delivered the latest body blow and I could no longer dismiss the limitations that this country would inevitably impose upon me.

Had I been truly courageous, I would have insisted that we make our way to the United States, where I could have pursued my career in 'the big league'. The prospect of competing against so many established builders and developers was daunting, however, and ultimately we chose to settle in Australia, which by all accounts would offer more immediate opportunities. Our knowledge of the land 'down under', sparse as it was, was provided by Sarah's uncle, Mr London. Sarah, Iris and I would settle initially in Perth, where the London family now lived.

In September of 1956, as Israel was preparing to enter into war over the Sinai and wrest control of the Suez Canal from Egypt, my small family boarded an Air France flight from Tel Aviv to Perth via

Rome. The affairs of state that occupied the news in Israel were so far removed from the outpost to which we were now heading that we were completely unaware that the Olympic Games were about to be opened in Melbourne. Even the presence of the entire Iraqi national team on our flight from Rome, strange as it appeared, did not alert us to the fact that a major world event was taking place in our new home.

To a man approaching the age of forty, the prospect of embarking on a journey to start life all over again in yet another new country should well have been a daunting one. However, unlike my move from Poland to Israel, where the Hebrew language proved to be my greatest hurdle, my years in Damascus with the British had left me with a working knowledge of the language spoken in Australia. And unlike my move from Damascus back to Tel Aviv, where I arrived without a shekel to my name, the last few years had been good to me and I had been able to save a reasonable nest egg with which to establish my family abroad.

The newborn nation of Israel was jealously guarding its money reserves. Although it was now illegal to move money out of the country, I was told that the ultra-orthodox Mizrahi Bank was able to do so, within certain limits. I had been introduced to a manager at that bank, a blindingly religious, God-fearing man. He agreed to arrange for the transfer of £9000 to a contact of mine in New York. From there, the money would be forwarded to me in Perth. Upon our arrival in Rome, however, I called New York, only to find that no money had been sent across. My friend wired through five hundred dollars to keep me going, but I was furious.

'I'm going back to Israel immediately,' I told Sarah, 'and I am going to cut off that bastard's balls.'

'If you want to go back, you go,' she replied. 'I am going to Australia.'

'What are you talking about? We have nothing and we have to set up in a new country.'

'Abba, you do what you want. I am out of that country and I have had enough. Now I am going on to Australia.'

We travelled on, but the issue was not yet done with.

Throughout 1956, Nasser's Egypt had intensified its campaign against Israel. By June, Nasser had made his intentions clear: to regain the rights of the Palestinians by force. Between July and September, Egyptian-trained *fedayeen* assaulted Israel from bases in Gaza, Jordan and Syria. During this period, many Israelis had contemplated leaving, and it seems that many more had attempted to get their money out. What was a concern for some was clearly an opportunity for others. And if my case was the rule and not the exception, the Mizrahi Bank made a lot of money indeed. Ironically, it was the Sinai campaign that provided me with the opportunity to recover some of my funds. It was around that time that the Israeli government decided to take action to curb the flow of the millions of dollars that were streaming out of the country. If caught, the penalties would be severe. On hearing this news, I made contact with the crooked bank manager. I informed him that I would provide detailed accounts of our transaction to the Israeli authorities. I would see him sent to prison just for the sake of it. I had nothing to lose—I was on the other side of the world. He assessed the risk and we negotiated, eventually settling on a payment of £4500.

The journey to Australia was tedious and uncomfortable. The Air France flight was inadequately staffed, and apart from having to care for my airsick wife and distraught twelve-year-old daughter, I found myself looking after an elderly woman who was violently ill for the duration of the trip. In an attempt to calm her down, I suggested that she had nothing to worry about since she had already regurgitated about twenty-five years' worth of whatever lay in her stomach.

'I am travelling to Sydney to stay with my nephew,' she told me. 'He is also an architect. I suggest that you continue on to Sydney to meet with him. He will be waiting for me at the airport. Perhaps you have heard of him. He is very well known.'

I listened patiently. The woman was offering sound advice in appreciation of my efforts to nurse her. But, in my arrogance, not only did I reject her offer, but I also took offence at the comment about her nephew's fame. After all, *I* had been well known in Tel Aviv.

'I don't know him,' I snorted. 'But perhaps *he* knows *me*.'

Her nephew's name was Harry Seidler. And he was, and is, perhaps Australia's best known architect. Years later, during the mid 1980s, he would support my attempts to organise a biannual competition for pre-established projects to be selected by the Institute of Architects.

As we flew into Darwin, the first port of call in our new country, an announcement came over the intercom: 'We apologise for the turbulence. It appears that one of our engines has failed. But we are more than capable of landing safely using the second engine.' And so, after a journey of more than 24 hours, our crippled aircraft limped into

Australia. It was somewhat appropriate. Still concerned about the bank fiasco, about starting a new life at the age of forty in an alien land and in an almost penniless state, I felt like a shipwrecked sailor being washed up on the shore. A refugee.

We had to stay in Darwin for two days until the engine was repaired. The airport consisted of little more than an airstrip. There were no buildings and we were housed in a huge tent together with the rest of the passengers in transit. Upon our arrival, we were ushered to the cafeteria, where we were presented with what appeared to be a fabulous meal: soup followed by chicken and vegetables, and finally a fruit platter. It was our first taste of Australian food and as we began to eat, Sarah and I looked at each other in bewilderment. Despite its sumptuous appearance, the food was almost completely tasteless. As if in anticipation of our horrified reaction, we were informed by our hosts that Australia was a free country and we could use as much salt as we wished.

'Sarah,' I exclaimed, 'had you been supplied with these ingredients, you could have cooked up a feast, a banquet.'

Despite the food, our two-day sojourn in Darwin was an enchanting, almost magical experience. We were surrounded by jungle, an exotic blend of tropical plants and wildlife. It was a lush and fertile landscape with new and unfamiliar sights and sounds at every turn, a richness of colour and light. Iris was excited about seeing her first kangaroo, and Sarah and I were happy to have arrived in such a beautiful country.

A few days later, we were politely warned that the single engine was adequate to fly to Melbourne. There we bid farewell to the elderly woman from the plane, who seemed upset that we decided against travelling on to Sydney from Melbourne. Sarah had said, 'Abba, we have train tickets to Perth, and I would like to see my uncle and thank him for sending us the entry permits.' Without further thought, we boarded the train to Perth. Had I known that the trip across the continent would take another three days, compared with a few extra hours travelling to Sydney, my decision might have been different. And indeed that might have saved us not just three days, but more than two years.

We arrived at Sarah's uncle's home, which was situated in the leafy Perth suburb of Mount Lawley. Mr and Mrs London opened the door to find the three of us standing there, bags in hand. Their expressions were less than welcoming. For two weeks they housed us in their 'lean-to', a small and crude construction built onto the side of their house. There was barely enough room for us to sleep, and sleep was impossible anyway because of the summer weather. It was a most uncomfortable experience made all the more distressing by the lack of any attempts by our hosts to conceal the fact that they did not really want us to be there.

Mrs London was Sarah's mother's sister, but as they had different fathers, there was little love lost between them. We soon came to realise that we were nothing but an inconvenience to her, and furthermore, we seemed to be an embarrassment to her children. The situation soon became unendurable. Sarah was relying on her aunt to teach her how to function in this foreign environment: to show her where to buy food and what to ask for. It was clearly a burden for her aunt and Sarah would return in tears each day.

'Abba, look where we are living. How we are living. When is this going to end?'

'Sarah,' I would reply, 'what are we supposed to do? We need somewhere to live.'

Finally, Sarah's uncle offered a suggestion. 'I am going to introduce you to Barakshek Kohn.'

Mr Kohn was a gentleman, a Russian-born Jew who offered us accommodation in his home until we could find a permanent place to live. We moved in, and while Sarah was still conscious that this was not her own house, our hosts were polite, our quarters were civilised, and the growing tension between Sarah and her aunt was no longer a factor in our lives.

I was fully aware that in order to establish myself in Australia, I would have to take two steps back in terms of my career. In Tel Aviv, I had spent years working my way up from building supervisor to freelance draftsman and finally to bona fide developer. Now I was looking for anything at all, and my break would come in the form of a drafting job for the Perth Council. The city engineer recommended me for membership to the Institute of Engineers and I sat a series of examinations in order to qualify.

After securing the council job, I found us a small house in Mount Lawley, and finally Sarah was able to feel comfortable cooking in her own kitchen and tending to her own garden. Iris was able to settle into school, but she had not been too happy about leaving her friends in

Israel and now she found it difficult to adapt to her new country. She did have one advantage, however. She had managed to learn some English while visiting her uncle in Chicago—albeit with an annoying American accent—and after settling in Perth she managed to become proficient in the language in a very short time. Her mother, on the other hand, found the prospect of learning English far too daunting, and would never apply herself to the task with any conviction.

I was working with a Dutch draftsman, Van Houten, who had lived in the East Indies, until the formation of Indonesia, before migrating to Perth. Through his council experience he had met most of Perth's small developers, and had soon established his own drafting service. Van Houten began supplying me with design jobs for home builders, which I completed after council hours. I bought a stool and a drawing board so that I could set up a convenient workplace at home. Soon I was producing between twenty and thirty designs per week.

I knew that the Dutchman was charging between five and ten pounds per job, and he was paying me three pounds. As I began to produce greater volumes of his drawings, I warned him that he should reassess my worth lest I go out on my own and charge the client six pounds. He told me that he did not want that to happen.

'You have an advantage over me, Ted,' he began. 'You are Jewish, and you Jews are smarter.'

'How can you suspect me of being smart,' I responded, 'when I am sitting here working for you for three pounds a drawing?'

To my advantage, I chose not to interfere any further with his convictions, and settled for a pay rise.

The extra money enabled us to live quite comfortably, but I was working extremely long hours, beginning each morning at nine and continuing through the night, often drawing plans until two or three in the morning. While the pay was reasonable, it was labour-intensive work, and there was a limit to how many drawings one person could produce. It was certainly not a long-term solution for me. In the meantime, the money had arrived from the bank in Israel but, determined to put the entire payout away for the future, we lived on what I earned and no more.

Our steady progress was interrupted just a few months later when Sarah fell ill and was taken to hospital. During her three-week recovery, I had to look after Iris as well as working the long hours. I was growing weary and I began to wonder what I was doing here at the end of the world, working like a dog at the age of forty. I had left a senior position in Tel Aviv and now I found myself, quite literally, back at the drawing-board.

My incessant struggle was catching up with me. With an infirm wife and a daughter who had found it difficult to adjust to a new country, I felt the weight of the world on my shoulders. Would I have to work this hard for the rest of my life? For the first time in my life, I was overcome with a deep depression, and entertained thoughts of ending my life then and there. It was as though once more I was being pulled down the channel at my grandfather's sawmill, but this time I was unable, or unwilling, to summon the energy to grasp the branch that protruded from the riverbank.

But Sarah was a particularly strong woman and her recovery within a few weeks helped to ease my burden. A devoted wife, she was once again capable and more than willing to do whatever was necessary to make my life more comfortable. But the long hours at the drafting board had taken their toll. I was emotionally and physically spent. One night, soon after her return from the hospital, Sarah heard a loud thud and ran into my office to find me collapsed on the floor. I had fainted and fallen from the stool. It was now my turn to spend some weeks in hospital, with what turned out to be a gall bladder infection. My gall bladder had burst and the bile was spreading through my system. It was a harbinger of death, and the doctors had to operate immediately. It was the first time in more than twenty years that I had been ill—since lying on the floor of my brother's kitchen with a fever after arriving in Palestine.

I recall very little of my time in hospital. By all reports I was well on my way to recovery when one of the student nurses, noticing that I was extremely thirsty, inadvertently gave me tonic water, rendering my condition worse and prolonging my stay. Sarah visited me daily, and upon arriving one afternoon to find two of the nurses administering a sponge bath, she angrily told them that my body belonged to her and that she would take all future responsibility for that task. I had always been the jealous one, and I must admit that on this occasion I found her jealousy somewhat comforting.

It seemed that the worst was over for Sarah and me. We had both spent time in hospital, had recovered, and were ready to press on with our lives with some renewed vigour. After a four-week recuperation period I was back at work. I even managed to secure a number of jobs that I found most satisfying. One of these, a project for the Perth Municipal Council, involved designing and constructing Australia's first concrete velodrome.

It was on this project that I suddenly realised I had skills that were scarce in Australia. At that time, construction in this country almost exclusively utilised structural steel and brick. Concrete was taboo—simply too unpredictable. But I had learned a great deal about concrete construction and form work in Israel, where alternative building materials were unavailable, particularly with *Tahal*, working on the construction of huge underground water reservoirs. The huge artificial lakes had to be circular or elliptical in shape and seamless in order to avoid leaks. Furthermore, allowances had to be made for the expansion and contraction of the concrete. It was indeed a science, and one that was in its infancy in Australia. I was extremely proud of my work on the velodrome.

Three months after my return to work, as life was beginning to take on some appearance of normalcy, Sarah was involved in an accident from which she would never fully recover.

Sarah loved to work in the garden. One evening, as it was growing dark, the telephone began ringing. I was indoors working on a drawing when I heard her cry out. Hurrying to get inside, she had turned past the corner of the house at full speed, hitting her head and knocking herself unconscious. I found her lying on the path; a deep cut on her forehead was bleeding profusely and it appeared that her right eye was badly damaged. It was oozing fluid.

I called an ambulance immediately and she was rushed to hospital. For the next eight weeks she had to lie in that hospital bed without moving her head; sandbags were placed on either side of her to keep it completely immobilised. It was a horrendous experience for her. The doctors had operated on the eye but were unable to save her sight. Almost ninety per cent of vision was lost in her right eye. Worse still, she was badly scarred and her right eye was now noticeably smaller than her left.

Sarah had beautiful eyes, and this disfigurement would cause her agonising and intolerable spiritual pain. She was a very attractive, and very vain, woman. She had been highly conscious of her appearance and was always well-groomed. She had invested considerable time and energy in maintaining her figure. Her beauty had always been of paramount importance to her, all the more so for a woman whose

Military exercises—continuous mosquitoes

This illustration was created during Ted's national defence service in the Negev Desert. Swarms of mosquitoes plagued the men while they worked and during their meal breaks. Despite the mosquitoes, the artist, a Dutchman, pleaded with Ted to continue posing for him. The Hebrew can be translated loosely as 'What a mess!'

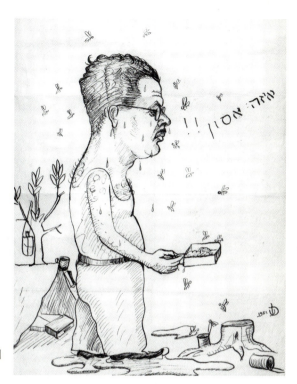

Enjoying a cold refreshment

Ted had been discussing business at an outdoor café in Tel Aviv, Café Atara, in about 1949. The temperature outdoors was at least 43°C. A street artist drew this picture without Ted's knowledge, and then offered it to him for a small fee.

Above: The Perth Velodrome, one of Ted's first projects in Australia *(See pp. 211–212)*

Left: Sarah, during a holiday in Australia, c. 1960

Below: Ted (lower left) playing bridge with friends (clockwise from left) Marion Bieldek, Vera Finkel, and Tony Murkies

Above: Ted (second row, fifth from left) with some of his bridge-playing friends

Left: Sarah Lustig and Marlene Blewett, during a trip to Europe on which Marlene accompanied the Lustigs

Below: The office building at 20/22 Albert Road, South Melbourne *(See pp. 244 ff., 256)*

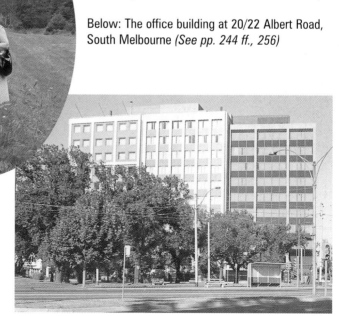

Left: Beginning of construction on Box Hill Central, 1983

Below: Box Hill Central shopping centre, c. 1983–84

Left: Chatswood Chase, Sydney *(See pp. 265, 268)*

Below: At the opening of The Pines shopping centre in 1986. Pictured are (l. to r.) Ted Lustig; the Mayor of Doncaster, Vernard B. Denford; Jeff Kennett (then Leader of the Opposition in Victoria); Julie Stainton, Centre Manager; Max Moar. *(See p. 264)*

The Grand Hyatt Hotel, Melbourne *(See pp. 284 ff.)*

Ted Lustig and Franco Casella *(See pp. 269 ff.)*

Kevin Lonie
(See pp. 278–279)

Ted Lustig with Bob Hawke and Iris Lustig-Moar

Above: Jay Moar with his great-aunt Hassia Schwartz, Sarah Lustig's sister *(See pp. 175–177)*

Left: Iris Lustig-Moar

Ted Lustig, Member of the Order of Australia

Above: Ted, with Nathalie and Guy, Iris's daughter and one of her sons

Right: (front, l. to r.) Jay Moar, Ted Lustig; (back, l. to r.) Max Moar, Iris Lustig-Moar, Guy Moar, Nathalie Moar, at Guy's graduation from Melbourne University in 1989

Ted and Heather Lustig

education was slight, and who felt that she had little else to offer in a social setting, especially in a country where she struggled to speak the language.

Upon her discharge from the hospital, she had been fitted with protective goggles. One evening, after returning home from work, I found her sitting in the bedroom, sobbing uncontrollably. That day, while nobody was home, she had finally plucked up the courage to look at her eye.

'I don't want to live any more. Look at me, Abba,' she wailed.

I did not have the courage to remove the goggles. I called for the doctor instead and he lifted them for me. As much as I tried to conceal my reaction, I was genuinely shocked. One eye was set about an inch below the other. At that moment I understood the full implications of what I saw, the devastating effect this was going to have on my wife.

'I will never go out in public again,' she cried.

From that time on, her sunglasses became a permanent appendage, even in the cinema when it was completely dark. Gradually, she lost her interest in life and slipped into a chronic depression. All of our surplus money was being spent on professional support for her psychological condition.

With my salary I was able to cover the rent of our small house and the food, and with a little creativity, I was even able to afford the cost of Sarah's medical care. But we were unable to save anything. I was a middle-aged man working as frantically as a twenty-year-old, and I was getting nowhere fast. Again I began to indulge in thoughts of giving up the struggle. Ending it all. In my more rational moments, however, one simple truth became clear: yet again, in order to advance, I had to start all over again. I could no longer stay in Perth. Nothing of any consequence was happening in Perth. All of the action was taking place on the east coast. We would have to move across the country.

I began buying the Melbourne and Sydney newspapers every day, even though they were two days old by the time they reached Perth. I wrote hundreds of job applications, and many of the companies did not even bother to answer. Those who did invited me to come to Melbourne for an interview. Naturally they would not hire me by correspondence. A handful of desperate companies were prepared to do so only because the jobs were situated in country towns, in the outback—the middle of nowhere. I did not want to move from one remote outpost to another.

I had to take my chances and hope for the best. I would not be able to secure a job until we had made the move. Fortunately, it would not take long for me to realise that I had made the right choice. My first day in Melbourne would produce an experience so bizarre that it could hardly fail to restore my faith completely. But for now, I was happy just to start afresh, and to close a most distressing and frustrating chapter of our lives.

24 Back to the Beginning

Where, unwillingly, dies the rose,
Buds the new, another year.
DOROTHY PARKER

WE ARRIVED IN Melbourne on Saturday morning; with our worldly possessions packed tightly into three suitcases and without the foggiest notion of where to go. 'An inexpensive hotel' was the instruction I gave the taxi driver, and he deposited us outside a dilapidated building in Spencer Street. As we entered the lobby—if you could call it that—it reminded me of one of those sleazy dives that so often appear in American detective movies, one of those hotels where you reserve the room by the half hour. The suite itself did nothing to dispel this image. It consisted of two old metal beds, a bedside table with a grimy lamp, and a festering sink. And we shared this questionable accommodation with another family—the crawling six-legged variety. Cockroaches.

After depositing our cases, we decided to take a walk around the city, to become familiar with our new surroundings. As we reached the city square, and noticed the hill ahead of us, Sarah decided that she wanted to sit down and rest for a while. She wasn't tired; she simply wanted to soak up the atmosphere of the metropolis—something she had missed in Perth. I looked at her and saw her radiant with happiness. Perhaps here, things would finally turn out all right for us.

What happened next would dramatically restore my faith in our future. The sheer improbability of the experience would leave me with no doubts that fate, or God, had dictated that we should be in that place at that time.

'I don't believe my eyes,' I said in amazement to my wife. 'Isn't that Ephraim Lifshitz?'

It was perhaps not all that miraculous to run into someone I knew on my first day in Melbourne. Large numbers of Polish Jews had settled here after the Second World War. But of all the people I could have met in this strange city, 'Fishel' was the very last person I expected to see. Not merely an acquaintance, but a man who had been so closely involved in so many chapters of my life. We had studied together at the Haifa Technion and lived together in the abandoned office block. We had worked on the wharves together. I had saved him from the Palestinian police force by bringing him to Damascus—until he disappeared with two truckloads of steel. He had even spent time working with *Tahal* while I was there. Shortly before I left Israel, I read that he had disappeared and was last seen in Spain.

'Fishel?'

He stopped and looked around.

'Lustig,' he exclaimed, almost as bewildered as I, 'what on earth are you doing here?'

'I had exactly the same question in mind, but as usual, you beat me to it.'

'I am working here. Making money.'

'Fishel, I am here with my family. Sit down and have a coffee with us.'

He greeted Sarah in Hebrew and then turned to me.

'I wish I could, Lustig. But I am racing to catch a train. I have a ticket to Adelaide. Your wife will be all right here. Come and talk to me while I walk.'

'What are you doing here?' I asked.

'After the war in 1948, there was an opening at the Dead Sea Company. Believe it or not, I am now internationally recognised as an expert on different kinds of salts. I am working as a chief engineer for an Adelaide company involved in extracting salt from the sea. I am trying to teach these *shmucks* how to do it. I have to catch this train because tomorrow I am scheduled to leave Adelaide for Lake Eyre.'

'What happened in Israel, Fishel? I heard that you fled to Spain.'

'Oh, it's a long story,' he replied uncomfortably, keen to change the subject. 'When did you arrive?'

'We arrived in Melbourne today.'

'What are you going to do here?'

'I don't know. But I intend to stay here. I have had quite enough of moving around.'

'You'll have no problems here. You are an engineer. Apply for a job. Anybody who knows how to use a slide-rule can get a job here.'

'Are you going to stay in Adelaide?' I asked, hoping that he had plans to return to Melbourne.

'I don't know. I am still married but my wife is still living in Tel Aviv. So I don't see her. I am waiting to hear about a better job in Queensland, and when I have enough money, I will probably return to Israel. But I am not sure.'

Before bidding me farewell, he gave me his address and told me that he would be visiting Melbourne from time to time. I told him that I had no address, that I was staying in this flea-ridden hotel around the corner. He suggested I write to him; perhaps he could assist me.

Eventually I did write to him, but received no reply. Then, two or three years later, he sent a letter from Townsville, in northern Queensland. He could not find satisfaction. 'The job is bullshit ... the employees are absolute nobodies ... Even screwing is a problem here because everybody knows everybody ... don't suspect me of being sentimental just because I am returning to Israel.'

It was the last I ever heard from Ephraim Lifshitz. I was saddened by this news of his departure. Despite the fact that he was an arrogant bully of a man, despite the fact that he had robbed me in Damascus, despite the fact that he was always prepared to take more than he could ever give, he was a genuine character and I was fond of him. And strangely enough, I would miss him. Our friendship dated back more than twenty years, and my life of constant emigration had resulted in a dearth of such associations, adding to my feelings of remoteness and alienation.

But our chance meeting that day, my first day in Melbourne, signalled that I was not alone in this jungle. It gave me hope. I returned to the city square with the newspaper tucked under my arm. And as I sat drinking coffee with my wife and daughter, I scoured the employment pages with renewed enthusiasm.

Among the advertisements was a vacancy for a structural engineer at the architectural firm of Buchan, Laird and Buchan in South Yarra. I went across to the pay phone and called them. Within minutes I had organised for an interview on Monday afternoon.

In order to make the right impression, I had to be on time. But I had no idea how far South Yarra was from the city. So the following day—Sunday—I hired a taxi to take me to Buchan's and back. Although somewhat expensive, I considered it a necessary investment to determine travelling time.

The following day, I arrived on time. Buchan's was a substantial firm, occupying three double-storey terrace houses in leafy Park Street. I was shown to a rather dark but elegant waiting room. A young man emerged. A boy. He was very tall; a long, reddish nose being his most pronounced feature. He struck me as a very friendly fellow, though I detected in his voice that he was trying to sound more important than his position dictated.

'I am Andy Goldstone, the chief structural engineer.'

We sat in his office, where he fired a series of questions at me.

'Name?'

'Theodore Lustig.'

'Born?'

'Vienna.'

'Really? Very good.'

I could not help but notice how impressed he was with this answer. I knew that there would be no point in clarifying that I was actually raised in Poland. In a remote island like Australia, who would understand the complex nature of Europe, the wars and the changing borders? For the sake of simplicity, I settled on a half-truth. And Vienna seemed to elicit the appropriate response. Soon I would become known around the office as 'the new Viennese engineer'. It had a nice ring to it.

After a few more questions, I was given the job.

'What is your experience?'

I told him about Damascus and Tel Aviv, suspecting that he wasn't quite sure where these strange places were.

'All right, we will take you on a trial period for three months. You will have a bank account and we will pay directly into your account. When can you start?'

'Tomorrow. Unless you insist and I will start today.'

'Tomorrow is fine, nine o'clock.'

I returned to the hotel with the good news.

'I don't think we are going to starve,' I told Sarah.

Securing a job with a reputable firm within days of arriving in Melbourne was undoubtedly a good omen, and it would usher in the most wondrous and wonderful period of my life. Every opportunity led to another in what appeared to be a glorious chain of miracles. After all those years of struggling, I was now finally on a golden road to professional success.

I began my new life the following day, at the offices of Buchan, Laird and Buchan. I was placed in a room occupied by the civil and structural engineers; the architects were located on the other side of the premises. I was impressed with the number of employees—it appeared that this firm handled all aspects of the building process. And they were not small projects, but tendered jobs. My first job involved working on the Shell building on the corner of Bourke and William streets.

As soon as I arrived at work on my first day, I was introduced to a culture that was completely foreign to me. The morning was spent around the coffee machine, where a series of 'meetings' were held to discuss the weekend's sporting results. Being a new employee, and somewhat overenthusiastic, I could not help wondering when we were actually going to begin work. But while I knew nothing about the local sport scene, I enjoyed listening to the exchanges between my colleagues. After all, it was a breath of fresh air for me to be living in a country that wasn't obsessed with politics and nationalism, in a place where the most heated arguments of the day involved an umpire's ruling, and where a person's affiliation was identified by the football team he supported rather than an electoral preference.

Naturally, I was keen to move my family out of the dreadful hotel as quickly as possible and one of my colleagues suggested that I call Williams and Company, the local real estate agent in South Yarra. I spoke with a woman who asked where I worked and then found me a suitable apartment.

'I will meet you there tomorrow at one,' she said.

I had always been averse to the idea of using work hours to run private errands. It seemed particularly inappropriate now, since I had been in the job for just a few days. Reluctantly I told Andy that I would be away for about an hour. It was only after I left the building that I realised that the apartment in question was situated directly across the road, on Park Street. The agent had been right—it was perfect. A neat two-bedroom apartment, light and quite smart. When I heard that it cost nine pounds a month I was astounded. I thought this was daylight robbery. But after my three-month trial at Buchan's, I would be placed on a wage of fifty pounds per month—more than enough to justify the cost—and so I decided to take it.

The perceived advantage of living directly across the road from Buchan, Laird and Buchan turned out to have been a bit of an illusion. Indeed, having to wait at home until just before nine each morning before heading off to work nearly drove me to distraction. But we were comfortable in our new surroundings, and for the first time, Sarah and I were beginning to feel that our travels were over. Iris was settling into her new school, Mount Scopus College, and our family life began to take on an element of routine. Our weekly outing took place each Saturday morning, when we would walk through the Botanic Gardens together and across the city to the Victoria Market before returning on the tram with our shopping.

My family's transition to Melbourne life had been easier than I expected, and it was further aided when I happened to run into a very dear old friend—my cousin, in fact—whom I had not seen since leaving Poland in 1938.

Occasionally I would accompany my parents to the Drohobycz railway station on Sunday morning, where we would board the train for Boryslav to visit the Kaufmans, the family of Dr Herman Kaufman's brother. Indeed, Dr Kaufman painstakingly concealed the fact that he grew up in Boryslav and not Drohobycz. The Kaufman brothers were very different in physical appearance as well as in personality, and I can remember wondering how two such dissimilar people could have been born to the same set of parents. I had always been interested in comparing brothers, and the Kaufman brothers provided me with much food for thought.

Mrs Kaufman was my mother's best friend. Consequently, our families were close—we considered each other kin. And in fact there was a family connection, with the Kaufman brothers being related to Pachtman, my mother's uncle. That's how close things were in the *shtetl* environment of pre-war Poland.

The Kaufmans had three children: Edu (Edward), Lilly and Franca. Franca was the closest to my own age, and I spent the most time with her during our visits. I remember that she was always a very bright girl, clever and streetwise. It was a pleasure to be in her company.

When she was about fourteen, Franca fell in love with Ziggy Krantz, a Boryslav boy who was studying at the Sorbonne. His father was influential in the Galician oil business—indeed, he was the production manager for the entire Boryslav operation. Franca and Ziggy became inseparable, and they eventually married in 1939, soon after I left Poland for the last time. I would not see Franca again for more than two decades. By then, both our lives had changed in unimaginable ways.

Sarah and I had taken Iris into Sportsgirl to buy her a winter overcoat. As we looked over the range, we were discussing—in Hebrew—the various prices and possibilities.

'I speak Hebrew!' interjected a rather large woman standing nearby.

I was unmoved by this woman's revelation.

'That's nice,' I replied, hardly glancing in her direction before returning to the pressing family issues at hand.

Suddenly, another woman stepped toward us, obviously the larger woman's shopping companion.

'Tedek?' she whispered quietly, as if she had seen a ghost. I turned towards her and saw that she had tears in her eyes.

It was Franca.

It was an emotional reunion, and we held each other in tearful silence for quite some time before Franca began to ask a barrage of questions.

'Where are you living?'

'Park Street in South Yarra.'

'Are you sure you are giving me the right address? That is an expensive area.'

'Yes, I know.'

'And this is your wife, Tedek? And your daughter?' she asked warmly.

Up to this point, Sarah's face had remained somewhat impassive. She had always been a little wary of anyone from my past, but soon after I explained who Franca was, she visibly relaxed.

Soon after, Franca and Ziggy came to visit us at our home, and among other things, they told us of their flight from Europe during the war. They had escaped through Norway, and were very nearly captured. Although they had left Poland almost a year after me, they had no news of what had happened to my parents. Franca was now manufacturing clothes with her business partner, and Ziggy, who was trained as an industrial chemist, held a position with the CSIRO. In his spare time, Ziggy pursued his passion, sculpture. Like many others fleeing Europe at that time, they chose Australia because it is about as far from Europe as one can get. It was well known that it had a growing migrant population, was relatively tolerant of newcomers, and could provide excellent employment opportunities.

Over the next few weeks, Franca undertook to teach Sarah all she needed to know about living in Melbourne. She took her out, showed her 'the ropes', and introduced her around. She took Sarah under her wing, and it proved to be a terrific boon. Franca and Ziggy would become our closest friends and weekly bridge partners for the next thirty years.

While actively helping Sarah to get to know the city, Franca decided to help me as well by organising a function to introduce me to a group of Jewish developers. Despite Franca's extraordinary efforts, those present seemed altogether indifferent to this little fellow who had just arrived from Israel, via a couple of undistinguished years in Perth. Not only did they show no interest in working with me, but they made no effort to talk to me at all. Nevertheless, I always felt indebted to Franca for her help and her good intentions.

What I was able to glean from the get-together with the Jewish builders was that unlike Perth, Melbourne offered a developer tremendous potential. Subsequently, a year after joining Buchan's, I decided that spending all of my time at the drawing board would not allow me to take full advantage of the opportunities. I made the decision to move out on my own. My boss, John Buchan, told me that he could not understand my decision. I explained to him that I was not a young man, that I was wasting precious time, and that I had confidence in my ability to sell my designs better and faster than anyone else could.

With a little persuasion, he accepted my position. Ultimately John Buchan would prove to be a good friend, a close ally, and even a partner to me in business, from the early days when he helped to get my small business off the ground by supplying me with his overflow of drafting jobs, to much later on, when we joined forces in preparing tenders for larger projects.

Initially, I worked from home. As was the case in Israel, I had to learn how to crawl before I could walk, which meant establishing a business as a drafting service before growing large enough to own my own projects. I tried to convince some of my colleagues from Buchan's to join me, including Andy, whom I liked very much and who was kind enough to give me my first job.

Many years later, at a social function, a tall, good-looking woman approached me and introduced herself as Andy's daughter. 'Mr Lustig, it is a pleasure to meet you. My father always spoke very highly of you. Unfortunately, my father did not have the courage to join you. I always advised him to get together with you.' I was touched by her words.

Two of my colleagues did decide to work with me for a short time, including Alan Nelson, an architect who later went on to work on the design and construction of the Melbourne Arts Centre. I invited Alan to become my partner—I needed somebody who could introduce me to the city, to the people, and to the various institutions. He stayed with me for two years before moving on. At one time, four of my colleagues from Buchan, Laird and Buchan were working with me after hours. Sarah would prepare their dinner and they would work from five o'clock until ten at night before stopping. In fact, they were earning more money from me than they were being paid across the road.

I spent a great deal of time driving around the suburbs and studying the new buildings, particularly the luxury apartment blocks. It was important for me to learn about the local conditions. And I had to re-educate myself, for while my own speciality was concrete construction, I knew relatively little about working with brick.

Demand for drawings was high and we were kept extremely busy. Soon I had developed basic templates for my designs; the draftsmen were able to duplicate them or modify them slightly to fit the different sites. Apart from the Buchan work, which alone could have kept the business afloat, my enterprise received a boost as I became more widely known, particularly to the Jewish community.

One sunny Saturday afternoon, condemned to spend the weekend designing a block of apartments, I received a cold call. The voice on the other end of the line was abrupt and spoke in Hebrew. I immediately identified him as an Israeli.

'*Ata* Lustig?' [Are you Lustig?]

Somewhat taken aback by his manner, and feeling that it was inappropriate for him to address me in a foreign language, I responded in English.

'Who is Ata?'

There was silence.

'Yes, I am Lustig,' I answered, relenting.

'Hello. My name is Haber. Do you remember me?'

I did not, but considered it more polite to leave the question unanswered.

'What do you want, Haber?'

'I want to speak with you. *Yesh li avodah bishvilcha* [I have work for you].'

'Well, that is a different matter.'

'What is your address?'

I told him that I lived in Park Street, South Yarra, and within ten minutes, he was at my door. He told me the story of how he had to leave Israel because of insurmountable debts. He then explained that he knew of my work and had decided to seek me out when he heard I was in Melbourne.

'I have bought a piece of land in St Kilda,' he explained, 'and I want you to design a block of flats. The way you designed in Tel Aviv. They do not know how to do it here.'

I drew up a plan for four flats on the small block. He paid me fifty pounds, but only after I had obtained the permit. When I finally handed him the documents, I told him, 'This is the first and last time. Should you be stupid enough to come here again, you had better be prepared to pay me something in advance, or you can find another genius to design for you.'

Within a few weeks he had returned. This time, he came with the layout for a larger block of land. The following day I showed him a sketch that included twelve apartments. Naturally I did not release it to him, but to my surprise he immediately handed me £250.

Haber must have spread the word around, because before long I had received another call. Schwartz, an elderly fellow, was by all reports a very influential developer. He asked me to visit him at his home.

'You see this piece of land I bought? How many units can you put on this block?'

Seeing the dimensions for the first time, and without the opportunity to sketch out a plan, I took a guess.

'I could probably put eighteen units in—six one-bedrooms and twelve two-bedrooms.'

He looked at me in bewilderment. 'Lustig, if you can get me a permit for eighteen units, you have the job.'

I sensed that this man was as shrewd as a fox. 'Come on. You are a smart guy. You know that the building surveyor will not give me approval unless it is officially submitted.'

'I know that you will be able to fix it somehow. You will give me some proof.'

'All right, Mr Schwartz.'

Within two days, the surveyor told me that the plans were fine. But he could offer me no guarantee.

I pleaded with him. 'This is a matter of fees. He will not pay me.'

'Who is he?'

'Schwartz.'

He laughed. 'I see. He's picked on you, has he? He is unbelievable, that old bastard.'

I returned to Schwartz, but he refused to sign anything.

'Look,' I explained, 'the building surveyor would be happy to talk to you. He knows you very well.'

'Everybody knows me well,' he answered, momentarily thrilled with his notoriety.

It was indeed the case, and while that project never came my way, Schwartz did try to assist me by introducing me to an architect by the name of Ernest Fookes at a company called Multiplex.

'If I have a complicated job,' Fookes told me, 'I will call you. Are you a builder or a designer?'

'It depends what you prefer. If you want me to be a builder, I will be a builder. If you only want design, I will be a designer.'

Our conversation proved to be academic, because shortly thereafter I was approached by Henry Rosmarin, a rag-trader from Flinders Lane with a taste for property development. He and his two partners, also in the clothing industry, were about to commence a string of projects, and they wanted me to become involved. Consequently, I would join forces with these 'three musketeers' to pick up my career where I left off in Israel—as a budding developer/owner rather than a designer and draftsman.

It was a successful partnership that would last for more than eight years. The success was based on a number of advantages I had over my competitors. Firstly, my experience in Damascus, and later in Palestine, had taught me the British system of quantity surveying. This was particularly important—my ability to accurately measure the costs involved in any construction and, crucially, to gauge the cost effects of any variations to the original plans, meant that I had a significantly tighter control of projects. Furthermore, without the need to hire the services of a quantity surveyor, I would save both time and money in the preparation of plans and tenders. Very few builders, let alone developers, possessed this knowledge.

Secondly, I was well versed in the requirements for comfortable, European-style apartment living, which was unfamiliar to the Australian culture at that time. Thirdly, I was Jewish. And finally, while word was spreading that I was committed to producing work of high quality, nobody actually knew me. They heard I had come from Israel, but nobody in the community, on that vast grapevine of gossip and information, was able to enlighten anybody else as to who I was, where I had come from, or what I had done in the past. I was an enigma, and this was of great benefit to me.

I had spent two fruitless years in Perth. Now, within two years of arriving in Melbourne, I was able to regain the ground I had lost. And finally, it all seemed worthwhile.

25 Home at Last

The fellow that owns his own home is always just coming out of a hardware store.
KIN HUBBARD

SARAH AND I had been married for almost twenty years. She had supported me through the good times and the lean—and the lean times were by far the more plentiful. She had been determined to leave Israel, and our years in Perth had proved to be disastrous. After two years in Melbourne, we were beginning to feel settled. We had found a place that had something to offer us. It was time to buy her a home she could call her own.

I had not touched our nest egg, the £4500 that I had fought so hard to recover from the crooked bank manager. I approached Williams and Company and told them that I was in the market for a house. They found me a property in Darling Street, South Yarra, one half of a neglected duplex. The interior was in a terrible state; you could shake hands with someone through the holes in the walls. But I was told it was a bargain—just four thousand pounds.

At the time I was unsure as to whether this was a good price or not, and anticipating that Sarah would want to see it before the purchase, I decided not to sign the sale document on the spot, but rather an intention to buy. Ultimately, we purchased the property, with the intention of renovating it before moving in.

Over the next six weeks, Sarah and I worked every night and weekend to make the house livable. I went to McEwans in the city, Melbourne's leading hardware store, to buy some machinery, including a polisher for the timber floorboards. The shop attendant was packing the equipment when it dawned on me that I had not been told the prices.

'How much does it cost?' I asked warily.

'Don't worry,' he replied. 'You don't need to pay right now.'

I was stunned.

'You are new here, aren't you? Where do you work?'

'Buchan, Laird and Buchan.'

'Let me explain, sir. You buy and we deliver. Later on you will receive an invoice. But you still don't have to pay. Then you will receive a statement.'

'What is the statement for?'

'I know this is difficult for you to understand. But it is a good system.'

'When do I have to pay?'

'Maybe thirty days, perhaps more. It depends. If we trust the client, we don't push for payment.'

I was never one to buck the system, and I was certainly not about to begin now. I asked the fellow if he knew of any tradesmen who might be able to assist me. He recommended a plumber and a painter. The equipment was delivered to Darling Street and we began the job. I assisted the tradesmen with the structural work, while Sarah set about cleaning and polishing the floors.

The renovation was nearing completion. One day, as I was working on the exterior at the front of the house, I was approached by a young real estate agent.

'Are you the owner of the house?' he asked.

'Yes.'

'I will make you an offer.'

'I am not selling.'

'Don't you want to hear the offer?'

'Sure.'

'I will give you five and a half thousand pounds.'

It was tempting.

'My wife is inside,' I explained. 'I will have to consult her.' I went inside alone.

'Sarah, there is a young man outside who is offering us five and a half thousand pounds for the house.'

'Abba,' she replied, 'I trust your judgment. You know what you are doing. If you want to sell, then sell. If you want us to move in, we will move in. But you know how excited I have been about moving in.'

I returned to the agent.

'She is not happy,' I said.

'Okay. I will offer you an extra hundred. Five thousand six hundred pounds.'

'Who is the buyer?'

He turned around and motioned towards an elderly gentleman across the road.

I recognised this man. He had kept a close eye on our progress, wandering past each weekend, enquiring about our new additions and commenting on how nice the property was looking. I approached him.

'Why do you want to buy it?'

'I am a retired gentleman from Hong Kong. I like to watch you work. The work is very good. I do like the house, but most of all, I like the walnut tree.'

'Are you serious? I am also fond of the walnut tree.'

He bought the house and we became very friendly.

Having made a profit of £1600 in a matter of weeks, I felt like a king. I had work, I had cash, and my confidence had returned.

With £8000 starting capital, I was ready to begin developing. Were it not for the credit 'squeeze' imposed by the government during the early 1960s, which prevented the possibility of borrowing money from the bank, I might have been able to go it alone. But I needed partners, and Henry Rosmarin and his fellow 'rag-traders' from Flinders Lane provided me with just that.

Rosmarin, a Warsaw Jew, rang me one evening at home. Speaking in Polish, he introduced himself and explained that he and his two partners wished to develop a block of flats in Camberwell. I recognised his name at once—indeed it was a very well-known name in Poland. A man named Rosmarin had been the only Jewish senator to the Polish *Sejm* (Parliament).

The terms of our initial arrangement meant that I would provide the design and construction as well as sell the units. I would be paid £1500 plus a percentage of the profits. As the only experienced builder and developer in the group, I would have control over the project, from the selection of land to the quality of construction.

After studying many of the new blocks that were being constructed at the time, I had developed strict specifications regarding the quality of work I wished to produce. The credit restrictions and high costs of construction had led many developers to seek ways of cutting their expenses. The trend had escalated to such an extent that developers were beginning to show signs of genuine irresponsibility, 'cutting corners' almost to the point where the walls didn't join. Even if I had wanted to compete with them on this level, I could not. There were no corners left to cut. Instead, I decided to abandon the idea of competing, and run my own race—even if it cost more and resulted in a higher price for the buyer. Quality had to count for something. This philosophy would bear fruit, especially when it came to developing apartments in Caulfield and St Kilda that were aimed at a European, predominantly Jewish market.

I accompanied Rosmarin around Camberwell in search of a suitable site. I was particularly interested in the Camberwell area. Having spent most of my life in the flat lands of Drohobycz and the arid cities of Israel, I saw the lush, green, hilly suburb as a residential paradise. I finally settled on a corner block that attracted me primarily because of two magnificent willow trees that stood on its grounds. I would leave those trees in place and proceed to build around them.

The design stage of this project would pose me little problem. After all, I was already in the business of producing drawings. The actual building process, however, was a different story. Building costs were high since there was generally a shortage of labour, and securing the services of a good building crew was one of the keys to success. Here I drew upon yet another small dose of my good fortune.

Leo Simon was an influential builder and developer, as well as a lecturer at the University of Adelaide. I had been acquainted with his brother, who lived in Haifa. When I realised that I was about to begin developing again, I made contact with him. Leo was a great admirer of the city of Melbourne and upon our meeting, we took a drive along Alexandra Avenue, beside the Yarra River, and on to the Dandenongs. Along the way he showed me his own work, as well as a number of historically important developments, in what became a 'crash course' in the architecture of Melbourne. As we stood atop Mount Dandenong, looking down over the entire metropolis, he broached the subject of my own career.

'If you have a good crew, Ted, you will be okay.'

'I am just beginning my first project. I am hoping that, in time, this will come.'

'Look, Ted. To be honest, I don't know you very well. But you seem trustworthy. Right now, I have a spare team of twelve men—bricklayers, concreters, builders, labourers. They are yours. But you will have to find the carpenters yourself.'

I was most obliged to Leo for providing me with a ready-made team of workers. In time, I would develop my own crew, headed by one of the men who worked for Leo. But in the meantime, Leo's gesture would enable me to embark on the Camberwell development with the greatest possible opportunity for success.

The building crew was made up entirely of Italian tradesmen and workers. I was most impressed with their work, and particularly their work ethic, and in the years to come my own teams would consist largely of Italians. Rosmarin could not believe that I, as a Jew, would work with non-Jewish builders and developers. I could never agree with that view, for a number of reasons. Firstly, my experience in Israel, as well as in Damascus, had taught me to be wary—for various reasons it was easier to work with the non-Jewish firms there. The vast majority of builders in Melbourne were not Jewish, and I saw no reason for saddling myself with the inevitable haggling and protracted negotiations that were a consequence of working with Jewish firms. Furthermore, I was almost completely ignorant in the use of *schwartzgelt*—the cash economy. I was, according to the Israeli expression, a 'clear pisser'. An infant: naïve and stupid.

I spent every day on site supervising the construction work, and even slept there overnight on numerous occasions. As the apartments neared completion, I was approached by a woman dressed entirely in black. She expressed an interest in making a purchase and I escorted her into one of the ground floor units. The woman, who was recently widowed, produced a cheque for £6000 and bought it on the spot. It represented a significant profit for us. The woman then suggested that she could sell the remaining apartments for me. She was not an agent, but she was extremely enthusiastic, and I hired her for the task, based purely on commission. Within weeks, the entire block had been sold, and the development proved to be a tremendous success. Her achievement in selling the apartments was all the more notable given that the idea of own-your-own apartments was still relatively new to Australia. The vast majority of apartments were leased at that time.

This development was a launching pad for me. It convinced me that I did not need to guess on the costs of construction; I could accurately estimate the costs myself. My experience with tendering and procurement, as well as with finances at *Tahal*, was a very good training ground for costing these projects. Furthermore, the Camberwell development lent support to my theory that a quality product would always sell.

Almost twenty years later, a young gentleman entered my office, claiming he had come on behalf of his mother, who had purchased one of those apartments all those years ago. The owners had decided to throw a party and they wanted me to attend. They were united in the opinion that the builder of their block had been a cut above the rest. After twenty years, there were no signs of cracks or settlements—no problems at all. One by one, they thanked me, and expressed their feeling that they had indeed got something special for their money. I felt most heartened. Their sentiments were perhaps the greatest honour I could ever have received.

The success of the Camberwell development catapulted me into a frenzy of activity over the next ten years. At times, I would have six to eight apartment blocks under construction concurrently. I had no problem coping with this workload in terms of producing designs and supervising construction. But I soon realised that the business was becoming too big to manage from home—I needed work space for a number of draftsmen in my employ—and I needed help with the administrative side of things. I mentioned this to a client of mine, an industrialist who had hired my services for the refurbishment of his family home, and he recommended that I meet a young lady from London who might be able to help. She came to see me in my newly established office in the bayside suburb of St Kilda.

'Mr Lustig, my name is Marlene. I believe that you are looking for a typist.'

Before me stood one of the most beautiful women I had ever seen. Her physical appeal was more than matched by her effervescent personality and radiant eyes. In what was one of the shortest job interviews in the history of mankind, I decided to give Marlene a chance.

Three days later I came into the office to find Marlene in tears.

'I am sorry, Mr Lustig. I cannot stay. I have cheated you by pretending that I had typing and shorthand skills. I am not a secretary, or anything else. I was so sure that you would ask me about my qualifications, but you didn't.'

'I had no interest in seeing your résumé. I wanted to see your performance. And you are not that slow.'

'But I was dishonest,' she insisted tearfully.

'Listen, Marlene, when trained properly, anyone can learn typing and shorthand, and then use that knowledge. Suppose you leave. Where are you going to go? If you go to another office, you will last another three days, without pay. I suggest that you give this some thought.'

The next day Marlene arrived at work as usual, and stayed for the next thirty-five years. While I cannot say that Marlene was ever a particularly skilful secretary, she became invaluable to my company in many other ways. With miraculous powers of recall, and capable of enchanting the men around her, Marlene became more of an account manager than a secretary. It was not unusual to discover that the odd client, sales rep, council member, or contractor had fallen head over heels in love with Marlene. While adept at diverting the attention of various tradesmen seeking payment at the wrong time, she also proved to be my conscience, frequently imploring me to consider their position. 'But Mr Lustig,' she would say, 'this man has a family to feed.'

Marlene and I formed the basis of the company: between the two of us we managed the entire operation. While I had always encouraged my partner, Rosmarin, to take a greater interest in the proceedings, this would never eventuate. He would remain 'silent'.

Many of the projects we embarked on during the early days were located in Caulfield and East St Kilda and, unlike the Camberwell project, were aimed squarely at the Jewish market. For the most part, I targeted an older sector of the community: those whose children had grown and left home, those who were looking to sell the family house and move into a more convenient, smaller dwelling. I had been raised in Europe, where apartment living was the norm, and when studying in Israel, I had taken a particular interest in the more 'psychological' considerations involved in creating apartments that were 'livable areas.' In Australia, for the European market, I would incorporate many of those influences into my work. I had soon developed a style of my own, one that spoke to the practical as well as the aesthetic concerns of the buyer.

In terms of floor plan, a number of factors were paramount. My apartments had to be slightly larger than the norm. A two-bedroom flat, for example, had to contain ten squares rather than the usual eight. The extra space would make a significant difference in terms of comfort, as well as provide sufficient scope to build a separate room for the toilet. Most developers saved space by placing the toilet facility in the bathroom. I felt that this was a violation of aesthetic and privacy standards.

It was certainly to my benefit that in learning my craft in Tel Aviv, I had experienced dealing with the most difficult type of client in the world—the Jewish–Israeli woman.

'What is *this*?' would come a piercing shriek from the bathroom as the client inspected the new apartment. 'When I am in the bathroom, I need to see myself from head to toe and from every conceivable angle. With this mirror I can only see myself from the front, and I can't see my shoes. I must be able to see MY SHOES!'

With a few minor adjustments—an extra mirror and a bit of creative design—the woman had what she wanted, and I had learned a couple of important lessons. Firstly, you must design for the way people actually live, not how you want them to live. And secondly, adding a little bit adds a lot. The key is in the thought invested in the design.

That is not to say that all of my successful innovations were the result of thought and planning. One Saturday morning, I was present as the real estate agent opened one of my apartments for inspection. For the most part, I felt that I ought to keep an eye on the agents. After all, by virtue of the market at which I was aiming, they had to deal with some of the most difficult clients known to man. On this occasion, an elderly Jewish couple came in to inspect the apartment. When the agent introduced me as the developer, the woman's expression immediately soured. Clearly, I was her nemesis and it was her job to catch me out.

The woman scrutinised every inch of the unit while her husband followed closely behind her, not uttering a word. I realised just how difficult this sale would be when the woman reached into her handbag, took out a handful of marbles, and placed them on the floor to test that it was level. Having ascertained that she would not have to serve the meals uphill, she then proceeded to inspect the bathroom. I suspected that I had all the bases covered with the inclusion of my special mirror system, but I was wrong.

'Why does the toilet door open outwards?' my adversary barked.

To my horror, I found that she had indeed caught me out—the builder had installed the door incorrectly. With no time to think, I retorted, 'Isn't it obvious? Take a look at your husband. He is elderly. If something were to happen to him while he was in there, God forbid, how would you get inside to lift him out?'

'Mr Lustig,' she announced, 'I would like to buy this apartment.'

A number of innovations also characterised the buildings themselves. First, I held a strong conviction that each apartment should provide the owner with under-cover parking for at least one car. Consequently, I introduced the Israeli idea of elevating the building so that the ground floor became a car park. Many of the other developers scoffed at this idea. In areas where height restrictions came into play, they felt that this was a blatant waste of space. 'How can he afford to do that?' they would ask. 'I wonder whose money he is wasting now.' I did not consider it a waste. Rather, it represented another convenience, one that added value to the apartments themselves. Another characteristic of my buildings was a security entrance, virtually unknown in Australia at the time.

During this period, I completed a development in Orrong Road, Caulfield, and one of the apartments would become our family home. There were four apartments in the block. I purchased one and Rosmarin another; the remaining two were sold off. This building had other unusual characteristics. In an attempt to create a sense of privacy, the feeling of four separate, self-contained dwellings, I designed each apartment with its own separate entrance. There was no communal stairwell.

As this building was being constructed, two competing builders sat across the road each day, notepads and pencils in hand, copying the design. Within twelve months, a replica of the building had appeared less than a block away.

Despite all the innovations and variations, one factor remained constant in my work: the quality. I was always prepared to spend more and maintain faith in the buyer's preparedness to spend the extra dollars. Naturally, I assessed each development on its own merits: the value of the area and the location and aspect of the land. But for the most part, my customers were seeking a relatively high level of luxury, and the blocks of land were selected accordingly.

Although my faith was justified, it did not follow that I was popular. The word around town was that Ted Lustig would charge the customer for every nail, but would provide quality work. And I always looked to confirm this rumour.

The 1960s would prove to be a period of huge demand and my business grew dramatically. There were difficulties, however. Owning your own apartment was a new idea in Australia, and this meant that unlike today, pre-selling was almost non-existent. Consequently, developing real estate was a risky business—the properties had to be sold quickly after completion in order to maintain profits. My properties tended to sell very quickly and at the time, I saw this as a matter of luck, one miracle following another. In retrospect, however, I can see that I had successfully identified my market, and provided them with exactly what they wanted.

My faith in the public's ability to recognise quality construction was bolstered with the development of a luxury block of apartments in the centre of affluence, Toorak. The location of the land justified my decision to spare little expense in creating apartments of the very highest quality, and this development remains one of the few pieces of work which, in its construction, truly achieved the high standards that I set out in my vision of its design.

The block of land in Balfour Street, Toorak, was owned by a woman in her fifties—herself a developer. She was haranguing the agent.

'I want (this) and I want (that) … You can tell him that he can build sixteen units here. I know what I'm talking about. I have the plans right here. If he is a nice guy, I will even give them to him at no extra cost.'

I instructed the agent to thank her for the advice, but I had my own ideas. I would build just six apartments: two three-bedroom flats at the front, and four two-bedroom flats at the rear. They would be luxury apartments with every attention to detail. The rooms would be large. The internal layouts would facilitate natural movement between the various functioning areas—the kitchen and dining room, for example. I paid particular attention to airflow, working with a mechanical engineer, Max Maier, to create natural cooling. Each apartment featured floor-to-ceiling windows and picturesque (and private) balconies. The property featured carefully designed and manicured gardens, a security entrance, and two car spots for each apartment.

Williams and Company held the auction on a Saturday afternoon. Despite the fact that the property had not been advertised at all, the street was filled with luxury cars: Rolls-Royces, Bentleys, Jaguars. My rationale in developing the block was that elegance and convenience would always sell, and this was the market I had aimed for: wealthy couples whose children had left home. By five o'clock all the units were sold. It was a phenomenal success. The smaller flats sold for £25,000 and the larger ones sold for £30,000. While I had already completed a large number of developments, this was a special project for me—every detail was built to perfection without the burden of financial restraint.

Uncharacteristically, this job was completed three months after the date I had set for sale. A number of problems had arisen with the joiners who were producing built-in furniture. Since by this time I was developing a substantial number of apartments around Melbourne, I decided to establish my own factory for furniture manufacture.

I had met a cabinet-maker from Tel Aviv and I approached him with the proposition.

'Abram,' I said, 'I will provide the space, the machinery, and the timber. Do you need anything else?'

'I need two men,' he replied.

'Look, you don't need the two men to begin with. Let's commence operations and we will look at hiring men later. Let's see how we go.'

'You have nothing to worry about, Ted. When I do it, you will be at the top in Melbourne.'

'Take it easy, Abram. If we start at the top, we have nowhere to go.'

The joinery workshop was located behind my office in High Street, St Kilda. While we made provisions to soundproof the area, the noise of the machines could be heard out front. Indeed, the machines had to be shut down whenever I was meeting with clients. Despite these difficulties, the factory was a tremendous success. We were producing a high volume of kitchen cupboards and wardrobes. Before long, I realised that despite the fact that my own developments were becoming larger and more numerous, I could not produce enough apartments to cater to the output of furniture being manufactured, and so began selling furniture to other developers.

It was around this period, the mid 1960s, that my daughter Iris married, and our small family of three became a small family of four. Iris had completed her schooling and was being pestered by all manner of boys, from young Jewish architects to non-Jewish football players. While it never really mattered to me whether Iris married out of her religion, Sarah was determined that her daughter marry a Jewish man. Indeed, my wife suffered continual anxiety at the prospect of Iris 'marrying out' and so was more than relieved to hear that Iris had decided to return to Israel.

I, too, considered this to be a good idea. Iris was only twelve years old when we left Israel, and while the move was a bit of a disruption for Sarah and me, it must have been extremely hard for Iris to leave her school friends behind and start all over again. She had been popular at school, and she stood out for her platinum hair and Nordic beauty. She had voiced her despair about leaving at the time, and at times since had been a little unforgiving, but I understood that leaving Israel represented a huge loss for her.

My cousin in Tel Aviv, Alex Yaron, assured me that he would provide Iris with a job and organise accommodation for her. Three or four months later, she met Max Moar, and shortly thereafter I received a telephone call from Alex.

'Something's cooking with Iris, Ted,' he began. 'There is this fellow; very intelligent in fact. His grandfather was a Chief Rabbi. There may be a real opportunity here, but I will not look after it myself. You will have to come over. But make it fast—they are both on fire.'

I went quickly. I went by myself, and Sarah did not like it. I explained that it would cost us a small fortune for both of us to go and besides, we did not know whether it was worthwhile for her to come. As it turned out, Iris and Max had been seeing each other for a month already, and soon after my arrival, I realised that I was in Israel to attend a wedding.

I had my reservations. After all, I knew nothing about the boy she was marrying. All I could glean before walking down the aisle with my daughter on my arm was that he was an Israeli boy. I had known enough Israeli boys in my time to warrant a good deal of apprehension. But my daughter wanted to marry Max. Iris was happy and I would not stand in her way.

I suffered on the day of my daughter's wedding. The primary symptoms were tears, a feeling of suffocation, and an unremitting pain. It was a pain I had never experienced, a strange and potent cocktail of joy and despair.

On the occasion of his marriage, the groom's father gifted him with a small apron factory. This might have been construed as a generous gesture, providing the young couple with a financial benefit as they started their life together. But it turned out that the business was in debt and the creditors wanted their money. I soon found myself bailing out my young son-in-law. Still, I would never presume to cast aspersions on the son for the sins of his father. One never knows when such an imputation might come back to bite one on the backside.

It soon became apparent to me that Max and Iris would have a better chance of achieving their goals in Australia, and I finally convinced them to try it for twelve months. By early 1966, Iris and Max were living with Sarah and me in our Caulfield apartment.

I negotiated a job for Max with McEwans, the hardware store, with whom I had developed a wonderful relationship dating back to my first building job—our first home in Darling Street. McEwans had surprised me then with its generous purchasing terms, and it had continued to be my supplier through the early days of my expanding business. They supplied almost every nut, screw and hinge that went into my apartments, as well as all the fittings. The only things they didn't supply were the timber, glass and bricks. Indeed, I credit much of my early success to this working relationship.

My reasons for sending Max to work at McEwans were simple. He would be working with Australians, learning the correct English terms for the various building items. He would also become accustomed to imperial measurements in preparation for working on building sites.

Max stayed with McEwans for three or four months, but from the very start was looking for ways to generate extra income in his spare time. On his first weekend in Australia, I supplied him with a station-wagon, a wheelbarrow and a broom and took him to a block of apartments I was building. His job was to clean the concrete droppings from the apartments.

'I have a very lazy labourer,' I explained, 'who is able to clean four of these apartments in eight hours. But you are a young, strong and determined fellow. You should be able to do at least that well.'

I left Max to his task, and when he returned home that evening, his hands were bleeding badly. He had worked extremely hard, and had managed to clean three of the four apartments. It was not until we sat down to dinner that I came clean to my son-in-law. The lazy labourer I had referred to earlier was really able to clean only one or two apartments in the time it took Max to clean three.

Within weeks, Max's hands had calloused and his work rate improved. And he had begun to take some interest in the construction business.

I would have liked Max to study construction, to provide him with a theoretical and working understanding of how things are organised and how the buildings could be sold. But Max preferred to learn on the job. He had an insatiable appetite for the outdoors, and so chose to spend his time on the building sites, learning from the tradesmen and labourers to supplement the knowledge he obtained from me.

The opportunity for Max to leave McEwans and take up a full-time position in the construction industry came towards the end of 1966. I was involved in developing two blocks of apartments and was approached by a Yugoslavian fellow named Pecek who was interested in doing the concrete work. I asked him to work with Max, and set up a plan by which my son-in-law could cut his teeth on the finances of the operation.

I was determined that my Max should not be dependent upon me. Rather than employ Max myself, I preferred this arrangement, in which he and Pecek went into partnership, creating a concreting company called 'Pemoar' and employing a crew of Italian workers. In establishing a separate business, Max would learn to handle his own finances and quotations. I hoped that in time, and as my own company grew, Pemoar and Lustig would join forces on larger developments. It was always going to be advantageous to be in business with a concreting firm, especially if it was in the family. It would then be in everyone's interest to get the job done on time and at the right price.

By the late 1960s, I was taking on much larger jobs. A residential project in Moorabbin involved the construction of roads and the development of infrastructure, and included more than 100 apartments. It represented a departure from my usual formula, as it was aimed toward the lower end of the market, providing rental accommodation for the numerous families of immigrants seeking their first dwelling. At the time, these 'New Australians' were considered a risk to landlords, and many were finding it difficult to secure rental arrangements. It was a much more substantial project than I had ever attempted before and it proved to be an outstanding success.

Pemoar made its debut with the Moorabbin development, pouring the footpaths on the freshly built roads. Before long, Max had identified a rather unique niche in the market. He began to pick up a lot of work with the Jewish developers around town, who had never come into contact with, nor even heard of, a Jewish concreter.

Max's big break came from one of these Jewish clients, a clever man who took great pride in not having spoken to his own brother in more than twenty-five years. He was developing a number of factories in South Yarra, and after experiencing some water seepage problems, he decided to sack the builder. Pemoar was given the job of building the 600,000-square-foot premises, and completed it in less than six months. Max soon earned a healthy reputation among the community.

With the success of Pemoar, Max's partner began to let things slip. He was living it up and neglecting the work. The opportunity to offload Pecek came with the unfortunate event of a concrete collapse in

Brunswick. Pemoar had hired a great deal of formwork and most of it was damaged and lost. Pemoar lost the job and a considerable amount of money. Pecek gladly backed out, leaving Max to pay all the creditors. Pemoar recovered, but within a couple of years Max had decided to focus his efforts elsewhere. He sold half of the business to his brother and the balance to two of his foremen.

Iris had been keen for her husband to leave the concreting business and join me in the development firm, and in 1970, Lustig became Lustig & Moar.

Through the first ten years of my own business, prior to the birth of Lustig & Moar, the majority of projects were conducted in partnership with Rosmarin and the 'three musketeers'. A few others had been completed for other developers, who hired my services as a designer and builder. Joint venturing *per se* was an unknown quantity for me. Toward the end of the decade, a young man came into my office requesting a meeting with me. Tom Spry was a member of a very wealthy and established Melbourne family.

'I have a piece of land in Darling Street, South Yarra, Mr Lustig,' he began, 'and I would like you to provide me with a sketch for the development of apartments.'

'Please sit down,' I motioned.

He handed me two drawings. One was the layout of the land; the other, a sketch provided by another architect. I looked at him in astonishment.

'You consider this to be a good design?'

'I consider it to be a design, but I am not sure that it is good.'

'To be honest, financially, this design is wasteful. It represents loss.'

'If you can provide me with a better design, Mr Lustig, I would appreciate it. How long would it take?'

'You can have it the day after tomorrow.'

When he returned, I handed him a sketch. I had altered the layout, the distribution to the main aspect, the nature of the entrance, and the general quality of the apartments.

'I must say, this does look like a better design, Mr Lustig. Would you give me a price?'

I hesitated.

He continued. 'You know, as a family, we own one hundred and twenty apartments in Toorak and South Yarra.'

'Really,' I replied, 'I do not want to know what *they* look like. But with this development, I know that you have a good proposition.'

While I had not included these details on the sketch, I had calculated for myself the cost, the land, the construction, and the interest.

'As you have told me,' I continued, 'you don't want to sell. You want to lease. So we are basing the value of this project on your return on the cost. A percentage.'

He listen intently without uttering a word. I hoped I was not telling him too much.

'I think that we may be able to do some business, Mr Lustig,' he finally said. 'I will speak with the family.'

Two days later he returned.

'What is the price?'

I told him the price. He continued, 'You say that you will be able to lease on a good percentage.'

'Of course.'

'I will be satisfied with, say, seven and a half to eight per cent.'

'Look, Mr Spry, I do not work on that kind of net percentage. It would be a minimum of ten per cent, but more realistically, we are looking at around twelve per cent.'

'That sounds fine to me.'

We shook on it.

'I trust you,' I said to him as made his way to leave, 'but if worst comes to worst, I will remove you from the picture and take it over myself.'

Tom and I became good friends during the course of the project, which turned out to be a successful one. Soon after its completion, I was invited to their office in South Yarra, where I met with a number of family members. They had purchased a substantial piece of land on St Kilda Road and were planning a large development. They wanted me to come in on the project with them. As I contemplated their offer, they sent me a considerable packet of their company shares. Almost sixty thousand dollars worth.

'Mr Lustig,' they explained, 'we are very happy with your work. The family is very keen to do business with you and we would like you to accept this share package.'

I was very wary of shares. It seemed wise to avoid being tempted by the offer, in any event, despite the fact that there were no strings attached.

I also decided not to become involved in the St Kilda Road

development. Nevertheless, I was flattered by the Spry family's offer. I had been concerned that the sheer size of the venture was enough to flood the market and push the prices down. Then, as the point was under discussion, the market collapsed.

By the end of the decade, the bottom was falling out of the residential market. Every man and his dog were developing property—greengrocers who thought they were builders had mastered the art of copying reasonable designs without understanding them, and then replicating them in substandard buildings. Glossy façades were selling, regardless of what was underneath. It seemed that price was fast becoming the all-important factor. The market was largely ignorant and I was struggling to convince buyers to pay more for quality they could not immediately see. The costs of construction were increasing dramatically and I was not prepared to compromise my standards; nor was I willing to sell my quality work at lower prices. I came to the conclusion that eventually I would be cut out of the market.

This became painfully clear to me as I completed my final residential project, a sizeable subdivision in Caulfield. I had purchased the land from the local church and built Whitehall Court, a small cul-de-sac with five apartment blocks around it. At sale, the two-bedroom apartments were fetching around $6000 each. Twenty years earlier, in Camberwell, my two-bedroom apartments were selling for 6000 *pounds*. Naturally I came to the conclusion that I would have to be crazy to stay in this game.

While it was time to change tack, the work that I had done through the 1960s laid the foundations for my professional future. After half a lifetime of moving around, of starting over, of battling to maintain hope for the future, the last ten years had brought my share of good fortune, professional success, emotional stability, and a modicum of wealth. Though I had already flown past the age of fifty, I looked upon the past decade—my forties—with fondness, as my youth, my golden years.

26 How To Make a Million

Chance is always powerful. Let your hook be always cast. In the pool where you least expect it will be a fish.
OVID

SARAH SPENT MOST of her week tending to the housework, cooking and cleaning. My work involved long hours, and Sarah never questioned my absence. I appreciated that she never complained, but left me alone to my work.

On the weekends, we would take afternoon drives together. It was an opportunity for us to talk about the week, and it also gave me the opportunity to look for blocks of land to develop. One Sunday afternoon, we were driving down St Kilda Road and as we passed Albert Square, I pointed out the BP building, commenting on its architectural appeal. I had always considered this area to be prime real estate, not only in terms of its central location, but in terms of its aesthetics. Sprawling parklands lay across St Kilda Road to the one side, and Albert Park Lake and its surrounding gardens were on the other. More immediately, the small island that formed the centre of Albert Square boasted some splendid greenery.

As we passed the intersection, I noticed a row of three terrace houses to the far side of the square. One of them housed a small café and we decided to stop for refreshments.

The café was empty and the two young Greek proprietors were delighted to see the arrival of the day's first customers. We were seated and brought two cups of excellent Turkish coffee. Naturally, a conversation ensued. Despite my complete lack of knowledge regarding the zoning of these properties, I decided to get straight down to business. I enquired about the properties and learned that the three houses were owned by these two young men, who were brothers, and their mother.

'I wouldn't mind buying these houses,' I told them. 'Would you sell?'

'How much will you pay?'

'Look, the houses belong to you and your mother. That means that it is your property. When you serve me a cup of coffee, you tell me how much I am supposed to pay for it. You don't ask me how much I am prepared to pay for a cup of coffee.'

Unable to counter such an argument, one of the brothers simply replied, 'We had better speak with our mother.'

'If you wish, but perhaps it would be better if *I* spoke with your mother. No doubt she would tell you that you are young boys and ought not interfere in big business.' I hoped that I had not overstepped the mark.

'Okay,' replied the elder brother. 'We will organise it.'

My abrupt and somewhat patronising manner had proved effective, and I decided to continue along similar lines.

'Look, either you wish to sell or you do not. I am here and I am an interested party. I will be frank. I will be here on Tuesday morning at eleven, and if you are interested, make sure that your mother is here.'

Sure enough, when I arrived the following Tuesday, their mother was waiting for me. The middle-aged European woman was dressed in black, and I had to fight to resist the temptation to enquire about the whereabouts of her husband. That was none of my business.

'Who are you?' she asked.

'I am a developer,' I replied, 'and I am interested in developing this land. I would like to do something good with it.'

'I will speak with my lawyer.'

A bad sign.

'Well,' I replied, 'that is always very bad. But if you insist, that is fine. The reason I say that it is bad is because lawyers always want to justify their charges. And it always turns out to be a lot of money. So he will keep on generating correspondence, as will my lawyer. As far as I am concerned, this has nothing to do with lawyers.'

She was silent. Silence was good. I decided to move in for the kill.

'Look,' I continued, 'it's lunchtime. Would you like to join me for a meal?' I rose and gestured invitingly to the chair opposite mine.

'No, Mr Smart Guy.'

This was not the response I expected. I thought quickly.

'I am not so smart, just a little hungry. Would you like to be my *guest* for lunch? *I* am inviting *you* for lunch.'

'This is *my* restaurant.'

'Okay. Then *I* am *your* guest!'

'Guests don't pay.'

A battle of wits. Such thrust and parry.

'Oh, boy. You seem to have all the answers.' And then it came to me. 'Look around you. Look at these people sitting in your restaurant. *They* are your guests. Are you trying to tell me that they don't pay? I'm sure you are a better businesswoman than that.'

'Okay, you, sit down.'

I had won the first battle but the war continued to rage.

She opened with: 'Are you buying the house, or are you buying the land?'

'What do you mean? I am buying the land. I want to do something big. By the way, how many square feet do you have here?'

'How should I know? I bought a house. I didn't buy the land.'

'Wait a minute! You bought the house *and* the land.'

'Land doesn't interest me, never has …'

This was sounding very good indeed.

'… But I want ONE HUNDRED AND TEN THOUSAND DOLLARS!'

She was good. Very good.

'Oh,' I murmured, slightly out of breath and still reeling, 'that's a lot of money.'

'That's what I want! You want to buy, so you pay me *one hundred and ten thousand dollars.*'

A brilliant strategist. Having observed my physical reaction to her asking price, she had immediately repeated it, thereby completing the 'one-two' punch combination. I was breathless but by no means down for the count.

'I have a proposition for you. You want one hundred and ten thousand dollars. But I need to know how much land I have here, and I need to know what I can build here. So I need time. I would like to take an option.'

'What's an "option"?'

'I will pay you some money. Regardless of what happens, you can keep it. It is yours. In return, I have six months to find out what I can build here. At the end of the six months I will either buy it or not. If I decide to buy it, I will bring you a cheque for *one hundred and ten thousand dollars.*'

Her silence was encouraging. I could almost see her mind ticking over: money for nothing, money for nothing. I continued.

'I will give you one hundred dollars right here and now. Just for the option.'

'Oh, no,' she replied, 'one hundred dollars is not enough.'

Clearly I had underestimated her.

'Okay, one hundred and fifty. It's money for nothing.'

'Done!'

Over a good, strong Turkish coffee, we drew up an agreement. She signed it and I handed over a cheque.

I left the café feeling proud of myself. I now had control over the site for six months. My only concern was my ability to generate the $110,000. While my residential business had grown quite sizeable, and while I was still involved in a significant development in Caulfield, I knew that I could not draw such a large amount of money from the company.

I went to see my lawyer, Arnold Bloch, and told him about the deal I had just completed.

'This looks good, Mr Lustig.'

I was possibly his only client with whom a relationship was conducted on a surname basis. Everybody else called him Arnold and he addressed them by their given (or borrowed) first names.

'I must advise you, Mr Lustig, to draw up a proper contract. This casual agreement simply will not suffice.'

'I will do that. But more importantly, if I decide to take up this option, do you have any idea where I might be able to get one hundred and ten thousand dollars?'

'Don't worry yourself about that. If you can arrange to buy on the right terms, it will not be a problem. If necessary, I will lend you the money. Tell your wife not to have sleepless nights. There will be enough of those once you have started the development.'

At that stage I had no idea about the possibilities of development on that site. I discovered that the area was zoned to allow for almost any type of development, residential or commercial. I had gained a level of expertise in the residential arena, but knew little about developing office blocks.

I did know something about *building* office blocks, however. Just two years after arriving in Melbourne, I was approached by a colleague of mine, an architect named Popper, who wanted my assistance in constructing a three-storey structure on the corner of Elizabeth Street and Flinders Lane in the city. We joined forces—I was to draw up the schematics and in doing so, improve on his plans free of charge—and won the tender.

The land was owned by a Jewish property developer named Faiman, who would later join forces with George Herscu and Maurice Alter to form 'Hanover', the high-powered shopping centre development company.

During the negotiations, Faiman insisted that penalty payments would be applied for each day after the specified deadline that the job was completed.

'Fine,' I said, 'but that means that you pay me the equivalent daily rate in bonus payments if I finish the job early—since you'll have your income earlier.'

Reluctantly, he agreed.

It was my first experience in supervising a central city site, and of the unique problems that accompanied this type of project. Due to the traffic restrictions in the city, materials could only be brought in late at night, and the crew on this shift worked into the small hours of the morning. One night, very early on in the project, I drove out to the site to inspect the incoming materials. It was pouring with rain, and I could see that this was slowing the work crew down. I raced back home and helped Sarah to prepare any and every piece of food we had in the house—sandwiches, sausages, chicken, fruit—to give to the workers. I grabbed a bottle of cognac and the picnic basket and returned to the site.

We shared the food and the drink, and then we all went to work. I set the example and they followed. From that moment on, they worked like hell, and over the next few weeks, my nightly banquets became a routine. I even invited the council inspector to join us, which he did on a number of occasions. I created a positive and efficient working environment and Popper was thrilled with the results. I delivered the Practical Completion Certificate early and earned the bonus payments from Faiman.

While this project gave me some practical experience in building office premises, I was effectively working as an engineer and project manager for another developer. With the Albert Road site, *I* was the developer, which meant that so many extra factors had to be considered. This was new territory for me.

I sought advice from a number of my old friends, particularly those from Buchan, Laird and Buchan. Alan Nelson introduced me to the finance director at Jones Lang Wootton, who assisted me in calculating the financials, taking into account the height restrictions that were in place. My research revealed that there was little to impede me in developing my first office block, and consequently, I would certainly take up the option on the site. In doing so, a casual Sunday morning enquiry at a coffee shop would ultimately earn me my first million dollars.

One afternoon, soon after the option on Albert Road had been negotiated, Marlene came into my office and informed me that a real estate agent was waiting outside to see me about the Albert Road property.

Mr Hamilton introduced himself as a real estate agent with a colourful past. In what was perhaps an attempt to strike a note of solidarity between us, he explained that he was Polish, and that he had been attached to the Royal Air Force as a Polish pilot. His name, Hamilton, was an anglicised version of 'Newnisky'. When he mentioned that 'many of his best friends were Jews', I knew that I was dealing with a dedicated anti-Semite.

'Mr Lustig,' he said, after concluding the pleasantries, 'I understand that you are very lucky and managed to make a deal in Albert Road. A *very good* deal. Well, I have a buyer, and I am prepared to pay you one hundred and thirty thousand dollars.'

Twenty thousand dollars profit. It *was* a good deal.

'I'll have to speak with my lawyer,' I replied.

'Okay. Who is your lawyer?'

'Arnold Bloch.'

'Very good.'

'Do you know him?' I asked.

'I have heard of him.'

Good, I thought to myself. He is lying again. He hasn't heard of him, but he does recognise the name as a Jewish one.

I called Bloch.

'Mr Lustig,' Arnold Bloch said excitedly, 'don't dare commit yourself to anything. Twenty thousand dollars is nothing; you'll pay half of that out in tax. You haven't agreed to anything, have you?'

'Nothing.'

'Good. I think you will do well out of this. Of course, I would have paid less for the land but it is still looking quite good. Congratulations.'

'Thank you.'

'You can tell this agent to forget it,' he concluded.

'You're offering me peanuts!' I told the agent when he called back that afternoon.

'Okay,' he replied, 'leave it with me. I will speak with my client and get back to you.'

He called back the following day.

'Mr Lustig, you are a very smart man. I know that we can work together. My client is willing to offer you one hundred and fifty thousand dollars.'

Forty thousand dollars profit! My mind began racing. What am I going to do with this money? I had to make the deal. After all, I still had no idea where I was going to find the $110,000. And it would take a long time to make that kind of money selling own-your-own apartments.

'Okay,' I replied.

That evening, I called Bloch, and told him about the latest offer.

'Please, Mr Lustig, I have already instructed you not to sell, nor even discuss the matter. You should understand yourself that if the buyer is returning with an offer for one hundred and fifty thousand within twenty-four hours, then the land must be worth two hundred and fifty thousand.'

'What did Bloch say?' asked Sarah.

I told her.

'I am not interfering, Abba,' she said, 'but I see how worried you are. Instead of having some happiness, you are unable to sleep at night.'

She was right, of course. Selling the land would indeed solve my problem of having to raise cash, as well as providing me with a very handy windfall. I had just one concern, and I broached it with Hamilton the following day in my office.

'I'm afraid I cannot proceed until you tell me the name of the buyer.'

'I cannot tell you that, Mr Lustig. I swore that I would not reveal the name.'

'Then I cannot tell you whether I will sell. I will not deal with unknowns. Your client may well be pulling your leg, and then we will all lose out.'

'Believe me, this is the best buyer you could have.'

'Understand me, Mr Hamilton. Unless you tell me who it is, I am not selling. It is as simple as that.'

'Okay, Mr Lustig. But please don't tell anybody that I told you.'

'I would be crazy to tell anybody. Is that the impression you have of me?'

'No, no. I can tell that you are a gentleman.'

He hesitated slightly. I could tell that it was difficult for him to disclose the information.

'The client is AMP.'

'Really! AMP?' I said in surprise. 'What does AMP want with such a small piece of land? It is an enormous company.'

'As a matter of fact, they want to construct an office building. Perhaps you want to think about presenting a package deal—land and building included.'

Two days later, I was invited to the offices of AMP to discuss the possibility of a package deal. I would provide the land, the design and the construction, and AMP would buy the lot. It was a tremendous opportunity for me.

I met with two company representatives, one of whom was a Mr Porteous, the man in charge of real estate. He had instructions to provide a good-quality, inexpensive office block on, or just off, St Kilda Road. My site was considered more than adequate. They wanted no involvement at all in the building process, apart from the presence of a single company representative, a clerk of works. I was familiar with the concept of a 'clerk of works' through my work in Damascus with the British army. As the interview proceeded, my knowledge of the procedures they described seemed to strengthen their confidence in my ability to get the job done. I was most impressed with their straightforward approach and the degree of trust they showed in me as I presented my ideas of how such a deal should be constructed.

They made it clear to me that they intended to buy the finished office block and provide me with a contract accordingly. I called for tenders. The plans were prepared by Joshua Pilar, an extremely bright young Jewish architect. In lieu of sketches, Joshua calculated everything on a slide-rule before producing the actual design. For construction, I would employ Santilli Primavera, the premier concrete construction firm in Melbourne at that time. It would be the first time I had worked with contractors rather than a 'gang' of concreters, and this would prove a revelation to me. Primavera were professionals who took responsibility for the quality of their work. Furthermore, I discovered that by employing contractors rather than hired labourers, I could minimise potential union problems.

The negotiations for a contract with AMP continued for some weeks. Arnold Bloch was able to construct an agreement that was not only clear and precise, but also totally acceptable to AMP. In an extremely positive atmosphere, we co-signed a contract that would pay me almost one and a half million dollars for the complete package. I had specified that the job would be completed in two years, though I suspected it would not take more than twelve to fourteen months. While they expressed their feeling that two years was a little long, they preferred to be conservative rather than suffer a late completion. This worked out in my favour, for they were prepared to offer me bonuses for an early completion.

The time bonuses were not the only source of the extra income that was ultimately generated through the course of the project. As it turned out, AMP had become increasingly concerned about the extremely low price they were paying for the building. They were not accustomed to such a low cost per lineal foot. Before signing the contract, they had asked to see plans for the air-conditioning unit. I had priced this element of the job at $135,000. Their reply from Sydney claimed that they would have approved a price of $185,000. Consequently, they felt that the work would have to be closely monitored. They had doubts about me, and the last thing they needed was a bankrupt developer on their hands.

In a sense they were right. With my limited experience in office block development, I was not sure how much the job was costing me. I had figured that, in a worst case scenario, I would lose a couple hundred thousand dollars—but I would have gained valuable experience, and an exceptional client.

I learned soon after that AMP had not taken seriously my quoted price of one and a half million dollars because they themselves had estimated that the job would cost almost two million dollars. It prompted them to add in a large number of variations on the job. I had very little trouble gaining approval to handle these variations myself because of the unusual relationship I had with AMP's clerk of works.

Since AMP had little experience with construction procedures, I was invited to assist them in appointing someone to the position. There were three candidates: an Australian, a Dutchman, and a German. Hans, the German, clearly had the most impressive résumé, but AMP was not sure whether I would be willing to work with him. After all, he was German and I was a Jew. They seemed satisfied when I agreed that he was the best man for the job. And I was satisfied, suspecting that a little unspoken emotional blackmail would result in this German clerk of works eating out of my hand. Suffice it to say he approved my quotes for each and every variation on the building.

The extra work and time bonuses would ultimately push the price of the building up to $1,850,000. On a building that ended up costing a little over $900,000 to build, it represented almost one million dollars profit.

It was the first time I had made a decent amount of money, and this presented me with a new set of problems. First and foremost was the question of income tax. My accountant, Graeme Bancroft, came to my office looking particularly concerned.

'You have made a profit of a *million* dollars, Mr Lustig, *a million-dollar profit*. How am I supposed to handle that?'

It had never really occurred to me that making a million dollars was a problem.

'You're the accountant. You tell me.'

The solution was a simple one. I had to keep building, and avoid selling. Like all successful developers, I was now condemned to a lifetime of building.

The enormous success of the AMP project would propel my business to new heights. Before the completion of this building, I had commenced work on two similar projects and this would usher in a string of large shopping-centre developments. At last I was beginning to fulfil my financial goals. I was already fifty-five years old—some might say I was a 'late developer'.

Through the ensuing period of my life in the 1970s, Sarah's and my social life was restricted to occasional outings to the cinema and was populated by a small number of friends and acquaintances. But from time to time, Max and Iris would invite us out to dinner with the children. Being creatures of habit, we would almost always end up in Chinatown, and always at the same restaurant, 'our restaurant', where we would be greeted with a familiar 'Hello, Mr Lustig' or 'Good evening, Mr Moar'. Indeed, we were such important patrons that we qualified for the owner's special treatment, which included using the possessive: 'your table' and 'your waiter', as if we were directly responsible for their existence. This accompanied the usual selection of jovial references to our frequency of custom. 'Mr Lustig, the dividend cheque is in the mail!' 'Mr Moar, you have a buyer for the restaurant. Ha ha!'

On one particular occasion, Max's friend Manu, who was visiting from Israel, joined the family for dinner. 'Our' waiter for the evening was a young Melbourne University student, a tall, slim fellow and the epitome of obsequiousness. He began to take the orders, and finally came around to me.

'May I recommend the fish, sir, it is very good tonight. It is a fillet of blue-eye, lightly steamed, with ginger, shallots and soy,' he intoned. He paused, pen poised.

Now, had he not recommended the fish, I would have probably left the poor boy alone. But suppose I was allergic to seafood? Or suppose—as is the case—that I simply didn't like fish? Furthermore, I could not help wondering whether he had recommended the fish simply because everybody else had ordered it.

I allowed him to complete his detailed description and complex analysis of the dish, fixing him with an earnest gaze, before asking my question. 'Young man, I have a concern regarding the fish.'

'What is it, sir?'

'My companions are confident that they will enjoy the fish. But will my fish be of the same gender as their fish?'

That threw him.

'I beg your pardon, sir?'

'Gender. Will my fish be of the same gender?'

'I am sorry, sir. I do not understand the word "gender".'

For some strange reason, my explanation of the word served only to cause more confusion. Now that he was familiar with the question, he found himself unacquainted with an answer.

I still wanted a response, and assured him that I would be happy with the fish if only he could vouch for its gender.

There ensued a flurry of activity, correspondences in Chinese whispers between waiter and owner, owner and chef, chef and waiter. Finally, the proprietor approached our table wearing the broadest smile he could muster under the circumstances.

'Mr Lustig …' he began.

I interrupted, fearing the commencement of a major oration.

'Look, I believe that in "our" restaurant, I am entitled to ask whether the fish that is destined for my plate is male or female.'

He scuttled away. The family was starting to get a little agitated. After all, we had come to eat, not discuss zoology. Then the proprietor reappeared, this time directing the chef to our table, after which I was offered a lovely beef dish (of no specific gender). Waiter, chef and owner retreated, with some degree of obvious relief.

I noticed a smile on Manu's face. My embarrassed family knew that I was just playing a game, but only Manu seemed to recognise the prize for which I was truly angling. My specially prepared, premium-grade steak dish was only going to cost me the same price as that lousy piece of fish!

Some years later, I was visiting Israel and was invited to dine with Manu and his family. Ever the polite host, Manu was the last to order. As he selected the gefilte fish he gave the waiter a sly wink, and when his meal arrived it was steak. When I caught his eye he gave me the same knowing smile as the one I saw that night in Chinatown.

27 Shopping Around

When the going gets tough, the tough go shopping.
MODERN SAYING

WITH THE SUCCESS of the AMP development, I felt confident of my abilities to replicate the results elsewhere. Even before the first office block was completed, I had managed to negotiate the purchase of two adjacent properties on Albert Square—numbers 16–18 and 20–22. Naturally, I had to pay more for each property, but the interest shown by AMP had convinced me that the location was a promising one.

Indeed, it was AMP who suggested I buy the adjacent block in case they needed more space. The only problem was that they did not have the funds available to finance the second building. Instead, they arranged for me to meet the manager of the military forces superannuation fund in Canberra. He was more than willing to throw money at me.

'You come highly recommended, Mr Lustig. How much do you need?'

'About a million dollars,' I replied.

He wanted to give me more than that. In fact, I did not even need the million dollars, since the cost of the second building was being covered by the progressive payments I was receiving for the first. I had an oversupply of funds.

One Friday evening, as I was sitting down to the Sabbath meal with my family, preparing to break the bread, there was a knock at the door. I excused myself from the table, where Sarah, Iris, Max, and my two young grandchildren Guy and Nathalie were about to begin their first course. When I opened the door I was confronted by the sight of two Italian workers, still dressed in their overalls. I knew one of the men; the other was a stranger to me.

I couldn't believe my eyes. It was a most inopportune moment for them to arrive. Reluctant to create a scene in the doorway, I ushered them into my study, which was Iris' old bedroom.

'Friday night!' I said. 'You arrive at my door unannounced on the Sabbath. Marco, are you stupid? It is the holiest day for us Jews. We starve all bloody week because we like to eat on Friday night. Tonight, we like to eat a lot. And I have just sat down to do so.'

'I am very sorry to interrupt you, Mr Lustig. But,' he said, gesturing to the man next to him, 'this is Bruno Grollo.'

I had heard this name before.

Before me stood a man covered in dust and spattered with globs of viscous concrete setting before my very eyes.

Sarah called from the dining room. '*Abba*, what is going on? Who are you talking to?'

'Try to keep me some fish. I will be in shortly. If the children want something to eat, let them begin. These gentlemen have had an accident and they need assistance.'

Grollo said nothing apart from a few grunts. When I noticed that he was about to sit down I told him to wait until I had put a towel over the chair.

'Can't you wash yourself after work?' I asked, rather irritated.

There was no reply.

Marco proceeded to tell me the story. Sensitive to the fact that my family was waiting for me at the table, he spoke at breakneck speed. It seems that Bruno had been involved in a disagreement with a Jewish developer who decided not to pay for Bruno's work. Now Bruno was in financial trouble. He was obviously very upset, because tears were rolling down his cheeks, leaving sodden tracks through the concrete. He had come to me for a job.

I expressed my sorrow for his pain, and asked the men to return the following day. Grollo arrived alone the next morning.

'If you are going to do a job for me,' I began, 'you must understand that it will be done *my* way. I will show you how *I* believe it should be done.'

I had always held the strong belief that it was advantageous to hire tradesmen who were not yet masters of their craft so that I could take it upon myself to train them to some extent. I introduced Bruno to Primavera. They were established tradesmen and were working with prominent architectural firms—like Buchan's, for example—on big, tendered jobs. Together, we instructed Grollo in the art of formwork, a skill I had learned in Israel.

When I was satisfied that Bruno was willing to adopt the techniques, I decided to contract him to build the second office block on Albert Square. He was grateful for the opportunity and he attacked the job with gusto.

It did not begin well, however. Shortly after Grollo's men had laid the slab, there was a violent storm, and a substantial amount of cement was lost. We had to establish whether we could continue with the slab or else pull it up and start again. Luckily, the cement was still fresh and we could simply add another layer instead of starting over.

After the shaky start, Grollo settled into the job and performed admirably. Indeed, Bruno seemed determined to reach the same level of quality as we achieved with the AMP building next door. I wanted the second building to be finished as quickly as possible; the workmanship did not have to match up to the first. I promised Bruno a certain amount of money and to his credit, the building was completed in a very short time.

Bruno and I soon developed a close working relationship. His firm built the second and third buildings on Albert Square, and we would continue working together throughout. We undertook many of the larger projects as partners. The benefits were obvious. As a partner, it was in Grollo's interest to finish the job on time and at the right price. Consequently, Grollo was prepared to sign a contract on the basis of a fixed price, and with the inclusion of a penalty clause for overdue deadlines. This meant that as a partnership we were able accurately to assess the costs involved in any given project.

In later years, Bruno was to become one of Australia's most successful developers. He and Max would work together closely, and my role would change to that of a fatherly mentor. For Bruno, our relationship represented a continuing education supported by a most powerful business arrangement. For me, Grollo's involvement offered its own benefits. Among Bruno's strengths was the loyalty of his workers, a powerful tool at a time when relations with unions could pose some challenges.

I had enjoyed peaceful relations with the Builders' Labourers Federation throughout this period. I had first encountered Norm Gallagher—the BLF boss at the time—while working on the AMP building, and in the course of a number of conversations, I had won his confidence. There was considerable infighting when builders' labourers were elevated to the security of permanent positions—full-time with all the benefits. I promoted the idea that the builders' labourers should have three weeks' holidays with pay and found myself in the uncommon situation of enjoying the approval of the unions.

The office building projects on Albert Road proved a revelation to me. I sold the first building to AMP and kept the remaining buildings, which meant that a significant part of my business now involved ongoing commercial property management and ownership. It was a business that involved large sums of money, and a big-name clientele. The second building was leased in its entirety through the efforts of a young estate agent, a fellow no older than twenty-two, who had come to my office and told me he could lease the space to the Royal Australian Air Force. I admired his gumption, which proved to be supported by equal parts skill and performance.

My own *modus operandi* was to build, develop, and lease, and this is how my relationship with Jones Lang Wootton began. The JLW name had been around since the 1780s (as a London firm) and I realised very quickly that the presence of their letterhead on my submissions was most influential.

My association with them would provide me with a number of important opportunities. Upon completion of the third building, at 16–18 Albert Road, JLW managed to secure a single tenant for the entire building. The Federal Department of Civil Aviation would remain my tenant there for more than twenty years. During this period, I heard word that the then Prime Minister, Mr Malcolm Fraser, planned to relocate the department to Canberra. Naturally, I was not too thrilled with the prospect of losing my tenants, but I suspected that it would take a period of some years for the transfer to eventuate. I moved quickly to turn a potentially negative situation into a positive one. Joining forces with my former employer, Sir John Buchan, who had by then become a leading member of the Liberal Party, we travelled to Canberra to speak with the Prime Minister, and to campaign for the opportunity to construct the new building that would house the department.

The proposed size of the development was 450,000 square metres, a large project even for Canberra. The idea was that the government would lease us the land for a price and we would develop the offices, which were required in eighteen months. Everything was moving along in Canberra until a number of new demands were made. They included provision of a hotel and a casino. The casino idea was an attempt to keep the public servants in Canberra over the weekends rather than see a mass exodus from the capital every weekend, often including the Friday. I wanted to explain that it would be less risky to develop offices only rather than adding the hotel and casino. The Canberra Super Fund for the Armed Forces was prepared to finance the entire project. Including the hotel and casino, I prepared a package with the condition that I would not pay rent for the land. This obligation would be met instead by the casino and hotel owners.

It was during these negotiations that I learned that it was important when dealing with the government to have everything written on a single page with the signature on the same page—all clearly, simply and unequivocally spelled out.

At a meeting with the Ministers for the ACT and Agriculture, and the Head of the Prime Minister's Department, John Buchan was asked if we had the money. I could not help thinking that this question would have been unnecessary had they had the decency to read the one-page document in front of them. Suddenly, a shrill alarm rang through the chamber, an almost deafening bell. I was sure that something was ablaze. Except for John and myself, everyone stood up and ran out of the room *en masse*. Somewhat stunned, I asked a staff member what was the nature of the emergency. 'The Prime Minister is to make an announcement,' was the response. I was swept along and found myself seated in the chamber behind the leader of the ALP, behind the Opposition front bench. Fortunately there was no vote taken, so despite my acute embarrassment at being in the wrong place, my presence was, quite probably, not even noticed.

It took five years for the planned development to eventuate, by which time I was in my mid sixties and had lost the drive and fight to maintain this constant pressure. After years of protracted negotiations, we failed to win the contract. The government did not accept my proposition. Nevertheless, the episode illustrated the importance of keeping an ear close to the ground, of keeping abreast of the developments involving tenants of the political kind.

The success of the Albert Road development meant that I had the finances to look at a number of larger projects, and I chose to move into the area of commercial property development: shopping centres. The rapid expansion of Melbourne's suburban area resulted in increasing opportunities for developing centres. These were not the massive 'regional centres' like Chadstone; there were very few developments of this type going on. We were developing smaller centres on the shopping strips—'local centres'. Throughout the 1970s and early 1980s, my business was dominated by these developments.

The site of my first such development, in the inner Melbourne suburb of Richmond, became available while I was still working on the Albert Road sites. I was approached by two very elegant gentlemen, one about sixty-five and the other in his early fifties. They were real estate agents, though they never made this fact known. They were freelance operators. There was no company *per se* involved, and all dealings were treated as purely confidential.

The block of land was situated at one of Richmond's busiest intersections—Bridge Road and Church Street—and was owned by a recently bankrupted construction company. I was most impressed with its size—around 100,000 square feet—and I purchased the block at auction. After discussions with JLW, we built a shopping centre and office space.

Grollo had just completed the third Albert Road building and began working on the Richmond site. By this time, Max's concreting firm Pemoar had been sold to his brother and Max had come in as my partner. Lustig & Moar was born. Initially, his stake was 25 per cent, but within a few years we were on a fifty-fifty basis.

I did not have a son, Iris was very busy raising a family, and Max was the natural successor to the business. I wanted him to work in the office so that he could learn all aspects of the operations, but Max preferred to stay on site. (I joked that perhaps that was because I was in the office.) Taking up the position of manager of the Richmond site—and while trying to keep up with Grollo—I endeavoured to teach Max the basis of securing production, and gradually he absorbed the lessons. Before long, Max was 'King of the Site'.

It was in Richmond that I established a new headquarters for my company. Over the next ten years, I would take an almost perverse pleasure in having clients and associates who were accustomed to spending their time in the plush surrounds of Collins Street trudge through the fruit and vegetable market en route to a meeting.

While the Richmond shopping centre was under construction, I received word that a large block of land was available in Boronia, and that the local council wanted a facility built to compete with 'Knox City', the AMP-owned shopping centre in neighbouring Knox. I then discovered that Hanover, the major player in the regional shopping centre game, had informed the town clerk that they would not be bidding for the land. This interested me.

The following Friday night, after the Sabbath meal with my family, Max, Sarah and I drove out to inspect the area. As we headed towards the foothills of the Dandenong Ranges, the fog became thicker and the rain became heavier. By the time we reached our destination, we could see virtually nothing at all. I was still in the dark as to why Hanover had passed on the project.

On Monday morning, I went to see the town clerk. It turned out that the council wanted a suitable area for a medium-sized shopping centre and would assist in the purchase of the twenty-four houses on the selected site. I had to agree not to pay more than a specified amount for each block.

So this was, as much as anything else, an exercise in consolidating an area of land. It would prove to be a great challenge, and a most valuable experience for me. It was important to learn how people would react to this sort of thing. I could only assume that Hanover had withdrawn from the project because they doubted whether it could be achieved.

Twenty of the twenty-four sales proceeded smoothly; three took a little more work. But there will always be one holdout, and eventually we began excavating around him. He finally vacated after I offered him a nice painting on top of the price for his house.

Richmond and Boronia were built concurrently. The success of these projects would depend on a number of factors, none more important than securing a major tenant. This was the key to developing shopping centres. The big retailers would generate the traffic and the smaller boutique shops and retail chains would gravitate towards that traffic. My relationship with the then joint managing director of the Coles group would prove integral to my success.

L.R. Robinson, a leading-edge retail administrator who brought about the marriage between Coles and Kmart, came to see me soon after I had submitted plans for development to the Richmond Council. Coles already had two stores in Richmond but was looking for a third location, and could not pass up the prime position of my shopping centre.

I was well aware that my performance at Richmond would determine my future relationship with Coles. I was more than confident of my ability to provide a quality building to their specifications, but I had a lot to learn about the principles of developing a successful shopping centre. The types of considerations that were important in the design and leasing of the centre were completely new to me. Consequently, I was 'all ears' when it came to learning about the needs of retailers and ways to maximise the performance of the shops within the complex. The managing director of Coles thus became my mentor in the shopping centre business.

On one occasion, I was considering a purchase of land in a bayside suburb for a medium-sized development. It was an extremely pretty location—right on the beachfront in fact. When I took L.R. Robinson to inspect the site, he turned to me in horror. 'Ted,' he said, pointing straight out to sea, 'who's going to come in from that direction?' I only needed to be told once, and I was most grateful for the input.

The relationship I enjoyed with the Coles Group, and particularly with the Kmart chain, would form a rock-solid basis for my future shopping centre developments. It was cultivated at Richmond, consolidated at Boronia, and then cast in stone at the Whitehorse Plaza in Box Hill.

At Richmond, I impressed the Coles management with my ability to complete the job on time, to specifications, and to budget. Boronia featured both a Coles and a Kmart—the first non-free-standing Kmart store in Australia.

The Kmart administration in the United States was very particular about its store specifications. During the course of construction, there was some confusion about the air-conditioning systems that were being installed.

As usual, I had hired Cor Stastra and Alan Page, a couple of bright young engineers, to design the electrical, mechanical, and air-conditioning systems. I considered their work superior to the standard Kmart specifications. While many developers would have sorted out a misunderstanding by correspondence, I immediately flew to Kmart headquarters in Ohio to meet with them personally and clarify the issue. I see this as one of the most important decisions of my career. I presented my case and by the time the meeting was over, the Americans had requested permission to adopt the Stastra & Page designs as their new standard. From that time on, I enjoyed an extraordinary relationship with them, and they became my major tenant in every shopping centre I developed.

The relationship was cemented further with the development of the Whitehorse Plaza Shopping Centre in Box Hill. It was important to work strictly to deadlines so that the tenants could organise their business around the opening of a new store. Massive amounts of money were expended advertising the 'Grand Opening Sale', and an inability to open—for whatever reason—would have amounted to disaster. At Box Hill, union trouble threatened to push the completion date past deadline, and I had to act swiftly to avoid such a scenario. The site was being guarded and I needed to get the escalators inside. One night, I fortuitously managed to bribe a crane operator to get them off the semi-trailers and onto the site for installation. The Coles administration felt that I had delivered a miracle, and indeed, of the five new centres that Coles was opening at the time, only two of them were completed on time.

While forming the basis of my success in developing shopping centres, my relationship with the Coles group brought a number of other more obscure benefits. The Rubenstein brothers owned three supermarkets, in South Yarra, Richmond, and Balaclava. They were good operators—the two brothers and their brother-in-law each managed a store and staffed it with their family members. They had a plan to renovate the premises and sell them off to Coles. And who better to renovate them than someone who knows how to build to Coles' specifications, and has a 'hotline' through to the managing director? Lustig. It was a clever move on their part and eventually they achieved their aim of selling the properties to Coles.

Jones Lang Wootton were specialists in commercial real estate (office blocks) and had very little experience with shopping centres. Subsequently, I organised the shopping centre leases myself. Later, Max would take over this role and perform the job with aplomb. He developed a tremendous sense of all things retail, particularly of how to organise the leasing such that each of the tenants benefited from their particular position within the centre.

Following the success of the Richmond and Boronia shopping centres, larger developments were completed, one in the Latrobe Valley (at Morwell and Sale), as well as The Pines Shopping Centre in Doncaster, Whitehorse Plaza in Box Hill and Greensborough Shopping Centre. With the developments becoming progressively larger, we needed partners. Usually, we teamed up with Grollo, but on occasion there were others. We were invited into partnership with the Gandel-Besen Group on the Greensborough project, and later we took in Morrie Alter as a partner to develop Chatswood Chase in Sydney.

There were few major developments where the owner of the land was himself the financier, developer, builder, and salesperson. But this was the case with almost all of our projects.

In theatre parlance, Lustig & Moar was the producer, director, writer, production designer, and financier (albeit in partnership) of each project. The only task we did not perform was the 'set construction', which was Grollo's job. And since he was usually the partner, this meant that between us we had complete control over the project. So on the basis of decent 'houses' (tenancies), we could maintain a clear view of our potential profits.

The ability of Lustig & Moar to control all aspects of its projects had its source in the fact that I was both a developer and an engineer. Very few developers of the day were able to both manage finances and read and understand blueprints and schematics. Furthermore, my background in quantity surveying meant that I could cost the work precisely without having to hire someone specifically to perform that task. In addition, my expertise lay in the area of concrete construction (the stuff of modern construction) and it is understandable that I was often in a position to pay a little more for the land. I would always be able to build for less than my competitors, and had the expertise to build to a superior quality as well.

I designed the first large shopping centre at Richmond, but having decided to tender for the development of a shopping centre for the Victorian Gas and Fuel Corporation, I felt that it could be in my interest to take an architect on board. I approached Llew Bawden, an excellent architect and an old colleague of mine from Buchan, Laird and Buchan. Ordinarily, a firm of its standing would have considered itself above developing shopping centres, but Buchan's was a little short of work at the time and welcomed the opportunity. Indeed, they were keen to establish a branch of shopping centre business for themselves. While we didn't win the Gas and Fuel job, Llew came on board for the development of Boronia Shoppingtown and would work on all of our subsequent shopping centre developments. It was a period where none of us had very much knowledge about shopping centre design but gradually, side by side, we learned the game. In time, Llew gained a reputation that would see Buchan's completing similar jobs for other developers, including Hanover.

Through this period of shopping centre success, Lustig & Moar was responsible for a number of important innovations and achievements. Boronia Shoppingtown was home to the first multi-deck car park in any shopping centre in Victoria. The Kmart store at Box Hill was the first Kmart in the world to be part of a multi-development shopping centre. Whitehorse Plaza was the first shopping centre in Australia to have moving walkways, and together with Coles, Lustig & Moar designed a special lock on the shopping trolley wheels so that the shopper could travel on the walkways. Whitehorse Plaza was also the first building in Australia with a glass elevator.

It was during the construction of the Whitehorse Plaza Shopping Centre that I was approached by a young man who introduced himself as J.F. Kennedy. When I asked him if he was related to the legendary American president, he told me that their matching names were purely coincidental. Mr Kennedy represented the Australian Industry Development Corporation (AIDC), an organisation established by the Whitlam Government with the task of aiding in the funding of various industries. The AIDC had lost millions of dollars on mortgages and loans to failing concerns, and its future was in doubt. In what was an attempt to recoup some of the lost funds and maintain its existence, it had decided to fund a number of real estate development projects that guaranteed some degree of success. Consequently, Mr Kennedy offered us a loan for the Box Hill project. We received the funds within a few weeks, and continued to work with them on future projects. Effectively, the AIDC became our bankers. And the success of our projects ensured that organisation's survival. While real estate could have been considered outside their lending brief, it soon formed the basis for their successful portfolio.

I received an invitation to attend a luncheon at the AIDC headquarters in Canberra. On my arrival, I was greeted by the head of the organisation and soon discovered that the luncheon was in my honour.

It was someone from the AIDC who approached me with the information that David Jones had purchased an excellent block of land—more than six hectares—on the north shore of Sydney, and was looking to develop a huge shopping centre. As a rule, a population of fifty or sixty thousand people in the surrounding areas was sufficient to justify the development of a shopping centre; the business it could generate would not exactly set the world on fire, but it could be profitable. Two hundred thousand people could ensure a thriving centre. The Sydney site had the potential to service almost a million people, and I knew that more than a few other developers would want to get their hands on it.

The AIDC had refused to lend the money to David Jones. Their attitude was 'If you can't run your retail operation, how do you expect to handle the development of a shopping centre?' But they were prepared to back me on the project.

We flew to Sydney immediately to meet with the David Jones management. In the green boardroom sat the CEO, the company chairman, the David Jones manager in charge of the project, and an architect who had been appointed to the job. I quickly understood that I had to make a deal on the spot. Their idea had been to develop the site themselves with our assistance as consultants, but since the AIDC was not prepared to lend David Jones the money directly, it was agreed that we would design, contract and develop it.

They wanted me to make an offer. But I couldn't give them a price—I had no idea yet of the development possibilities.

'When I come into David Jones to buy a dinner set,' I began, 'can I offer you any amount of money I like for it? No, the price is on the dinner set. So you give me a price: five, six, ten million dollars?'

I valued it at between fifteen and twenty million.

They offered me the site to develop for $11,000,000.

'But we don't require any assistance,' I said, looking towards their project manager.

'No, no,' the manager said. 'This must all be controlled and supervised.'

'We don't need anything from you,' I insisted.

I turned to the chairman.

'I have it on good authority that this manager sitting at the end of the table is out negotiating with a number of developers right now. I tell you that after I sign this agreement and hand over eleven million dollars, I expect absolutely no interference.'

'Mr Lustig,' said the chairman, 'do you know what you are saying?'

'My dear sir, of course I know what I am saying, otherwise I wouldn't say it. The reason I have the courage to say it is because I am convinced that this is the correct way to proceed.'

The meeting broke up for a few minutes and when we were called back the manager had gone.

'As you can see, the manager is gone. He may well take you to court, but we are reluctant to do business with people who make statements of that sort.'

This was only to scare me, because soon after they suggested that we continue. I knew then that it was all settled.

During the weeks that I was negotiating the details with David Jones, I received a telephone call from Frank Lowy of Westfield, the largest shopping centre developer in New South Wales at the time.

'Ted, we are in Melbourne and have a couple of hours to spare. We would like to have a yarn with you.'

I gave him my home address and he was there within half an hour. His partner John Saunders accompanied him. We sat down to an impromptu lunch. Lowy did the talking, while Saunders paced up and down my rather lengthy hallway.

I had told Max that they were coming to offer us payment for withdrawing from the deal. 'We may have a nice "little hit", or we may lose our site,' I had said.

Lowy tried to convince me that I didn't have the right construction people to develop successfully in Sydney.

'How much do you want?' he asked.

I replied that it was difficult to gauge.

'Come along with some ideas.'

'Perhaps I will ... perhaps not.'

'Ted,' Lowy continued, changing tack, 'I can see that you like trouble.'

'I like so many things, Frank, but if you knew me better, you would know that trouble is not one of them.'

In the end there was no trouble of any kind. I never did approach him with any ideas. Instead, I went ahead with the Chatswood Chase Shopping Centre development and it was, and remains, a resounding success. I believe that to this day, it remains one of the best shopping centres in Australia.

The situation surrounding the Sydney development was simply unbelievable. It was the first major 'regional' shopping centre I had ever attempted and remarkably it was completed successfully on a patch of turf that was not my own. Had external events not propelled me into such a position, I would never have dreamt of attempting such a thing.

Years later, I ran into Lowy. 'Ted, I still don't understand how it is that you managed to slip so quietly into our back yard. Bravo, Lustig!'

28 To Be Frank

There are formalities between the closest of friends.
JAPANESE PROVERB

Of my friends I am the only one I have left.
TERENCE

AFTER MORE THAN eighty years, I find that there are very few people who have left a lasting impression on my life. My father is one, for his moral fortitude and his unwavering dedication to the pursuit of knowledge; Doctor Kaufman, for his movie-star persona and his unashamed devotion to money and the benefits it offered; my mother's cousin, Bruno Schulz, for his belief in unrequited love and his celebration of melancholy; Ephraim Lifshitz for his brutal courage, the strength of his self-interested convictions and his absolute *chutzpah*. Franco Casella was another who left a lasting impression. But it was for altogether different reasons.

I first met Franco Casella on the worksite at 16 Albert Road, as the building neared completion. I would visit the site twice a day, once in the morning and again in the late afternoon. One afternoon, I noticed a short, stocky fellow rushing around, barking orders in every direction.

'Move it. Push it. Stop dreaming. Do you want a kick up the arse?'

I turned to my foreman, George Grey.

'George, who is that fellow?'

'Ah, he's just one of those crazy *eye*-talians.' George always placed the emphasis on 'I' when he said Italians.

The following day I saw him again. And once again, he was working at a breakneck speed, pushing his men in a manner I had never seen before. Men of his temperament were extremely rare, and normally the unions would have dispensed with such a man.

I turned to George.

'Would you call him over please? I would like a word with him.'

George did not leave his spot. He simply yelled in the man's direction.

'Hey, Frank.'

Franco was visibly upset about being interrupted from his ongoing barrage of orders.

From where he stood, he shouted back, 'What do you want?'

George answered from his own immovable spot. 'I want you to speak with Mr Lustig.'

'Who? Who is Mr Lustig?' His tone was contemptuous. Clearly, this was going to have to be important to justify such an abrupt intrusion on his time.

With unconcealed impatience, he stormed over to us.

'What do you want from me?' he snapped. 'Can't you see I'm busy with all these men?'

'I would like to speak with you,' I explained calmly, trying in vain to bring some civility to our exchange.

His mania would not be so easily quelled.

'So speak! I have no time.'

George broke in with his own attempt to provide Franco with some perspective.

'Frank. take it easy. This is Mr Lustig. The owner of this building.'

Even this knowledge did not temper his urgency.

'Oh, the owner. What do you want?'

'I would like to talk with you,' I repeated. 'Perhaps I would like you to work for me.'

'Why?'

'I like the way you drive these men.'

'What's your name?'

He knew my name. I wondered whether this man was 'short of a quid', or whether he was trying to make some obscure point. It turned out to be the latter.

'My name is Lustig,' I said slowly.

'Lustig. Lustig.' He sighed briefly before snapping to attention as if he had suddenly come to a realisation. 'You are not paying me! No, no, no. I work for Grollo.'

'Okay,' I said. 'I will speak to Bruno about you coming to work for me.'

'I don't want to work for you,' he screamed before turning his back and walking off. 'I want to work for Bruno.'

That afternoon, I called Bruno.

'Ted,' Bruno said, 'he's crazy, the little fellow. You want him? You know he's crazy.'

'I like the way he expresses his madness, Bruno. I like it. It is the first time I have seen somebody move around the site like that. And he wants the others to move in that fashion. He doesn't let them daydream.'

'Okay, Ted. I will tell him to go work for you.'

The following day, I was at the site again. The foreman called him over.

'What do you want? You are interfering with my work.'

'I have spoken with Bruno,' I explained. 'He told me that he wouldn't mind if you came to work for me. When do you want to start?'

'I have to tell Bruno that I am coming to work for you.'

'Sure. Speak to Bruno. When do you want to start with me?'

'I don't know. How about Monday?'

Franco was unpopular with everybody on the building site: the cleaners, labourers, tradesmen, operators. His tone was the same when addressing them all. 'Move. Or maybe you want me to move you?'

Franco had never been officially placed in charge of anything. He was simply a labourer, but despite this, he was blessed with extremely high standards and expectations of himself. He was never happy with the job he was doing because he always felt that he could do better. He was incredibly dedicated and motivated, despite the fact that he had absolutely no standing or official position. I liked his direct manner. He spoke with the owner of the building in the same tone with which he spoke to his co-workers. Even Grollo had respect for the owner. Not Franco. He never suspected for a moment that this may have been considered offensive.

Despite being in his mid forties, Franco was a single man with no children. He was happy to work seven days a week because he had nowhere else to go. At that time, I was involved in a number of projects, and I suggested that Franco work on several sites. Obviously, he would need a car, and I offered to buy him one.

'I want a sports car, Mr Lustig, so that I can look good when I go out on Sundays.'

He wanted to impress the Italian girls as he drove up to the Veneto Club. I offered to assist him in buying the car, but he insisted that he do it himself. He would buy what he liked. He would buy what he wanted.

Before long, I had transferred him to the building site at Heyington Place, Toorak, where we were constructing two houses—one for Sarah and me and the other for Iris, Max and the children. Work was progressing relatively slowly, and I needed someone to 'live' on the site—to oversee the work on a full-time basis. Franco was the perfect man for the job.

He had his own ideas on construction methods, but generally they were erroneous. On numerous occasions I had to argue with him, 'Please, Franco, don't do it this way. Do it the way I told you.'

One evening, he approached me and made a request.

'Boss, I would like you to teach me how to read plans.'

'Good,' I replied, 'but we don't have time now. We are too busy. We are going to have to finish this in the dark if we don't hurry. Remind me later.'

I hadn't read the expression in his eyes.

Years later, he turned to me and said, 'You were too busy, Boss, to teach me. And I know how to run the job. I know how to do it. I do it faster than anybody else. But you didn't recognise that, so I have not advanced in my career.'

It saddened me to hear these words. He was right. I regretted not having had the time to teach him. I thought a lot of him, and I had let him down.

Within a year of hiring Franco, I had raised his wages. Shortly after this, my secretary Marlene approached me on the subject of Franco.

'You know, Mr Lustig, Franco's family back in Italy are extracting every cent he is being paid.'

'What's going on, Franco?' I enquired.

'Ah, I don't need the money. I don't need anything.' He looked at me. 'Maybe I should save some money for a house?'

'Look, Franco. You are earning good money here. Make arrangements with Marlene. She will open a bank account for you, and all of your money will be placed directly into it. We will give you only what is necessary for you to live on and you can save the rest.'

And so it was.

Gradually, Franco was needed everywhere by Lustig & Moar.

Everybody disliked him, but everybody respected him. He knew it, and he enjoyed it.

Towards the completion of the Box Hill shopping centre, we discovered that somebody was coming into the car park at night and vandalising the machinery.

'What do you think?' I asked Franco. 'Should I call the police?'

'No police,' he replied. 'No good. Leave it to me. I know what to do.'

'Don't do anything stupid, Franco. It will cost me a fortune.'

'Don't worry, Mr Lustig. Tomorrow night I will camp at Box Hill.'

'Won't you be cold?'

'Mr Lustig, I will not be cold. I know what I am doing. You are treating me like a boy.'

The following evening, while Franco was hiding in the shadows at Box Hill, a group of youths arrived and started tampering with the machinery. They were moving it out of the way in order to gain access to an open area that was being prepared for a concrete slab. When more boys arrived soon afterwards, with a group of girls in tow, Franco realised that they were simply looking for somewhere to 'make out'.

He came into the office the following day to report his findings.

'Look,' I said, 'I am going to finish this once and for all. They may cause us problems. Let's call the police.'

'Please, Mr Lustig, leave it to me.'

That night he returned to the site, and when the youths arrived, he threatened them with a crowbar. They contemplated attacking him, but luckily realised that he was barking mad and had no fear. They fled the scene and Franco went directly to the police station.

'They have run away. I want the police stationed there.'

It turns out that the youths were local troublemakers and were well known to the police. Franco became the hero.

The following day I received a call from the police chief.

'Mr Lustig, please explain to Franco that we are here for this purpose. He should not worry himself because sooner or later they will beat him up and you will have Franco in hospital.'

It was a waste of time talking to Franco.

When we opened the shopping centre, each tenant had a fixed number of car spaces allocated to them in a specific area. Soon we realised that the staff were parking wherever it was convenient for them, thereby reducing the number of available car spots by about thirty or forty places. Franco took it upon himself to deal with the problem, and I received a call from the police.

'Tyres have been slashed, Mr Lustig, and we know who did this. You have to control him or there will be trouble.'

The Richmond shopping centre was opened and customers started arriving in large numbers.

'You control the movement of people in the car park, Franco. They seem to be ignoring the arrows, so I want you to direct them, and let them know what is and is not allowed.'

A few days later, I received a call from the town clerk of the Richmond Council.

'Ted, what's going on? You have some maniac in the centre.'

'What happened?'

He told me. The previous evening, his wife had tried to exit the car park. She was travelling in the wrong direction and in his inimitable fashion, Franco had scared the life out of her. 'Drive the way I am telling you to, Madame, or I will have to drive it for you myself!'

I had endless problems with the police. Franco has beaten somebody up. Franco has arrested somebody for parking in the wrong spot. Eventually, I managed to keep him under control.

Franco finally told me that he was going to buy a house. He purchased a dilapidated weatherboard cottage in Thomastown and renovated it into his very own Italian-style *palazzo*. He invited Sarah and me around to see the job. It was meticulous work. Over a drink, he began to tell us about his past. As an orphan, he was taken in and raised by a group of monks. At the age of fourteen, he was instructed to join the merchant navy.

'You should have seen me, Mr Lustig, when I was up on deck, ready for parade. Then I would serve the people in first class. I still have the uniform and the white gloves. I must use them. When are you having a party at home?'

I thought this was a fantastic idea. 'Yes, Franco. I would like to see that.'

He promptly disappeared, then came back wearing his uniform. Sarah began to laugh.

'Please, Mrs Lustig. Give me a chance. I would like to do something for you and your guests.'

We were sitting at tables around the swimming pool. Our live-in helper, Kevin Lonie, was preparing the barbecue meal and Franco appeared in his uniform, silver tray in hand, ready to serve the meal. He was meticulous, both in presentation and serving. He was so serious about his role that it was almost comical.

Six people were seated at each table. The conversation at my table was dominated by one self-important woman, who was prattling on about her travels around the world. Most of what she said was mindless drivel, but those listening were too polite to interrupt. We had all finished our meals, except for this woman, who was far too occupied to eat. Suddenly, Franco approached the table. He addressed her in an overly formal, somewhat stylised manner.

'Madame, would you *please* finish your plate. We are *all* waiting for you.'

Franco became the 'fix-it' man at Lustig & Moar. He did anything and everything. He was available any time, at any hour. He even took over Sunday lunches at our home.

It began one Sunday when he was invited to lunch with us. Sarah was busy preparing the meal when he turned to her and said, 'Mrs Lustig. That is no way to prepare macaroni. Let me show you how. You will love it.'

Naturally, a fight ensued.

'Let him do it,' I broke in. 'What's the problem?'

'You don't like my food? Franco is good enough for you and I am not?'

From that moment on, Sarah stopped cooking Sunday lunches and Franco took over. And to be brutally honest, they were the best lunches I ever ate!

At his home, Franco grew his own vegetables and herbs. Every day after a long day's work, he would go straight to the garden to tend to the plants. He loved his plants, and in his own way, he was a natural nurturer. In this respect, it was a shame that he didn't have children. I admired these qualities in Franco, as I admired his love for the simple things in life, and his willingness to be contented, to be happy. Unconditionally happy.

Indeed, Franco was a very sentimental fellow. I would often broach the subject of girls, whereupon he would respond, 'Maybe you could help me'.

I approached countless numbers of Italian tradesmen who worked on my sites. I went to the Veneto Club and pleaded with the manager. 'We must find a woman for Franco. For Pete's sake.'

Eventually Franco did marry. Carmel was an extremely attractive Italian woman who suffered from complete deafness. The love they had for each other was impossible to describe, and the communication between them was extraordinary—they often understood each other without any exchange. While she could lip-read a certain dialect of Calabrese Italian, she and Franco successfully created a language of their own. Franco was prepared to do anything and everything to help his wife, to make her happy, and this was further proof of the quality of this man.

Franco worked for me until the day he died, in 1990. He was working on the refurbishment of Austral House when he suffered a brain aneurysm and collapsed.

One day, Franco had turned to me and said, 'You wouldn't believe it. A cousin of mine died, and I have inherited a house on this island, south-east off the heel of the boot of Italy. One day, we will go there, you and I, and I will show you what the good life is.'

At that moment, I realised why Franco had come to mean so much to me, why I loved to have him around. It had taken me quite some time to hit upon it, perhaps because I had little experience of it. Franco Casella was my friend.

29 My Love Lost

It is ... less difficult to die than to watch the dying.
Patrick White, The Tree of Man

Eskell Goldberg has been my general practitioner for more than twenty years. He is a competent doctor and a caring man. When I suffered a car accident in the middle months of 1981, he came to see me in hospital, visiting as a friend rather than as a doctor. Sarah and her sister Hassia were also in the room at the time, conducting a conversation in Hebrew. I did not suspect that he was paying attention to their exchange.

Later that evening, I received a telephone call from Max. He seemed very upset. One of the children was unwell and Dr Goldberg had been called out to the house. During the house call, he had pulled Iris and Max aside to speak with them about a sensitive matter. He explained that he had overheard the conversation between Sarah and Hassia, and he suspected that Sarah may be suffering from an Alzheimer-type illness.

The doctor's concerns came as a complete surprise to the family. True, none of us had any knowledge of Alzheimer's or its effects. But more than this, Sarah's personality, her feelings of intellectual inferiority and her tendency to remain naïve and childlike, leaving all the decision-making to me, further obscured any signs of the symptoms normally associated with the disorder.

On reflection, the signs had been there. I had recently made some attempts to finally teach her to play bridge. It had remained a favourite pastime of mine, and hosting a weekly game after Friday night dinner was a cornerstone of our social existence. Little had changed since the early days of our marriage in Damascus. I would settle down to the game with a few friends, while Sarah played the perfect hostess, serving refreshments and generally viewing the proceedings from the 'outer'.

When she tried to learn the game, she found that she was simply unable to retain all the rules, and was even less competent at remembering the cards that had already been played. Her frustration grew, and eventually she gave up trying. I had attributed her lack of success to a lack of patience, much like her unwillingness to learn the English language upon our arrival in Australia. It had been 'too late', and considering that she was now approaching her late sixties, perhaps it was simply too late for her to learn the game of bridge.

I was wrong. Dr Goldberg's trained eye had detected something more—a degradation of her short-term memory. In the conversation with her sister, Sarah had often repeated herself in a manner that suggested she had no memory of having spoken those words moments before. This suggested that Sarah was, in fact, fast approaching the advanced stages of the disease. Her sense of frustration when unable to learn bridge, some time earlier, had suggested that things were going wrong. Her mind was slipping, but not yet to the extent where she was unaware of the changes. As I learned later, this was a characteristic of the early stages.

By October of 1981, Sarah had been diagnosed with Senile Dementia of the Alzheimer Type (SDAT), a manifestation of Alzheimer's disease that occurs in later life. With Sarah already at an advanced stage of this degenerative disorder, the prognosis was not good. Indeed, over the next few months, her health deteriorated rapidly. Her emotional outbursts became more frequent and more irrational. Her sense of time and place all but disappeared, and her short-term memory function failed. I was forced to install deadlocks on all the doors of the house to ensure that she did not walk out and disappear without trace. The need to protect her from herself meant that she became a prisoner in her own home. Witnessing Sarah's dramatic decline was a devastating experience for the whole family. By the end, we were hardly recognisable to her.

I was extremely fortunate to have had Kevin to help care for Sarah through these trying times. Kevin had been working for us at the house for many years. Over the years, his duties saw him in the roles of butler, cook, driver, housekeeper, peacekeeper, babysitter, gardener, and now nurse. But more than that, Kevin had become an integral part of the family. He was a true gentleman and a professional who loved his work and, in an old-world manner rarely seen today, took great pride in the results. He was very fond of Sarah, and was unfailingly there for her when she most needed him.

Hassia had agreed to come and live at the house while Sarah was suffering from her illness. Hassia and her husband Ziggy Schwartz had left Israel and arrived in Melbourne just six months after we did. While Hassia and Sarah had remained close, we saw little of them socially, since Ziggy and I were not the closest of friends. I had always considered Ziggy to be rather an ill-bred oaf, and Ziggy had always seemed intent on competing with me in any way he could. His main activity was developing factories, and when he died in the mid 1970s, he left Hassia a number of income-bearing properties.

In May of 1982, just six months after her illness was diagnosed, and after forty years of marriage, my wife passed away.

A couple of days after the funeral, Kevin came into my study carrying a small kitten. 'Mr Lustig, this is such a big house and now you are alone here. I thought you might want some company.' He was a good man.

This sad and difficult time was made all the worse when Kevin was diagnosed with cancer soon after Sarah's death. The illness was too advanced to control, and just months after losing my wife, I lost our very good friend. As was the case with Frank Casella, I found in Kevin a compassion and loyalty I had rarely encountered before. Kevin was always a willing listener and a provider of sensible advice. I would miss him greatly.

It was no surprise that I could not see Sarah's illness coming. Ironically, it was Sarah's innocence and naïvety that had attracted me to her in the first place. Our marriage had been built on pure romance. More than that, it had been predicated on my perception of her as a 'damsel in distress', locked in the tower of the terrible Maslovaty. I had been the white knight, and my arrival had heralded the rescue she had been waiting for. The fact that she was three years my senior served to reinforce my self-esteem further. After all, I had, at the time, fallen into a position of seniority with the British army that saw me in charge of men twice my age. A young boy with a man's job was surely a man—as was one who managed to save an older woman and ride off with her into the sunset. The control and strength that I felt in taking on this role may have assuaged a yearning that resulted from the loss of Suza, and perhaps even the loss of my mother, over which I was unable to exercise any control at all.

It did not take long for me to realise that this was a shaky foundation for a marriage. In keeping with my romantic notions, I immediately assumed complete responsibility for our combined well-being, and it was a responsibility that Sarah was more than willing to abdicate. In the absence of any real form of professional guidance in my career, however, I found the task difficult and it would be a long time before we felt any sense of financial or emotional security.

My progress toward my goals had been somewhat slow, especially on our return to Tel Aviv. With so many problems in the world around me, I saw my family as an oasis of stability, and saw no reason to alter the status quo. My insecurity, coupled with a tendency to be ultra-conservative about change of any sort, manifested itself as a reluctance to have any more children after the birth of Iris. I think that this upset Sarah who, having been raised in a Sephardic home, would have been inclined to raise a large family. Each time she broached the subject, I responded that we simply could not afford to support another child.

My wife suffered from *minder wertigkeitsgefühl*—an inferiority complex—based on a lack of formal education. And I suspect that our marriage did little to ease this feeling. From very early on, she sensed that there was little common interest between us, a lack of intellectual compatibility, and she surmised that I did not enjoy her company. This manifested itself as a profound insecurity. She frequently expressed a fear that I would leave her—it seemed to be permanently on her mind. She made constant efforts to please me; indeed, sometimes she would try too hard. When she realised that even our cuisine cultures were also miles apart, she dedicated herself to learning how to cook Galician food.

In Australia, the situation worsened. Her unwillingness to learn English limited her opportunity to make new friends and establish a social life for herself, as well as for us as a family. Apart from the weekly bridge game at home, she remained largely passive in terms of social contact. Naturally, the accident in Perth had not helped matters. Indeed, the potential longer-term effects of losing her eye, of her perceived disfigurement, came into play, creating all sorts of problems. For a woman who equated her self-respect with the way she looked, it was understandably a shattering blow.

Our sex life suffered immeasurably following her accident. Her fears that I no longer found her attractive slowly and insidiously became self-fulfilling prophecy. As her refusals became ever more frequent, our intimacy gradually ground to a halt. Concurrently, as my business began to develop, I spent less time at home and more time working. Indeed, I would soon be arriving daily at my office before breakfast and often working late into the evening, well past dinner. I was having three meals a day in the office. I was spending far more time with my 'support staff' at work than with my wife and family. For Sarah, this fact soon became a justification for her suspicions concerning my fidelity, and this would drive us even further apart.

I recalled the spirited and vivacious woman I first gazed upon all those years ago, whose affections I had sought and won. We were star-crossed lovers: the damsel in distress and the hero, at her behest, whisking off his prize to the other side of the world. What followed were the years of real life, the part the fairy tales neglect to explore: the day-to-day realities of making a living and finding one's place in the world. I set about the latter task with gusto. But Sarah felt her place was only by my side. After her accident, this became increasingly so; she was scared, unhappy and insecure, and if she was unwilling to negotiate a social and communal life of her own before, she was unable to do so now.

The final tragedy was in the last months of her illness, when her physical state was such that she truly did not know herself, or recognise her own immediate world or anyone in it. My only consolation is that this proud and passionate woman was unaware of the loss of Sarah. Iris and I and those who loved her were living the daily anguish for her. It was the price we paid for her not knowing.

My wife was the cornerstone of our small family and her death placed a strain on my relationship with Iris. Naturally, my work had kept me away from my daughter while she was growing up, and it was always going to be difficult to compensate for this shortfall. But my work always took priority. When I was a child, my mother used to sing to me. Among her favourite tunes was a duet that was popular around the cabaret clubs of Vienna. A woman's voice begins, singing something along these lines:

Sei doch gut, Sei doch nett, Sei doch lieb...
(be kind, be sweet, be a darling ...)
... und kauf mir:
(and buy me:)
ein schönes kleines Auto achtzig H.P.
(a nice little car with eighty horsepower)
und eine kleine Villa am See
(and a nice little villa on the seashore).
He answers:

Sonst, hast Du keine Schmerzen?
(Apart from this, you have no other pains?)
Liegt gar nichts am Herzen?
(and nothing more in your heart?)
She interrupts him:
Oh Ja, Ein kleines Perlen–collier...
(Oh yes, a little pearl necklace)
And it continued in the same vein.

It was a song that became etched in my memory, for better or for worse. And as I grew into manhood and began to recognise the world of discontent that was my parents' marriage, the words of the song rang true to me. I saw my mother's frustration grow as my father failed to deliver her from their middle-class existence to the aristocratic life she so desperately craved. She most certainly loved my father. But he had different values, and had neither the drive nor the desire to change them to suit her circumstances. Her disappointment was about money and the power it brought, and nothing else.

As a man and as a husband, I was determined to do everything in my power to avoid causing that same misery. At any cost. As a father, and later as a grandfather, I would find myself singing this same song, as a lullaby.

Now, in Sarah's absence, Iris and I would grow further apart. When Max and Iris' separation a number of years later resulted in a protracted series of negotiations, I felt deeply for Iris' suffering, but I was in a difficult position. Being Iris' father, and Max's business partner, I felt that it was inappropriate for me to become involved. I wanted to be kept away from it, which did little to help my relationship with my daughter. Instead of being able to turn to me, she turned instead to her lawyers. Gradually, the swimming pool that separated our homes became known as 'The Pacific Ocean' and represented the vast gulf that had sadly grown between us.

Shortly after Sarah's death, I joined the cause of helping to raise funds for Alzheimer's research. Each December, I would host a garden party at Heyington Place. The first such event, just eight months after Sarah's death, had a guest list of one hundred people. Over the coming years, the parties would grow in popularity and support and by the late 1980s, more than 400 people were attending, including the then Prime Minister Mr Bob Hawke and other eminent politicians and international diplomats.

The success of these events was all the more remarkable given that I had little, if any, experience of hosting social functions. Apart from our weekly bridge games, our social life had revolved entirely around the family: Friday night dinners with Max, Iris and our three grandchildren, and the occasional Saturday night outing to the pictures with Iris and Max. The only official function that had taken place in our home was a dinner for opera diva Dame Joan Sutherland. On that occasion, I employed the help of Marlene and her good friend Heather Wood to take care of the arrangements. Heather had accompanied Marlene to our home one evening to make up a fourth for bridge. When I realised how good her game was, I asked Heather to teach my wife to play, and they became friends in the process.

After Sarah's death, as a man approaching my seventies, I realised I was in need of companionship. There followed a string of relationships. I was a wealthy man at the time, and there was no lack of interest from women, including some who were ten or more years my junior. I would not remarry, however, for another twelve years, when I became reacquainted with Marlene's friend Heather.

Years earlier, when she first arrived at my home to play bridge, I was immediately struck by her physical presence. She came in wearing a long, field-blue overcoat that gave her the appearance (from the neck down, of course) of an impeccably tailored senior officer in the French army. Some months later, she reappeared at one of our dinner gatherings. At one stage during the evening, another of the guests, Mr Alec Ranoschy (the headmaster at Mount Scopus College) quizzed Heather on an issue concerning the Hebrews of the Old Testament. This was strange considering that Heather was the only gentile seated at the table. To my amazement, Heather proceeded to tackle the question head-on, demonstrating a remarkable degree of knowledge. Once more, I could not help but be impressed.

In the intervening decade, Heather had been married and widowed. Now we were both available, and it was an inevitable pairing. We shared many interests and we more than matched each other intellectually. Indeed, in contrast to my first marriage, I found Heather's assertiveness to be more than challenging—sometimes downright daunting. With her ability to make friends and her extraordinary talents as a host, my own social life soon soared to new heights. In Heather, I found the companionship I sought for so long after losing Sarah.

30 Raising the Stakes

If you owe the bank fifty thousand dollars, you have a problem. If you owe the bank fifty million dollars, they have a problem.
FROM THE FILM 'ROSALIE GOES SHOPPING'

MY FELLOW DEVELOPER, Morrie Alter, once asked me, 'Ted, why on earth did you build the Grand Hyatt Hotel?'

'I am surprised that a businessman of your calibre would ask me such a question,' I replied. 'Don't you know that as the owner of that hotel, I am eligible for a 50 per cent discount!'

'But,' said Alter, 'look how much you spent on it, Ted. Surely you should get the room for free!'

In terms of risk, it was certainly a colossal step to move from shopping centres to hotels and central city office blocks. Shopping centres involved minimal risk: the major leases were negotiated well in advance of laying a single concrete block. And since I enjoyed a fruitful relationship with Coles, Target and Kmart, I could be assured of filling the surrounding spaces.

Developing hotels and particularly vast commercial spaces was an altogether different proposition, one fraught with dangers. But it was the 1980s—a building boom, and the 'silly season' for developers. More than that, I still had something to prove. Sure, I had been successful in developing residential properties in the 1960s, and then some small office blocks and shopping centres in the 1970s. I had made my first million, and subsequent millions. But it was not enough.

I wanted to establish the name of Lustig as a major developer in Australia—and that meant big city buildings. It meant leaving the legacy of at least one architectural landmark, a work of beauty, and the shopping centres would never offer such kudos. Without this, I felt that I would always be the 'Little Lustig' who got his first break in Tel

Aviv by being mistaken for 'Big Lustig.' Now I had to know that I had finally become 'Big Lustig.'

The early and mid 1980s would be the busiest period of my professional career, with Lustig & Moar involved in a number of major projects both locally and abroad. Most of the attention at home centred on the top end of Collins Street. Plans for the construction of the Grand Hyatt began as early as 1981, with the hotel eventually opening in 1986. Negotiations to acquire the land, situated on the corner of Collins and Russell streets, Melbourne, were complicated and protracted. Indeed, with some of the existing tenants it took up to three years to strike deals for their departure. After securing options for ten or fifteen properties in the vicinity, we eventually consolidated the entire site of the planned development.

Two problems ensued: where to borrow the money, and what to do with the site. The plans involved offices, retail space and a hotel. We had absolutely no experience with hotels, but our partner, Grollo, had already been negotiating with the Regent chain of hotels, as well as the Carlton Group. Ultimately, we decided to deal with the Hyatt Group.

During 1984, a meeting was held at my home to organise the deal. Representatives from the Hyatt Group, the State Government, the Melbourne City Council, real estate agents, and the AIDC (our third partner, and financier) joined Bruno, Max and me for a buffet dinner. In all, twenty-two people were present.

I had three people working on the agreement: Max, a young lawyer by the name of Joe Gersh (who had been assigned the job by Arnold Bloch), and our financial consultant Reg Jebb.

Max had continued to work on site, looking after construction, through the progress of all of the shopping centre developments. By the time we began work on the Chatswood Chase centre in Sydney, I had finally convinced him to come in to the office to learn the finer aspects of the business.

'Look, Max,' I explained. 'As a construction manager out there, if your work is not up to scratch, you can be fired. But as a director and project manager, you cannot be dumped unless the company is dumped.'

The Grand Hyatt Hotel would be his first project in this capacity. Reg Jebb had been working for a city firm that handled the financial side of a number of our projects. Some years prior to the hotel project, I agreed to employ him for twelve months as a precursor to his opening his own firm. Reg's work was outstanding, and within a year, he had made the transition to self-employment. After that, he became our consultant.

Soon after establishing his own business, Reg was contracted by National Mutual, who were investigating the purchase of the Sheraton Wentworth Hotel in Sydney. Reg gained a degree of expertise in the hotel business, and this would prove invaluable in the Hyatt negotiations.

While Joe Gersh was relatively young, he was eager to learn about the construction business. Studiously, he acquired skills in reading and understanding architectural plans.

I was sixty-seven years old by this time, and for the first time in my career, I decided to take a back seat and leave the details of this project to these three young men—particularly Max, who had already been vocal about my perceived unwillingness to delegate responsibilities to him.

The designs for the project were submitted by Burratinni, an Italian architect, and Reg went to work establishing the minimum cost of constructing the building. Initially, we planned to reserve the upper four floors for high-class suites, luxury serviced apartments, allowing us to pre-sell or secure long-term tenants. Additionally, this meant that these floors would not have to be completed until such arrangements had been made. After investigating this idea further, however, we decided to abandon the concept and extend the hotel to occupy this space.

The price of construction was settled with AIDC at $115,000,000 and an agreement was signed. Some time later, during construction, it became apparent that the price was going to exceed this amount. AIDC then accepted the figure of $125,000,000 with the provision, 'If it ends up costing one hundred and twenty-five million and one dollars, Lustig & Moar will pay the one dollar.'

The Grand Hyatt site was little more than an empty lot in the early part of 1983, but it seems that the bulldozers made enough noise to bring the little developer Lustig to the attention of CRA, the giant mining company, who owned the acreage next door on Collins Street. It came as a complete surprise when I was contacted on behalf of CRA by a chartered surveyor and property consultant named Brian Baker, who invited me to lunch with the then chairman of the company, Sir Roderick Carnegie.

CRA had built its head office at what was then known as 95 Collins Street during the 1960s. It was the tallest building in Melbourne at that time, but unfortunately it was poorly designed, with small floor size being the major problem. In the early 1970s, CRA and Jones Lang Wootton conceived of the idea of developing the site and attracting other major mining companies as tenants. These plans were interrupted by the collapse of the leasing market in the central business district in the mid 1970s, and were not reviewed again until the market improved towards the end of the decade.

This time, however, CRA did not want to be a developer, nor did the company want to carry any development risk. Its objective, initially, was to use the strength of its leasing covenant to add value to its site. After numerous reports and stop/start, on/off moods from CRA, it was decided to invite two parties to submit proposals for the site. The parties were Lend Lease Corporation, a major Australian public company, and Lustig & Moar.

The proposed site was a huge block of land immediately adjacent to our hotel, a vast area of more than 100,000 square feet of prime city real estate. Naturally, I was interested—a block of that size at the 'Paris End' of Collins Street would justify a construction on the scale of the Sydney Opera House. And the prospect of securing the land adjacent to the hotel was a case of two plus two adding up to something between seven and eight.

We convened a meeting. At lunch were Sir Roderick Carnegie, John Carden (CRA's finance director), Brian Baker, and myself. I was subjected to the usual line of questioning: where had I come from and what had I built? I knew this to be my Achilles heel, for I had no major city office blocks to my name—just three small office blocks on Albert Road and a few shopping centres. And a hole in the ground that would later become the Grand Hyatt Hotel.

My limited résumé did not prove to be too detrimental, however. I presented CRA with a number of proposals, including one plan presented as a joke but with a serious expression on my face, to develop an office block with a concert hall—a second Carnegie Hall (which appealed to Sir Roderick to some degree). Ultimately, the proposals I submitted, consisting of various designs by Daryl Jackson, were preferred by CRA to those offered by Lend Lease and designed by Harry Seidler.

The proposed deal was to be based on our paying a minimal

amount in cash in order to secure the site for clearing and developing, with the balance to be paid in the form of a ten-year lease of 45,000 square feet of office space suitably equipped, and within a quality building. Despite my efforts, no official agreement was signed.

As I felt my position strengthen with CRA, and with the knowledge that I would be leasing office space at the CRA site, I decided to purchase another property, across the road at 90 Collins Street. Effectively, I was protecting myself on one side of Collins Street against any other developer who might build offices on the other side. And, with this purchase I would have control of the exclusive 'Paris End' of Collins Street, which would satisfy my commercial ends and, I must admit, my ego. Perhaps I would prove to be the 'Big Lustig' after all.

I bought the old three-story building at 90 Collins Street from National Mutual for $11,000,000. Shortly after I paid the 10 per cent deposit, I concluded that the purchase was wasteful. Our second Box Hill shopping centre development was coming in well over budget—as well as being late—and I was staring at another 10 per cent payment in thirty days and the balance in one hundred and twenty. I knew that there would be no money left for construction. I looked for a way out.

National Mutual had agreed to provide me with a vacant piece of land, but they were having trouble persuading one tenant to leave. The proprietor of a small shop that sold a wide range of sundry products wanted $25,000 to vacate. As it happened, I knew someone who knew this merchant. I made an offer.

'I'll give you five thousand just to stay for two more weeks. You'll still be getting your money for leaving. That's thirty thousand in total, with my five.'

Then I could return to National Mutual and say, 'Enough is enough. Contract off.'

But the offer came to naught. The apparently resolute trader left soon after with $10,000 from National Mutual. I was unable to get out of the deal, and found myself the not-so-proud owner of 90 Collins Street.

Within a few months, the adjacent property—a small, narrow tract of land at 88 Collins Street—went to auction. Because it was adjacent, I bid up to $3,500,000 on an almost unusable piece of land that sold for $5,500,000 to a well-known Melbourne developer. With such a small floor space, you couldn't justify building anything at all.

Some time later, my lawyer Joe Gersh received a visit from two gentlemen who claimed to be the developer's backers. They explained that the developer had assured them that Mr Lustig required 88 Collins in order to proceed with a development of 90 Collins Street, and would therefore be willing to pay them more than seven million dollars for it.

History had clearly demonstrated that whenever I purchased a block of land, I went ahead and developed it. I have never been one to speculate on land prices. I am a developer. Naturally, this colleague of mine assumed correctly that I would be looking to develop. His only miscalculation was that I did not require the tract of land. Joe Gersh rang me and after some brief negotiations, the backers were willing to sell for the $3,500,000 I bid at auction.

The 90 Collins Street purchase bore fruit much sooner than I expected—in about six months—when I was offered $27,000,000 for the site. I remembered Arnold Bloch's attitude while I was negotiating the properties at Albert Road, so I did not bother to go to him. Crazy profits meant crazy income tax. It was unnecessary. I did, however, agree to sell 50 per cent of the building for $13,500,000. Two and a half million up, and I still owned half the building.

My new partner was C. Itoh, Japan's third largest corporation.

In our partnership agreement, I was to be responsible for all decision-making regarding development, and they seemed to be quite comfortable with this. For a time. One afternoon, we met at my house. Seated around my dining room table were six Japanese representatives of C. Itoh, Joe Gersh, our general manager Peter Keogh, and myself. At one point, their lawyer insisted that the partnership agreement be amended, and the result of the amendment would have been the loss of all my decision-making privileges. I reacted immediately.

'You see these beautiful gardens and this swimming pool. It takes approximately three minutes to circumnavigate the pool. I am going for a three-minute walk. When I return, and if you still insist on these recommendations of your lawyer, then you will no longer need to waste my time. You will very nicely get up and get out.'

I didn't need to come back, because their most senior representative followed me outside. 'Please, Mr Lustig ...'

'Either you say yes, or you say no,' I said bluntly. 'Are you ready to come back inside?'

The deal was done. And with C. Itoh as my partners, I didn't just have my sights set on 90 Collins Street, but on the world. C. Itoh appreciated the way I worked and we enjoyed a strong relationship.

Throughout this period, I was touring the world six to eight times a year. Anywhere I went I would look, check, and compare during the day, then enjoy the nightlife in the evenings. But my business travelled with me as my most constant and watchful companion, and it was at a dramatic stage of its evolution, where one incorrect decision could have finished me off instantly.

I spent quite some time investigating opportunities in Taiwan. While attending a conference, I met a very pleasant-looking Taiwanese woman and we began to chat. As it turned out, she lived just one block away from me in Melbourne and we exchanged addresses. A few months later she invited me to dinner to meet the Chinese/Taiwanese high society. During the course of the evening, she began to tell me of the opportunities in Taiwan. Fortunately I was able to obtain an entry visa before dessert. I left for Taiwan the following day.

I had a lawyer in Taipei, the son of one of my very old friends and bridge partners Helen Finkel. He married a Taiwanese girl who happened to be a descendant of Chiang Kai-shek. His firm introduced me to the head of the Taipei district government. He was a rather hard man, but I won his heart when I showed him a photograph of a Chinese architect and his Taiwanese wife, whom I had met in Melbourne. Unbeknown to me, the woman in the picture was his daughter. He was so taken by the coincidence that he invited me out to dine with his new fiancée.

I wondered how and where to develop a major shopping centre in Taipei. I looked at a number of locations, including the old World Exposition site, which was government land under the military's control. But I lost interest when my friend at the council was promoted to Minister of Foreign Affairs. I would have had to establish a whole new set of contacts. At the same time, three large Japanese companies, one of which had done business locally before, took a keen interest in the proposed site. It was going to tender.

I also saw opportunities in Tokyo. But again, I did not get overly excited. I found it especially difficult because Max felt that these projects would never work, so I had no support. I went through Hong Kong, Taiwan, and Singapore with a lack of success. But then the work I was doing in Taipei was noticed in Hong Kong by the Pritzker family who owned the Hyatt Hotel chain.

Pritzker was prepared to take on Lustig & Moar as a partner in a large Hong Kong development: a shopping centre, residences and hotel on a large block on a Kowloon beach. We invested $2,500,000 on this site; Pritzker invested a similar amount. There were three partners: Lustig & Moar and Pritzker had 25 per cent each and the local developer had 50 per cent. The investors had put up $10,000,000 on a $450,000,000 project. (Is it any wonder that the banks went broke?)

At around the same time, I completed a very successful project in California. I had started travelling regularly to the United States after my wife passed away. I sincerely wished to know more about the American lifestyle, but the more time I spent there, the less I knew. Perhaps my fascination dated back to the old cowboy movies, or perhaps to the dream I had of really 'making it', which meant succeeding in America.

Eventually, I found something. Four local Jewish partners had been pulling in different directions. One of them didn't want to talk to me at all, and kept his distance. Another, according to the Russian classification, was 'soft shit'—a person of no consequence whatsoever. A third, a man by the name of White, wanted out of the partnership but wanted to stay in the action, so we became partners and he looked after the job. That way, I had someone with local knowledge.

The Los Angeles location was in the middle of nowhere. There were no houses; the suburbs were going to be built around the shopping centre. I thought the position was terrific—at sea level, in the San Fernando Valley—so I arranged for control of the site. We were successful in selling the units. Then I developed an office block in New York in partnership with Israeli twin brothers, jewellers who were establishing themselves in the Big Apple.

All of these developments were taking place around the mid to late 1980s. Indeed, Lustig & Moar was making great strides and I had every reason to feel proud of our achievements. Max and I were listed in the *Business Review Weekly* Top 200 wealthiest people in Australia, and Lustig & Moar occupied a similar position on the fastest growing business listings. One American colleague of mine suggested to me that if I really started running, I would be a billionaire within a few years.

It was not only on the 'rich lists' whose ranks I was rising through—I was beginning to mix with some very influential people. I never felt this more than the night I was seated between the Prime Minister of Australia and the Prime Minister of Hungary at a dinner held in the parliamentary dining room in Budapest.

As a small-time property developer in the 1960s and 1970s, I was involved in dealings with the building unions, and had come into contact with Bob Hawke, the ambitious young gun who worked with the ACTU and the Labor Party. I can remember one of our earliest encounters, at my home, when Bob launched into an exuberant trumpeting of the virtues of Golda Meir. Perhaps he felt that it was politically expedient to do so in the presence of a Jew. But Bob was unaware of my feelings towards the woman whose radical socialist policies had all but destroyed my career as a property developer in Tel Aviv.

It wasn't until the early 1980s, when I began hosting the garden parties in aid of Alzheimer's research, that our friendship was developed. Bob was a regular guest and speaker at the luncheons, even after he had become Australia's Prime Minister in 1983.

When Bob decided to take an official tour through Europe, I decided to join the Prime Minister's entourage. I had no official capacity—I just thought it would be an interesting way to visit the continent, and an opportunity to meet people I would not otherwise meet.

Our last stop was Budapest, and after a full day of sightseeing, we were invited to a state dinner for 120 guests. It was a rectangular table with sixty guests on each side. I am not sure how it came to pass that I was seated to Bob's immediate left, and directly opposite the Hungarian Prime Minister. But I was introduced as 'Mr Lustig, an immigrant from the old Austro-Hungarian Empire'.

After Bob delivered his speech, the Hungarian Prime Minister replied in broken English. As a third speaker, an Australian minister, stood up to address the gathering about financial issues, Bob turned to me and said, 'You will say something about tourism.' Sure, I was a hotel owner, but Bob had completely surprised me with his directive.

'What am I going to say?'

'I don't know, but use the opportunity.'

To this day, I cannot say with any surety what came out of my mouth that evening. Something about the importance of an exchange of tourism between the two countries now that the doors to Eastern Europe had been flung open.

I must have impressed somebody, because the following morning, I was summoned to meet with Peter Varkonyi, the Hungarian Minister of Foreign Affairs.

'I hope it is not too much of a risk to nominate you as an Honorary Consul for your state of Victoria.' He was trying to be humorous, but

I got the distinct impression that this was a well-rehearsed routine. In any event, when I walked out of the office twenty minutes later, I was officially the representative of the Hungarian government in Victoria.

What did this mean? I would provide an office and a secretary, and establish relations with the local Hungarian community. I would act as their agent in dealings with the Hungarian government, and I would provide ways and means of cooperation and business between the two countries. And in return? I was given a 'CC' number plate for my car— an exemption from having to pay parking fines (but only if I bother the Hungarian Minister of Foreign Affairs with a letter). But there were the kudos, the invitations to state affairs, and my inclusion within the network of Honorary Consuls of the world.

At this point in my life, it looked as if the sky was the limit. What I did not yet see was that there was a ceiling in the way.

First, the CRA deal fell through. Then I received the bill for the Grand Hyatt Hotel. Finally, the global economy collapsed.

Negotiations with CRA had continued for two years, and as time passed, the area of office space to which CRA was prepared to commit continued to decrease, from forty-five to thirty-five and then to twenty-five thousand square feet. I had negotiated with the AIDC to develop the CRA site. I wouldn't have dared to go into the site without them as partners, and they were prepared to build only if CRA took at least 25,000 square feet.

The board of directors at CRA eventually decided that they would not give me the obligation to lease. They did not see any reason why CRA should be based in Collins Street. They now wanted payment rather than lease terms. By this time, the building boom of the early to mid 1980s had resulted in an oversupply of office space. Leasing was drying up and it became clear to me that if I became involved in that land deal, without the prior commitment to lease, I could soon have found myself in very nasty trouble.

Furthermore, CRA still had not decided whether to develop with Lustig & Moar, or simply sell the land. When I became aware that a sale might be imminent, I sought to gain a last right of refusal on the site. It was not granted.

To my horror, I then learned that my partner in the recently completed Chatswood Chase shopping centre in Sydney, Maurice Alter, was being offered the CRA building at 95 Collins Street for an incredibly low price.

I rang John Carden, CRA's financial director, and told him that the land was being undervalued. As a result, a selective tender process was established. I no longer had a tenancy guarantee, so my two-and-a-half-year affair with CRA was over.

I failed with CRA and I took it very hard. It was a devastating blow given the amount of work that had gone into planning the development. But there was something more. As was the case with the proposed hotel and casino in Canberra, it seemed to me that these projects never got off the ground because I was not part of the old school. In Israel, my future was limited because I did not belong to *Mapai*; in Australia, I suffered from a lack of influence. And big business is all about influence.

With the CRA deal collapsing around me, I was left with the site at 90 Collins Street, an imminent saturation of office space in the city, and the knowledge that a huge office development was going to be built across the road. I wanted to move quickly and complete the office tower at 90 Collins Street before my competition at 101 could build theirs.

And then there was the hotel.

When the Grand Hyatt finally opened in November of 1986, the final bill for construction came in *way* over budget. The AIDC had warned me about exceeding the amount on our agreement, and duly withdrew from the project leaving Lustig & Moar and Grollo to raise money to buy them out. When Grollo too decided to withdraw, Lustig & Moar needed a saviour. The ANZ bank, with whom I had enjoyed a wonderful relationship for many years, provided the lifeline.

When the stock market crashed eleven months later, on that fateful day in October 1987, and interest rates suddenly doubled, I began an exhausting five-year battle to keep from drowning. I owed the bank a fortune, and the interest payments were astronomical.

The second Box Hill development also came in over budget, and when the market crashed, we were caught in the middle of the 90 Collins Street development. I had pre-leased the entire building to a group of stockbrokers—only to learn that after the crash, the companies had simply disappeared. To leave the building unfinished was pointless. I had to have an asset to sell or lease. And that meant spending a lot more money. I count myself lucky that I was able to secure three major tenants, including Nylex.

All of this was increasing our debt, the interest on which was now eating heavily into our assets. One by one, I watched them sold off: Albert Road, the shopping centres, our share in Hong Kong, and finally Chatswood Chase, which very nearly tore my heart out. I was so proud of that development.

Modern Melbourne had been building at that time without any explanation as to why and for whom. Many developers fell by the wayside at this time, and only a few recovered. The Kern Corporation, which ended up purchasing the CRA site in 1988 and developing 101 Collins Street, went into receivership soon after.

At least Lustig & Moar survived the storm. All was not lost. The performance of the Grand Hyatt Hotel was stronger than expected, even taking into account the horrendous effect of the nationwide pilots' strike of 1989. Eventually, Lustig & Moar was able to grow once more and now it boasts a second hotel: the superb Park Hyatt Hotel in Melbourne. Max's hotel. And with both my grandsons, Guy and Jay, having shown some degree of interest in the business, who knows how far it can go?

But back then, as I felt my small empire slowly crumble, I was able to take solace in just one thing—the Grand Hyatt Hotel. The cost may have been great, but I had my landmark building. I was 'Big Lustig'.

While it was common knowledge that I owed a lot of money, I also owned a beautiful hotel, perhaps the most beautiful in the city, and that hotel was worth considerably more than I owed.

In big business, it is necessary to be aware of all the various factors that influence the enterprise. Communicating involves seeking information while giving little away. It is almost like fishing: laying the bait of small tidbits of information in order to gauge reactions. Everything is very carefully controlled. But once you strip away the layers of intrigue, influence, secrecy and manipulation involved in the bigger games, it all reduces to the same basic principle: if you can produce the best quality product, at the best price, you will always be in demand. And the only way to achieve this is to be passionate and proud of your work. This principle can best be described in terms of the lowest common denominator of business: the Monday market. I am reminded of a Polish story.

Ivan owns a cow and a small paddock. The distance to market is possibly ten or fifteen kilometres. According to Polish military regulations, a soldier or battalion marching should cover between five and five and a half kilometres per hour. (The British are quite happy with miles and a slower pace, and I always wondered why Polish soldiers had to run faster.) Ivan and his cow would probably travel at a third of the speed of the Polish army, and so he would have to leave on Sunday night to arrive at market on Monday morning with his cow. He knows that in walking that distance, the cow will probably lose some weight, and her ribs may start showing. He will have to feed her very early on market morning, and then ensure that she looks her best for the market. He will brush her down and then dress her with the impressive collection of decorations he keeps for her. Ivan has his regular spot at the market and everybody knows that Ivan's cow will be there.

People pass and laugh about how much Ivan loves that cow. He is approached by a group of men, and one of them addresses him: 'I'll buy the cow, and I will pay you now.' Ivan doesn't answer, just listens. Another interrupts, 'This will be *my* cow. Fifty zlotys.' This is unheard of. You could buy two or three cows for that amount.

It is nearing the end of the day, and Ivan is tired. He still has to go all the way back home. But she is beautiful, Ivan's cow, and he simply shakes his head. They laugh at him.

Ivan knows that his cow is keeping him alive. Her upkeep is inexpensive and she provides him with milk to sell. And he can sell her manure. She is, in practical terms, extremely valuable. But this is not the only reason Ivan refuses to sell her. His motives go beyond mere economics. She has some indefinable quality that makes her different, special, more valuable and more prized than any other cow.

'So Ted, what is the price for the hotel?'

'I am not selling. This is the most beautiful hotel in the city.'

This is how the Grand Hyatt became known as 'Ted Lustig's Cow'.

Epilogue

The past is a foreign country. They do things differently there.
L. P. Hartley, The Go Betweens

After the game, the king and pawn go into the same box.
Italian Proverb

1998

I stood at the gates of the Himmel mansion, which was once the most elegant house on the avenue. The gardens, once resplendent with intricately balanced areas of orchard, forest and lawn, had long been reclaimed by the chaos of nature, and it was clear that the house itself had seen no maintenance in all the years I had been away.

This house had meant so much to me. It was here that I played as a child, that I first began to practise my art of storytelling. It was home to the first girl I cared for, and it was where I met the first girl I loved. It was also the house of our 'well to do' neighbours, and I had often wished it was mine.

I thought of Renata and Ziggy, the Himmel children, the rich kids. Ziggy had squandered his share of the family fortune years ago before taking his own life. Renata, on the other hand, had chosen differently. She was now living happily in modest accommodations in a poor area of New York, volunteering her services as a piano teacher to underprivileged children.

My mother had always told me that we Lustigs were special, something out of the ordinary—better than the next family. According to her, we naturally belonged in the same social circles as the Himmels. Now, at the age of eighty, I could see that I had spent my entire life striving to be special, extraordinary, something a little better than the common man and the run-of-the-mill. And the insight that suddenly overwhelmed me, despite my attempts to ignore it, was a recognition of my own ordinariness.

I looked up to the window of my old house at number 36 and saw the little boy sitting on the sill playing his violin, pining for the attention of the girl next door. I glanced out at the road, where Dr Kaufman pulled up in his pink sports car, and I saw the pipsqueak who was so keen to please, just for another ride. I saw the kid riding in the front seat, waving to me as if he was royalty. But he was just an ordinary boy. Despite my mother's claims to the contrary, we were just another middle-class family. Educated, and with some refinements, but essentially middle-class.

At one stage I had made it to the top. I had more money than most people could dream of, and I had earned the respect of my peers. But none of that protected me from the winds of fortune. When the world was ready to cut me down, there was nothing I could do about it. Had I really believed that riches would propel me above the human condition?

Despite all the successes I might have been considered to have achieved, in the face of all the wealth I had accumulated over the last thirty years, I stood in Mickiewicza Street at that moment and could not help but feel that I was somehow incomplete.

My success came late in life—the world had decided to keep Lustig moving until he was well into his forties—and so too did the lessons that success brings. Prosperity had come at a considerable price. It had robbed me of so much time: time to learn, time to reflect, time to be—especially with my family. I was just a passing blur as my daughter got older, and then again as my grandchildren grew into adults. I was always so busy, had so many people to see—and yet now I felt quite alone.

For solace, I found myself turning to friends from a distant past—to Ziggy Binstock and the boys in the band called Palma, with whom I rehearsed daily just across the way, above Dr Wilder's apartment. Ziggy had managed to track me down in Tel Aviv just after the Second World War. His mother and sister had perished in the Holocaust. Ziggy managed to survive in Poland, and then travelled into Russia at the end of the war to find his wife. Ziggy told me of the fates of the other band members: Staszek Wilder and Max Lambert were both killed during the war, and Gerry Galotti, an Italian Jew, was executed after being accused of spying for the Germans.

I did not see Ziggy again for almost twenty years, when I ran into him, quite by accident, in a Manhattan hotel. Sarah and I walked into the cocktail lounge, where I thought I recognised the fellow playing piano accordion. As he walked by, I whispered 'Ziggy?' in disbelief. He immediately stopped playing and turned towards me. The big bear of a man then proceeded to lift me off the ground in an almighty embrace and plant a succession of kisses on my face. 'Lustig!' he cried with pure delight.

Here was a man who had survived the war, a man who needed little out of life other than life itself.

Then there was my father, though my father did not survive. I walked through the park that stood between my family home and the King Jagiello school, taking the same route I travelled each day when I was a schoolboy. This was the same path that my father and I took each summer afternoon, discussing history, philosophy and all manner of subjects, where he had opened my mind to new ways of thinking, where we had shared our closest moments. I wondered what he would have thought, whether it would have all been different had my father lived. Again, I realised how very much I had missed Dr Samuel Lustig.

I left Drohobycz just eight hours after arriving. I had not wanted to remember my past. I had wanted to maintain control. I wanted to leave Drohobycz as the same man who arrived—as the man who reinvented himself for the umpteenth time upon arriving and settling in Australia. I wanted to remain the man I thought I was. And yet, I could not.

And as I departed, I regretted not having arranged to stay overnight. In retrospect, one more day couldn't have hurt any more than a few fleeting hours. I think I will go back.

An Ode to Ted Lustig

In days of old
When knights were bold
And chivalry was rife
A man's main aim
And claim to fame
Was to save a maiden in strife.

They rode around on steeds of white
Their silver armour shining bright
Their swords were ever at the ready
To wipe out any George or Freddy
Who even with a sideways look
Any lady's honour took.

Chastity belts were all the rage
And worn by females of any age.
Gentlemen were at their leisure
Devoted to giving their ladies pleasure.

To help a damsel in distress
And get her out of any mess
Was the honourable duty of any male
Tall or short, dark or pale.
Romance was the order of the day,
Men were gallant in every way.

That was many years ago
And chivalry is dead—
Why I do not know.
But in our midst here tonight
There is a star that shines so bright.
Although he's known to Esther and Abie,
He's not your typical Jewish 'Zadie'
And though his horse is in the stable
Without it he still is able
To attract the ladies young and old
And charm them all—that's what I'm told.

Always immaculate and debonair
He can cow a man with just one stare.
He really doesn't need his sword
One scream—and everyone is floored
And even his most fearsome foe
Will get itchy feet and want to go
If he decides them to regale
With a v-e-r-y v-e-r-y lengthy tale.

I refer of course to our friend
'Sir Ted'
For whom many hearts have bled.

We're gathered here to wish him well
Many more years of yarns to tell
Many more years in which to be well
Many more years of happy bridge
Many more years in which just to live
Many more years of clever wit
Many more years of brains to pit
Many more years of deals concluded
Many more years of charm exuded
No need for wealth
We wish you health and luck in every way.

Let's raise our glass
And wish dear Ted

A H-A-P-P-Y B-I-R-T-H-D-A-Y

—*Lee Hayden*
in honour of Ted Lustig on the occasion of his 75th birthday

INDEX

AIDC 268, 269, 287, 288, 295, 296
Albert Square offices 246–55, 258–60, 261, 297
Alexandria 100–1
Alter, Maurice 250, 265, 284, 293
AMP 253–5, 258, 261
ANZ Bank 296
apartments
    Melbourne 226–7, 231–3, 235–7, 238–9, 242, 243–4, 245
    Tel Aviv 183–6

Baker, Brian 288, 289
Bancroft, Graeme 255
Bawden, Llew 267
Beirut 101, 131–4
Betar 87
Bettingani and Quweitar 169–72
Beverley, Captain 162–4
'Big Lustig' 191–2, 195, 286–7, 290, 297
Binstock, Ziggy 38–9, 46, 95, 300–1
Blewett, Marlene 234–5, 285
Bloch, Arnold 249, 251–2, 254, 287, 291
Bodor, Ladislav 142, 144, 183, 197–8
Boronia Shoppingtown 263–4, 265, 267, 268
Box Hill Shopping Centre 290, 296
Brauder, – 85, 86
Brenner, Suza 49–52, 59, 60, 64–5, 76, 96–8, 100
British Army 136–45, 155–6, 157–64, 166–9, 198
Bruchner, – 142
Buchan, Laird and Buchan 219–21, 224, 225, 251, 267
Buchan, Sir John 224, 261, 262
Builders' Labourers Federation 260

C. Itoh 291
Camberwell apartments 231–34
Carden, John 289, 296
Carnegie, Sir Roderick 288, 289
Casella, Carmel 278
Casella, Franco 271–78, 281

Caulfield apartments 237, 245
Chatswood Chase 267, 268–71, 287, 295, 297
Chciuk, Tadek 21, 22, 27, 41, 93, 94–5
City developments 250, 286, 287, 290–1, 296, 297, 298
Coles Group 264–5, 266, 268, 286
concrete construction 214, 225, 267
Consul (Honorary Hungarian Consul) 7, 294–5
CRA 287–9, 295–6

Damascus 136–44, 145, 149, 153
David Jones 268–70
Diskin, – 130–1, 132, 133, 134, 156
Drohobycz
    anti-Semitism 6, 27, 57, 92–9
    discovering Judaism 24–32
    girlfriends 40, 43–52, 59
    going back 6–7, 92–9, 297–9
    growing up in 18–23, 29, 47–9, 53–9
    Holocaust 98, 99, 111, 112
    leaving 6, 59, 60–1
    school days 33–42
Dubienski, Stanislau 41

Efron, – 159–61

Faiman, – 250
Fauer el Fauer, Emir 165–9
Fogel, – 177–8
Fookes, Ernest 227
furniture manufacture 239

Gallagher, Norm 260
Gandel-Besen Group 266–7
Gersh, Joe 287, 288, 290–1
Goldberg, Eskell 279–80
Goldstone, Andy 220, 224
Grand Hyatt Hotel 286, 287, 288, 296, 297, 298
Greensborough Shopping Centre 266–7
Grey, George 271–2
Grollo, Bruno 259–60, 263, 266, 267, 272–3, 287, 296

Grossman, – 106–7, 109

Haber, – 225–6
Haganah 87, 89, 157, 184
Haifa 65–6, 69–78
Haifa Technion 57–8, 63–4, 73
 fortress competition 109–10
 politics at 84–91, 113
 student life 79–91
 vacation jobs 117–24
Hamilton, – 251–2
Hanover 250, 253, 263, 264, 267
Hawke, Bob 282, 292
Hebrew language 26–7, 73, 81–2, 88, 90, 100, 106
Herscu, George 250
Himmel, Renata 5–6, 20, 21, 22, 44–5, 96, 299
Himmel, Ziggy 20–1, 22, 96, 299
Histadrut 89, 197
Hong Kong 292, 293, 297
hotels 284, 285, 286, 294, 295, 296
Hyatt Group 287, 292

Janowsky, – 175
Jebb, Reg 287–8
Jerusalem 101–2
Jones Lang Wootton 251, 261, 266, 289

Kaminsky, Boris 156, 173–4, 177
Kaufman, Dr 23, 48, 106, 222, 271, 300
Kennedy, J.F. 268
Keogh, Peter 291
Kmart 264–5, 268, 286
Koch, – 63–4
Kohn, Barakshek 211
Krantz, Franca 222–4
Krantz, Ziggy 222, 223, 224
Kuhn, Marcel 142–3, 144, 150

Leder, – 64
Lerner, Abraham 40, 49–50
Liberal Party 261, 262
Libertowsky, – 85, 117
Lifshitz, Ephraim 86, 114–16, 118, 170, 172, 217–19, 271
'little Lustig' 191–2, 286–7
London family 182, 207, 210–11
Lonie, Kevin 276, 280–1

Lowy, Frank 270
Lustig, Anselm
 Haifa 32, 68–72, 73–8, 82, 103, 104, 105, 123–4
 Poland 13, 16, 24–5, 27, 28–32, 44, 47, 49, 57, 59
Lustig, Lucia 5, 6, 12, 13–14, 22, 23, 24, 25–6, 27, 29, 30–1, 32, 43, 47, 48, 53, 54–5, 58, 59, 60, 61, 63, 92–3, 96, 98, 104–5, 112, 284, 299
Lustig, Lusia 31–2, 69–72, 73–8, 82, 106
Lustig, Dr Samuel 6, 13–14, 20, 21, 22–3, 24, 25–6, 27, 30–1, 34, 40–1, 48, 54–6, 57, 58, 60, 61, 81, 91, 95–7, 98, 103–4, 111, 112, 156, 271, 284, 301
Lustig, Sarah 7, 145–54, 208, 211–13, 214–15, 222, 223–4, 229, 239, 240, 246, 252, 255, 277, 279–83
Lustig-Moar, Iris 154, 187–8, 211–12, 213, 222, 239–40, 243, 255, 263, 283, 284
Lustig & Moar 243, 263, 267–8, 274, 277, 287, 289, 292–3, 296–7

Maier, Max 237
Mapai 83, 84–5, 86, 87, 88, 102–3, 113, 197, 203, 296
Maslovaty, – 143, 144, 145, 148–50
McEwans store 229–30, 240–1
Meiri, Abraham 114, 116, 137, 145, 170
Melbourne
 arrival 216–19
 developer/owner 227–44, 246
 drafting service 224–5
 furniture manufacture 239
 Jewish community 224, 225–7
 Lustig & Moar 243, 263, 267–8, 274, 277, 287, 289, 292–3, 296–7
 see also apartments; hotels; office blocks; shopping centres
Mizrahi 87–8
Moar, Guy 258, 297
Moar, Jay 297
Moar, Max 240–41, 255, 260, 263, 266, 284, 287, 288, 292, 293, 297
Moar, Nathalie 258

Moorabbin apartments 242
Multiplex 227

National Mutual 290
Nelson, Alan 225, 251

Oberlander, Josef 75, 77
office blocks 246–55, 258–60, 261, 285, 297

Pachtmann, Dr 13–14, 16, 31
Page, Alan 265
Palestine 58–9, 72, 82–4, 87, 88, 119, 134
Palma jazz ensemble 38–9, 300
Palmach 157
Park Hyatt Hotel 297
Paynter, Captain 143, 155–6, 161–3
Pecek, – 242–3
Pemoar 242–3, 263
Perth 207, 210–12, 224, 228
Pilar, Joshua 253
Pines Shopping Centre 266
Poland *see* Drohobycz
Popper, – 249–50
Porteous, – 253
Primavera 253–4, 259
Pritzker, – 292–3

Richmond shopping centre 263, 265, 267, 276
Robinson, L.R. 264–5
Rosmarin, Henry 227, 231, 233, 235, 237, 243
Royal Air Force 125–7
Rubenstein brothers 266

Saunders, John 270
Schulz, Bruno 43, 271
Schwartz, Hassia 175–7, 279, 281
Schwartz, Ziggy 176–7, 281
Seidler, Harry 209, 289
Shell building 221
shopping centres 286
    innovations 268
    Melbourne 263–4, 265, 266–7, 268, 275–6, 290, 296
    Sydney 267, 268–70, 287, 295, 297
Simon, Leo 232–3

Solel Boneh 83–4, 125, 134, 156, 157, 197
South Yarra apartments 243–4
Spry, Tom 243–4
Stastra & Page 265–6
Stern, Arieh 84–5
Sydney 267, 268–71, 287, 295, 297

Tahal 197, 198–201
Taiwan 292
Tauchner, Milek 21, 40, 46, 47
Tel Aviv 72, 144
    building inspector 178–80
    property developer 190–8
    residential blocks 183–6
    Tahal 197, 198–201
Toorak apartments 238–9
Toorak house 229–31
Tyre 134–5

unions 260–1, 266, 294
United States 207, 293

Van Houten, – 212
Vandrov, – 178–9
velodrome, Perth 214
Vienna 11–16

war
    Palestine 58–9, 108, 112, 115–16, 156–7, 169, 180–6
    World War I 14–15, 33–4, 58, 87
    World War II 90, 93, 95, 98–9, 108–12, 125, 133–4, 136–7, 155, 160, 164
Weidenfeld 85–6, 181–2
Whitehorse Plaza 265–6, 268, 275–6
Wilder, Dr 19, 20
Wilder, Staszek 19, 38, 300
Wood, Heather 7, 285

Yaron, Alex 104, 184–5, 240
Yaron, Lonia 104–5, 106
Yaron, Shimon 54, 102–4, 106

Zakszewski, Peter 93, 94–5
Zinc family 106–7